DO I OWE YOU SOMETHING?

Also by Michael Mewshaw

Fiction

Man in Motion
Waking Slow
The Toll
Earthly Bread
Land Without Shadow
Year of the Gun
Blackballed
True Crime
Shelter from the Storm

Nonfiction

Life for Death
Short Circuit
Money to Burn
Playing Away
Ladies of the Court

DO I OWE YOU
SOMETHING?

A Memoir of the Literary Life

MICHAEL MEWSHAW

LOUISIANA STATE UNIVERSITY PRESS Baton Rouge

Copyright © 2003 by Louisiana State University Press
All rights reserved
Manufactured in the United States of America
First printing

12   11   10   09   08   07   06   05   04   03
5   4   3   2   1

Designer: Amanda McDonald Scallan
Typeface: Bembo
Typesetter: Coghill Composition Co., Inc.
Printer and binder: Thomson-Shore, Inc.

Library of Congress Cataloging-in-Publication Data

Mewshaw, Michael, 1943–
    Do I owe you something? : a memoir of the literary life / Michael Mewshaw.
       p.   cm.
    ISBN 0-8071-2852-4 (cloth : alk. paper)
      1. Mewshaw, Michael, 1943–   2. Mewshaw, Michael, 1943—Friends and associates.   3.
    Novelists, American—20th century—Biography.   4. College teachers—United
    States—Biography.   5. English teachers—United States—Biography.   6.
    Americans—Foreign countries—Biography.   I. Title.

    PS3563.E87 Z463   2003
    813'.54—dc21
    [B]   2002034040

The Anthony Burgess chapter first appeared in *Granta*. The Prologue and the George Garrett chapters first
appeared in *Sewanee Review*. The William Styron and Robert Penn Warren/Eleanor Clark chapters first appeared in *Southern Review*. Material concerning James Jones first appeared in *Texas Review*. A short excerpt
concerning Peter Taylor first appeared in *Virginia Quarterly Review*. An excerpt from the Gore Vidal chapter
first appeared in the journal of the Southwestern MLA. Material concerning Albert Erskine first appeared in
the *Dictionary of Literary Biography*.

The paper in this book meets the guidelines for permanence and durability of the Committee on Production
Guidelines for Book Longevity of the Council on Library Resources.♾

for my mother and father

CONTENTS

DO I OWE YOU SOMETHING?

PROLOGUE

G RAHAM GREENE claimed that a writer's childhood is the bank account he'll draw on for the rest of his creative life. When it dawned on me that I had no choice, no real alternative, I had to become a writer, I read Greene's comment with a sinking heart and feared I had been shortchanged. To have any chance at success, I thought I would need to switch banks or siphon off somebody else's account or do business in a different currency. For the patrimony I came into as a kid seemed to me inappropriate to fiction and unacceptable as fact.

Born in Washington, D.C., I was raised on the outskirts of the city, in Prince Georges Country, Maryland, in a precinct that one scathing sociological report referred to as America's first suburban slum. Our house, a red brick semi-detached unit identical in every respect to hundreds of others in the community of Templeton Knolls, had been built on rolling pastureland. To make the cookie-cutter construction process speedier and less expensive, bulldozers first knocked down the trees and skinned off every blade of grass. When we moved in, long before landscapers laid new sod and proud homeowners planted twig-like shrubs and trees, the neighborhood resembled one of those African villages whose inhabitants have scraped the ground clean of vegetation to protect against mosquitoes and poisonous snakes. In wet weather the red clay was the consistency of quicksand; during dry months it acquired a brittle ceramic crust.

Scant reminders of the development's rural setting survived at its fringes. Along one side of our lot, a clear ankle-deep creek separated us from a last remaining clump of trees on the far side. My brother and I played cowboys and Indians in the woods and caught frogs and turtles in the creek. But whenever it rained, the stream frothed with muddy runoff from the berm of the nearby Baltimore-Washington Parkway, and after one torrential storm, a five-year-old boy slipped into a whirlpool of cocoa-colored water. I was there and tried to save him, but failed. An hour too late, the fire department pulled his corpse from the creek.

Even in clement weather the parkway had the potential to bring cataclysm to our doorstep. Across from our house, the road took a deceptive curve, and inattentive drivers often crashed through the guardrail. At first, my whole family raced over to marvel at each wreck and count the number of killed or maimed. But eventually accidents became so commonplace, we didn't bother. We just called the rescue squad and let others reckon the death toll.

Blue-collar in population, Templeton Knolls was a place of hard drinkers, hard drivers, hard living and, all too often, dying. No sooner had families arrived than they started moving out, some in the middle of the night, leaving behind a rat's nest of unpaid bills and no forwarding addresses. Many of those who remained lamented that they hadn't gotten out before it was too late. People there were forever losing things—jobs, hope, loved ones, limbs.

Within a block of my front door lived a blind girl, and next to her a girl who had been hideously disfigured by fire. The blind girl tapped her way from house to house, singing "I'm Sorry" in imitation of Brenda Lee and begging for small change. The burned girl stayed indoors, out of the sun, while her skin grafts healed into a slick, livid brocade of scar tissue. There was also a little boy who had been hit by a car and hobbled along with his legs bound in metal braces. Another fellow breathed and squeaked words through a surgical tube in his throat, and a sad eleven-year-old attempted suicide with his father's .22 rifle and succeeded only in shooting off his lower jaw. One madcap teenager won a ten-dollar bet by letting a cherry bomb explode in his hand. The blast severed his thumb at the second knuckle.

He could count himself lucky. Many kids paid a far higher price for their pranks. A neighborhood boy, obsessed as we all were with cars, suffered such a deep compulsion that he started stealing them and, in the ultimate act of auto-eroticism, masturbating on the upholstery. When he hot-wired a moving van, the company pressed charges, and the kid ended up in Patuxent Institute for Defective Delinquents, where his fellow adolescent offenders badgered him so savagely he killed himself.

Despite—or perhaps because of—the local inclination toward extremes of behavior in most arenas, there was remarkably little tolerance for anything except the narrowest expression of sexual preferences. Infidelity among dating couples no less than among the long married prompted brutal and sometimes fatal retribution. One wife fled an abusive relationship and was hunted down by her husband, who beat her and their baby to death with a baseball bat. Another woman and child, murdered by gunfire, were assumed to be victims of domestic violence. No charges were ever filed in the case.

Nor were the police especially interested when a house was set afire while a clutch of kids looked on and cheered. The house's owner escaped with his life but little else. His wife had left him months before; he had lost his job and had taken to entertaining teenage boys who maintained that in exchange for beer he demanded blow jobs. That he got run out of the neighborhood struck everybody, including law enforcement officers, as rough and fitting justice.

At the time, none of this seemed to me extraordinary or particularly noteworthy. A malleable, protoplasmic creature whose shell had yet to harden, I assumed the shape of the space I occupied and accepted prevailing circumstances as my standard. I certainly didn't believe that the people I grew up with and the random events that unfurled around me constituted the raw material of fiction. All art existed for me in a vague ether, its provenance a profound mystery, its shimmering substance as inexplicable to this Catholic boy as water into wine, bread into body and blood.

Decades would pass before I realized that as aspiring author I had not been born a pauper. Far from it. I belatedly discovered I was every bit as well set up to be a writer as a Brooklyn Jew, ghetto black, or worm-ridden white boy raised in the moldering ruins of a Mississippi plantation.

In fact, such an embarrassment of novelistic riches rained down upon me that I had trouble sorting it out and deciding where to invest my wealth. It would have helped to have an assets manager, or what has come to be called a mentor. But while I was reared in an Ur-womb of fictional archetypes and universal themes, I knew nobody except my mother who read books and no one at all who wrote them.

Then new neighbors moved in next door. Obvious oddballs, set apart from the community by their accents—they hailed from New England—not to mention by their grammar and vocabulary—they were the first college graduates I'd met—the couple didn't drink, didn't smoke, and didn't own a television. What's more, the man never worked on his car, never even washed it, and had no interest in normal sports or in the local teams, the Senators and the Redskins. He described himself as a spelunker, and when he noticed that the word wrinkled our brows, he explained that his hobby was cave exploration. Every weekend he slung a coiled rope over his shoulder, clamped a miner's helmet on his head, and set off for some sinkhole or dank cavern.

His wife stayed home, and what she did alone during those days and nights seemed every bit as bizarre as her husband's subterranean forays. She stationed herself at the kitchen table and typed. In summer, when windows were left open, the clacking racket of her upright Underwood wafted from her house to mine and insinuated itself into my consciousness with the cryptic urgency of Morse code. First it made me curious, then it made me bold. I crossed the fence and stood on her back porch, staring through a door whose mesh screen diffused her solid bulk into a series of Benday dots. She might have been a newspaper photograph held too close to my face. I blinked to see her whole—a plain, plump, matronly figure dressed in pedal pushers and a man's shirt with the tails loose at her waist.

Sensing my presence, she glanced up from the page, fingers poised over the keys.

"What are you doing?" I asked.

"Writing."

"Writing what?"

"A short story."

"Can I watch?"

"Of course," she said. "Come in."

I fixed my eyes on her fingers and had difficulty comprehending their speed and dexterity. Words, phrases, whole paragraphs flew onto the paper, which one moment was empty and the next instant full of something that hadn't previously existed. The process gave me the same giddy sensation I got from watching a quarterback uncork a fifty-yard pass or a basketball player sink a shot from half-court. There were people, it occurred to me, who were capable of accomplishing the impossible. I wanted to be one of them.

I asked the woman why she wrote, and she said she hoped to break into *Cosmopolitan* or *Redbook*. That was the market to crack—magazines that paid a thousand dollars a story.

I didn't believe her. Nobody, no matter how foolish or rich, would fork over a thousand bucks for pages of words. That she maintained otherwise undermined her credibility and diminished some of the dazzling aura she had acquired in my eyes. Still, I didn't stop looking and I didn't stop listening as she continued talking and—marvelous feat!—typing at the same time.

There was big money to be made in writing, she swore. A woman like her, a housewife working in a kitchen just like this, had written a novel that transformed her into a millionaire. *Peyton Place*. Had I heard of it? No, it wasn't a book for a boy my age. But it showed what you could accomplish once you mastered the craft.

Her reference to writing as a craft put me in mind of braiding lanyards, weaving potholders or fashioning fans from Popsicle sticks—precisely the activities with which kids my age whiled away the dog days of summer. Her implausible claims about the financial rewards of publication interested me not at all. It was the magical luster of the act that appealed to me. I wanted to try something different, make something new. From the beginning I was in it for the art, not the money.

Hurrying home, I struggled to get started, but was stymied by the perennial search for a plot. Fortunately, an excellent source of material lay close to hand in my collection of comic books. Drawing narrative inspiration from the pictures and borrowing dialogue from the conversation balloons, I cannibalized the cartoons and produced a semblance of prose. By some strange process of alchemy, I found myself changing the settings, scenes, descriptions, even the sex of certain characters. More than mere whimsy, these changes, it seemed, possessed an organic inner logic, and they conferred a rare and heady power, comparable to nothing I had known except perhaps tearing the wings off Japanese beetles, re-

making creatures that God had created for the air into earthbound scut-
tlers. It is only now that I recognize how crucial the idea of control was,
and still is, to my concept of creativity. In a world where whirl was
king—where kids were blind or crippled or crazy, where houses burned,
cars crashed, and neighbors died with violent suddenness or killed themselves in calibrated doses—here at last was an opportunity for me to distance myself from immediate events and shape them into a pattern I
could live with.

But a few days of forging in the smithy of my soul was sufficient for
one summer. I soon went back to playing baseball, catching frogs, and
keeping abreast of news in Templeton Knolls, some of which made it
into the pages of the Washington newspapers. Police had unmasked the
neighborhood spelunker as a bigamist who, rather than rappel into caves
every weekend, retreated to a second wife and family at the opposite end
of the county. Thereafter, the term "spelunking" passed into local usage
as a synonym for the old adage that a wise fox fucks far from home. This,
I see now, was a story the woman might have profitably applied herself
to in the homey confines of her kitchen, but she never did succeed in
publishing in *Cosmo* or *Redbook* or anywhere else.

And so throughout my teens and into my twenties, I remained an
aspiring writer without a role model. In college, at the University of
Maryland, I signed up for creative writing courses. One was taught by a
German poet who smoked pungent cigarettes tweezed between his nico-
tine-stained thumb and first finger. The other was taught by an aging
spacey gentleman notorious for vatic pronouncements—"We live each
other's deaths and die each other's lives"—and for bringing his wife to
class to keep him from drifting off into fugue states. But since neither
gentleman, regardless of his other talents, had managed to get a book of
fiction into print, I considered myself to be operating at an unconscion-
able disadvantage.

When an English professor, a crusty old Texan, heard me complain
that I was like an actor who had never seen a play or a singer who had
never heard a song, he cautioned me that encounters with authors, even
famous ones, weren't necessarily what I imagined. "Writers are like
horseshit," he said. "If you spread them out over a huge field, they make
flowers grow. When you get too many of them heaped up in one spot,
they just stink."

This didn't dissuade me from my search, however. What follows is a chronicle of my efforts, frequently headlong and humbling, to meet writers and make myself into one. Whatever else they proved to be, the novelists I finally got to know make up a rare bouquet of figures responsible for some of this century's most significant bodies of work. They helped me, they influenced me, and frequently they consoled me both personally and by the example of their professionalism. Even after meetings that ended poorly or painfully, I emerged with a conviction that, as Saul Bellow put it, education is everybody's second prize, and I had learned hard lessons that wouldn't have come my way had I merely read their books and never met these people.

Of course, knowing writers doesn't make anybody a writer, and whether my own books, this one included, constitute horse manure injudiciously distributed, I'll have to let others decide. Although I wish it were otherwise, it's also self-evident that knowing famous people hasn't made me famous. If it had, I would be armor-plated against charges of name dropping or of pressing my nose against the windows of my literary betters. In my defense, I could contend that there's always value in seeing people close up and clearly as a corrective to the historical record and the distortions of rumor and rampant celebrity. But in the end I confess that for me, as I hope it will be for the reader, the pleasure of such company has been its own greatest reward.

GEORGE GARRETT

University of Virginia, Charlottesville

T HE summer after my senior year of college, whenever I wasn't hectically running in circles and chasing my own tail, I continued to harbor the fantasy of becoming a novelist. The question was how to go about it. The English department at the University of Virginia had offered me a four-year fellowship, but grad school, a common destination for feckless youths of my stripe, seemed too tame, too much like what I had already done and not at all what I thought I'd like to do. Rather than stay safely on track, I had an ungovernable impulse to jump the rails.

With forty dollars in my pocket, I caught a plane to Puerto Rico and hopped an inter-island ferry to the British Virgins, where I freeloaded off two fellows on Tortola who claimed to be shark fishermen. In fact they were a couple of drunks who had been hired to babysit the autistic son of an American millionairess. She had parked the boy out of the States to prevent her ex-husband from gaining custody. I might have remained in that sad menagerie a lot longer had I not been arrested for back-talking a very truculent traffic cop. After a day in a dungeon-like cell, I wired home for bail money and flew back to the States.

There I went to work as a hod-carrier at a construction site. Lugging bricks eight hours a day, I lasted exactly one week, after which I picked up my paycheck and lit out for Mexico with a friend in a VW Beetle. Taking turns at the wheel, we sped straight through to Acapulco and returned, all in ten days. This may make it sound like we were taking part in some sort of competition, a time trial or motor cross, but I can't hide behind that excuse. Nor can I claim that like Jack Kerouac I counted each mile as an aesthetic experience, a potential page in a future book. The truth is I didn't write a single sentence that summer, and it was sickness, not youthful exuberance, that kept me yo-yoing around. A shrink, I suppose, might have called me manic depressive and prescribed the same mood-leveling medication my mother took. But if I was sad and restless, suffering from an excess of adrenaline and no sense of direction, I ascribed this to the fact that a childhood friend had recently murdered his parents and been slammed into prison with a life sentence. Then, too, my college girlfriend had gotten pregnant by another guy. The draft board was also breathing down my neck, and I didn't view Vietnam as a good place to serve my writerly apprenticeship.

A month before I was due to register at the University of Virginia, I still hadn't made up my mind whether to go to grad school. When I read an ad in the *Washington Post* that asked, "Do you have what it takes? Have you got the brains, personality and competitive spirit to become a Junior Executive Trainee at AT&T?" I decided I might as well apply.

The first hurdle was an application form that might have been a fiendish exam designed by a sadistic professor. Since my real résumé would never suffice, I resorted to fiction, filling out the questionnaire in much the same way I would write a short story. After I pieced together a plausible narrative and concocted a more or less believable character— me!—through an accretion of bogus details, I gained the confidence to negotiate half a dozen interviews with the AT&T personnel department. The only shaky moment came when I learned that I would have to submit to the Minnesota Multiphasic Personality Index. While I feared the test would expose all the loose live wires of my circuitry, it somehow convinced AT&T that I was just the sort of JET they were searching for.

I started work on a Monday. By Tuesday afternoon I had resigned. The people responsible for my hiring pleaded with me to hang around at full pay and explain how I had hoodwinked them. But I declined. They would never have believed me anyway. How could I convince them that my life had been turned around by a rave review of *Do, Lord,*

Remember Me, a novel by George Garrett? Garrett taught at the University of Virginia. Finally, this was my chance to meet a published writer.

Arriving in Charlottesville, I didn't bother checking into the graduate dorm or stopping at the admissions office to collect my stipend. None of that mattered unless I got into Garrett's creative writing seminar. According to the course catalogue, advance permission of the instructor was required. So with a wad of manuscripts in hand, I tracked him down at the English faculty lounge.

On that sweltering September afternoon in 1965, the place swarmed with professors engaged in enterprises that have since become anachronistic. They smoked; the room reeked of cigarette, cigar, and pipe tobacco. There was another smell: The sweet scent of mimeograph ink empurpled the air, just as it empurpled the pages of class schedules that were run off on a clattering machine. With not a woman among them, the profs joked and razzed one another like frat boys in a locker room. Yet despite the heat and the horseplay, they wore coats and ties, as did all the students at Mr. Jefferson's academical village. This scene, summoned up from memory, has for me the peculiar fixity of a cave painting. None of it could happen today.

Short and stocky, dressed in a seersucker suit, George Garrett stood at the center of a small, rapt crowd . I can't recall what he was talking about. Specific subject matter seldom meant much when George held forth. His success as a raconteur depended on a raucous style reminiscent of the comedian Don Rickles. He mugged, he furrowed his high forehead into a ladder of quizzical wrinkles, he punctuated his sentences with histrionic hand gestures, he did different voices, acted out opposing points of view, and delivered his punch lines with explosions of laughter.

I prefer to believe I waited for George to finish. I want to think I didn't interrupt. But considering how self-absorbed and glistening with need I was back then, it's quite possible I broke in. "About this writing seminar of yours, how do I sign up?"

Garrett responded with a broad grin. "You're in. Just gimme your name." Shaking back his sleeve, he signed a permission slip and told me to present it to the registrar. "See you in class," he added and swung back to his audience.

Feeling let down, I left Cabell Hall and walked across the Lawn toward the Rotunda. I had expected there to be more to it—a test, an interview, a baroque selection process like the one I had lied my way through at AT&T. Given the ease with which I had gotten into his seminar and the offhanded way Garrett had dealt with my feverish aspirations, how could the course, how could the whole long delayed encounter with a writer, be worthwhile?

Following a brick path beside a serpentine wall, I strolled to the West Ranges and peered into Edgar Allen Poe's room. It looked as stark and forbidding as my jail cell on Tortola. I wouldn't have wanted to be stuck here any more than I had there. Come to think of it, Poe, too, had gone over the wall after a semester and dropped out of UVA. For somebody in my frame of mind, this seemed to suggest that prompt departure from Charlottesville was the wisest course of action.

By the next day there rang in my ears a noise as shrill as a burglar alarm. I feared if I didn't make a break right then, I'd be trapped. Better, I reasoned, to join the Army and take my chances of dying in Vietnam than poke along in this dull burg.

But before I made my getaway, I dropped in on George Garrett to tell him good-bye. And, oh yes, to ask a favor. Would he please read a sample of my work and say whether he saw the slightest chance of my becoming a writer?

Garrett's office was smaller but brighter and more welcoming than Edgar Allen Poe's cell. Taped to the wall above his desk was a headline clipped from a tabloid: LIFE WITH KIM NOVAK IS HELL. He had his coat off, his shirtsleeves rolled, and his tie at half-mast. Though he maintained an air of imperturbable cheeriness, he could not have been pleased to see me, or any student for that matter, dogging him so early in the semester. I was a writing teacher's worst nightmare, the kind of nincompoop who demands time and attention and believes that by off-loading his problems along with reams of bad prose, he has reciprocated a kindness.

When I told Garrett I was dropping out, he replied that he was sorry. When I added that I "simply" wanted him to say whether I could become a writer, he said, "Of course you can. That's the thing about writing. All you need is paper and a pencil. Nobody can stop you."

"I mean a published writer."

The furrowed ladder climbed his forehead. He smoothed it with the palm of his hand and pushed back his sparse hair. "That's a different question. No matter what I tell you, it's just an opinion. And you know the old saying. There are only two things everybody has—an asshole and an opinion."

"Your opinion is good enough for me. You see, I've never met a writer before. I'd like you to read my work and tell me whether I'm bullshitting myself."

Sliding open the bottom drawer of the desk, he propped his loafers on it and leaned back in a swivel chair. "Do you feel like you're bullshitting yourself when you're writing?"

"No. But afterward I wonder."

"Everybody wonders afterward. The key is whether you feel like a bullshitter while you're doing it. This isn't a science, you know. I might think your work is terrific. I might think it's terrible. Either way, so what? If you want to be a writer, nothing I say should stop you."

"But it might help me."

He picked up the manila folder of pages I had laid on his desk. He didn't open the folder. He appeared to be weighing it. Then he set it down gently. "Why are you quitting before you've even started classes?"

"I'm tired of school. If I could take your course and nothing else, I'd do it."

"Fine. Register part time."

"I can't afford to stay without a fellowship. And to keep it, I have to be registered full time."

"Wait a minute." He sat up straight. "You're here on a fellowship? A free ride and you're throwing it away? For someone who wants to be a novelist, that's nuts. Why not live off the university's money, stroll through your classes, and concentrate on writing until they catch on and throw you out?"

Garrett, I was beginning to gather, had the sort of iconoclastic cunning that regenerated itself and galvanized others. With balletic hand flourishes and bold body language, he dispensed advice in the same ebullient fashion as he confided a secret or recounted gossip or told a joke. We're in this together, he appeared to be saying, just the two of us, a couple of writers forced by circumstances to figure the odds and find the best way to finagle some free time.

As he talked, he shook a cigarette from a pack of Kools and lit up with a match from a box that carried the logo of the Chateau Marmont in Los Angeles. For Proust, the taste of a *petite madeleine* dunked in an infusion of tea unleashed a tsunami of memory and emotion. For me, the sight of that matchbox served the same purpose. Suddenly, Garrett found himself the repository of a sad tale that I told at lachrymose length about the girl

I loved who got knocked up by another guy. She moved to California and lived on North Harper Street, across Sunset Boulevard from the Chateau Marmont. I had followed her there, ostensibly to help her out of a terrible jam, in reality on the off-chance that she would change her mind about me. She did change it, several times. After some discussion, she rejected my suggestion that we get married and raise the baby as our own. Abortion was then illegal, and neither of us felt comfortable dealing with a back-alley doctor. So we settled on an improvised solution. We lived together for six months. Then she gave the baby up for adoption and dumped me. Which was part of what sent me spiraling off to the islands and Mexico, taking jobs and quitting them, planning to write but never getting around to it.

Hands clasped behind his head, Garrett listened and said little, only nodded and murmured an occasional sympathetic sound. As I achieved full narrative flight, he closed the office door, unlocked a file cabinet, and produced a bottle of Smirnoff vodka. He uncapped it, drank a healthy belt, and passed the bottle to me. Shutting up just long enough to chug a swig, I let the cold fire sizzle through my chest. Then I resumed talking until there was no more to tell.

"Know what I think?" Garrett said, sipping the Smirnoff. "I think you've got the makings of a novel there. I think you should sit tight until things stop spinning, then you should write it."

"You really think so?" I asked, eager to be convinced.

"I sure do. And I look forward to reading it." He gestured to my folder of stories. "I could read these, of course, but I'd rather wait for your best, your latest stuff. See you in class."

Set down in cold type, these words may not sound earthshaking or life-altering, but they had rippling consequences that carried on for years. Such was my shaky footing in the world and my susceptibility to advice from a literary source, that I stayed on in Charlottesville and completed an M.A. and a Ph.D. I met the woman I would marry. I wrote a couple of novels. And not coincidentally I received some much-needed help from the mental health clinic at the UVA Medical School. None of this would have happened had George Garrett not convinced me that I would never go anywhere until I stopped spinning my wheels and stayed in one place for awhile.

★   ★   ★

His seminar, it's no insult to say, was of secondary importance. His books, his personal behavior—a heartening example of how an author might negotiate a career in a world that was largely ignorant of, or oblivious to, literature—and his friendship mattered far more to me. When he chose to, George Garrett could play the conventional pedagogue. His lecture on Nathaniel West and his exegesis of unreliable narration in Truman Capote's *In Cold Blood* were among my most memorable moments in graduate school. But in general, he wore his learning lightly and disguised whatever disappointments he had suffered in life. Although he could be caustic, if wildly amusing, about other writers, he was no less severe with himself nor less likely to laugh at his own expense. Even at their most hilarious, however, his anecdotes had a subtext of seriousness and, at times, sadness.

For all his anecdotal genius, George rarely mentioned his own books. He certainly never bragged about them, nor did he, as many authors do, pepper his conversation with chronological references pegged to the titles of his publications and the dates of awards and prizes. With his trilogy of historical novels—*Death of the Fox, The Succession,* and *Entered from the Sun*—it became apparent that few Renaissance scholars could match his knowledge of Shakespeare and Marlowe, Elizabethan language, courtly love and doss-house ribaldry. Yet George continued to make no great claims for himself.

Instead he expended megatons of energy and hundreds of hours encouraging generations of students, touting the work of his contemporaries, and helping to arrange introductions to editors and agents. Decades later, his maxims still remain in my mind. Nothing is ever lost, he used to say of material that had to be deleted from one manuscript but might come in handy for another. That thought always consoled me—the notion that rough first drafts could be set aside and salvaged by revision, that even the worst mistakes need never be permanent. Garrett had played football at Princeton and boxed in the army, and he often salted his conversation with analogies to sport. About prizefighters, he contended that while rage and a desire for revenge against life's unfairness were what brought them to the Sweet Science, they had to learn to forget, or at least harness, these feelings if they wanted to become boxers. Anybody who entered the ring angry was likely to get knocked flat; a man who lost his temper usually lost the fight. The apothegm was reminiscent of T. S. Eliot's observation that poets had a tradition, not a personality, to express. If they hoped to become writers, people had to sublimate their private demons in the service of craft.

This bit of wisdom struck a resonant chord in me, and I recognized that if I continued to cut loose with the raw, hurt feelings I had hoarded up, they would curdle the most sympathetic reader's interest. At Garrett's urging, I returned to the story I had blithered about that day in his office, and George allowed as how the novel I produced wasn't half bad. He praised the Caribbean setting and said the scenes of skin diving and descriptions of weather and landscape reminded him of James Jones's *Go to the Widowmaker.* But he suggested that I detach myself even further from autobiographical events and the significance I had imposed upon them. After a cooling off period, perhaps I should recast this plot about a sensitive boy betrayed in love into a comedy about youthful self-delusion. This was a polite way of reminding me that if I intended to take writing seriously, I needed to start taking myself much less seriously.

Although Garrett insisted that nobody could make anyone into a writer—you had to do that for yourself—he did once turn me into Robie Macauley. This was more in the nature of a necessity than another of George's hijinks. Having organized a televised colloquium on the future of fiction, he discovered that a featured speaker had gone missing. Robie Macauley, longtime editor of the staid *Kenyon Review* and the newly appointed fiction editor at *Playboy,* didn't show up. Rather than cancel the program and lose rare publicity for the cause of literature, Garrett led me on camera as a substitute. Or to be precise, an impostor. The TV moderator, a middle-aged matron with a smile as lacquered as her hair, appeared not to notice anything anomalous about a twenty-three-year-old boy passing himself off as Hugh Hefner's latest hireling.

Buoyed by success, I remained in role and attended a reception later that evening wearing a bogus name tag. An old scowling man accosted me at the punch bowl. He leaned close, squinting at my face, then at my tag. In his right ear he wore a hearing aid with a thick pink wire that wormed down his neck and under his shirt collar. In confusion, he fiddled at the controls to this device as if to bring me into sharp focus by adjusting the sound level. As he groped, I noted his name tag—he was Malcolm Cowley, august man of letters, author of *Exile's Return* and *Second Flowering.* He had known Hemingway, Fitzgerald, and Dos Passos. He knew everybody—and now he knew me as a charlatan.

"You're not Robie Macauley," he roared.

I attempted to mumble an explanation, but Cowley didn't buy it. "You're not Robie Macauley," he repeated, so loud he silenced the room.

George rushed over to my rescue. I presume he managed to calm the irate Malcolm Cowley. I didn't wait around to watch. In ignominious retreat, I fled the reception, feeling for the first time, though not the last, the scourge of being unmasked as not the writer I wanted to be.

WILLIAM STYRON

University of Virginia, Charlottesville

IN April, 1966, William Styron was scheduled to give a reading at the University of Virginia from his long-awaited new novel. Already the subject of spirited discussion in *Harper's* and *Esquire* as well as in literary magazines and academic journals, *The Confessions of Nat Turner* dealt with one of the few slave revolts in the pre–Civil War South, a brief, bloody spasm of violence that took place in the Tidewater region of Virginia, not far from Styron's boyhood home of Newport News.

Since I was writing my master's thesis on Styron—indeed, I would go on to do my Ph.D. dissertation on him as well—it seemed a stroke of great good fortune when I was asked to pick him up at the airport, deliver him to his digs at the Colonnade Club, and escort him around Charlottesville if he so desired. The trouble was I didn't have a car. I did, however, have a girlfriend who not only owned an Oldsmobile convertible, but who was an avid fan of Styron's fiction. Hoping to meet him, Linda Kirby loaned me her car and planned to attend his reading.

Grateful as I was for Linda's car and her company, I had mixed feelings about her meeting Styron. Just a month before, she and I had had a run-in with James Dickey, the banjo-plucking national bard who had de-

scended on UVA with his sixteen-year-old son, Chris. Reading—no, he
did more than that—declaiming his verse in an amphitheater to a thousand boisterous listeners, Dickey broke off during "Sheep Child" to express disappointment at the paltry size of the crowd. He interrupted
himself a second time, during "Cherry Log Road," to sing out, "God-
damn, I forgot how great this poem is! It deserves to be heard by the
whole university."

Afterward, a passel of students and faculty repaired to the Colonnade
Club for refreshments and a chat with the great man. As Linda and I
came through the receiving line, Dickey paid me little mind. Years later,
in the film of his novel *Deliverance,* he would play a redneck sheriff. That
night he rehearsed the role. With a highball glass in his ham-sized fist and
a leer on his boiled-ham face, he hovered over Linda, leaning cozily close
yet speaking loudly enough to be heard by his son. Chris would go on
to become the Paris bureau chief of *Newsweek* and an author of his own
books, but that night he was just a boy listening to his famous father flirt
with a twenty-two-year-old girl.

"Honey," said the honey-voiced lout, "why don't me and you go to
a motel?"

Linda, God love her, attempted to paraphrase the putdown Paul
Newman unloaded whenever anyone implied that he wasn't faithful to
Joanne Woodward. "Why would I go out for hamburger," Newman de-
manded, "when I have steak at home?" But Linda had an endearing habit
of mixing metaphors, and she asked Dickey, "Why would I go out for a
Hershey bar when I have *mousse au chocolat* at home?"

"At least a Hershey bar's hard and has nuts," Dickey shot back, prov-
ing that you played word games with a writer at your peril.

Still, I imagined a clear delineation between poets and novelists, and
I refused to believe that anybody who wrote prose as gorgeous and high-
plumed as William Styron's could possibly be a drunk, skirt-chasing
churl. Of course, as a grad student, I had been schooled against commit-
ting the biographical fallacy. An author didn't need to be good in order
to be great. But in Styron's case, I had always had trouble separating the
man and his work.

The instant I opened his first novel, *Lie Down in Darkness,* I felt I had
reentered my childhood and become reacquainted with my tormented
family. In Peyton Loftis, the suicidal daughter of an alcoholic father and a
mentally disturbed mother, I saw myself, I saw my hard-drinking step-

father and bipolar mother. And when I learned about Styron's state during the composition of *Lie Down in Darkness,* I recognized some of the
same forces that drove me to write.

"The book was a form of self-psychoanalysis," Styron acknowledged
in an interview, "which freed me of any need to go to a shrink. At the
age of twenty-two, when I started that book, I remember being in a wildly unhappy state of neurotic angst. I had very few underpinnings. My
emotional life was in upheaval. I'd lost what little faith I had in religion.
I was just adrift, and the only thing that allowed me any kind of anchor
was the idea of creating a work of literature which somehow would be a
thing of beauty in the old-fashioned sense of the word and would also be
a kind of freeing for me of these terrible conflicts that were in my soul.
And by the time I got to the end of that tunnel I was a relatively happy
young man."

Published when Styron was twenty-six, *Lie Down in Darkness* was, in
Norman Mailer's words, "so good . . . one felt a kind of awe about
Styron. He gave promise of becoming a great writer, great not like Hemingway nor even like Faulkner whom he resembled a bit, but perhaps
like Hawthorne. And there were minor echoes of Fitzgerald and Malcolm Lowry."

Since his rocket-burst arrival in the literary constellation, Styron had
gone on to publish *The Long March,* a novella about the Marine Corps,
and *Set This House on Fire,* which some reviewers regarded as an unsuc-
cessful effort to transpose the Southern Gothic to Rome and the Amalfi
coast. But even in its excesses, it was an ambitious book, one that left me
longing to live in Italy, praying to publish a novel by the time I was
twenty-six, and eager to meet its author.

Among other connections that I imagined linked Styron and me,
there was his wife, Rose. An editor at the *Paris Review,* she had once
rejected a short story of mine. But rejected it nicely, encouragingly, ap-
pending a scrawled note to the bottom of a form letter: "These are two
well told tales, but I'm not sure they should be joined." At the age of
nineteen, I treasured that sentence, and in the absence of any tangible
evidence of talent, I clung to it. In my enormous naïveté, I believed that
to have a story accepted, or a novel published, would constitute a kind
of redemption.

How I had managed to maintain my innocence in literary matters
when cynicism ruled the rest of my life, I cannot explain. I knew that

writers could be venal, meanspirited, and as competitive as aluminum siding salesmen. I knew that publishers expected profits, reviewers were often splenetic and unfair, and that authors as different as Henry James, Fitzgerald, and Faulkner had suffered crackups, drinking binges, and stretches in loony bins. From research for my thesis, I knew that Styron himself had come under merciless attack. Critics accused him of laziness, complaining that he took too long between books and unspooled passages of purple prose whenever he had nothing original to say. In a pugnacious essay for *Esquire,* "Some Children of the Goddess: Further Evaluations of the Talent in the Room," Norman Mailer had lambasted the nine most celebrated novelists of his generation and saved his lowest blows for Styron. He claimed that bitterness had "poisoned [Styron's] reaction to everything," and "years of envy began to eat into his character." What's more, he wrote that Styron had betrayed his best friend, James Jones, by reading his books aloud at dinner parties and lampooning "the worst parts of *Some Came Running.*" Finally, Mailer dismissed *Set This House on Fire* as "a big maggoty novel. Four or five half-great short stories were buried like pullulating organs in a corpse of fecal matter. . . . It was the magnum opus of a fat spoiled rich boy."

Those three damning adjectives—fat, spoiled, rich—began to crop up in other articles and on the publishing grapevine. Since Rose came from a wealthy family that owned a department-store chain in Baltimore, Styron was presumed to be sponging off her trust fund. They lived in rural Roxbury, Connecticut—"Styron's Acres," Mailer dubbed the place—and had a summer home on Martha's Vineyard. Enemies carped that he spent too much time in glittering social circles. He had gone soft, they said, lost touch with his roots, turned into a snob and invested more energy in manipulating the press and prize-giving committees than in writing.

So as I sat waiting in Charlottesville's tiny air terminal, I decided that I had better bank my fires. Just because I liked the man's work didn't mean that I'd like him, nor that he would show the slightest interest in me. I was here to chauffeur him, I reminded myself, not court his friendship or curry approval.

When the plane landed, Styron disembarked in a state of moist dishevelment, his tie askew, his suit accordion-pleated at the knees and elbows, his face glistening with perspiration. Since Piedmont had cornered the market on air traffic into and out of town, this was often the condi-

tion of passengers climbing off small prop planes that had bumped
through the rough thermal currents over the Blue Ridge. But Styron
conceded he was also feeling rocky after rejecting the cellophane-
wrapped in-flight meal and consuming his lunch in liquid form.

We drove with the windows down. Warm spring wind rifled through
Linda's Oldsmobile. I may have asked about the weather up north or
commented on the dogwoods and flowering Judas blooming along
Route 29. On the ground beneath every tree, bright coin-sized blossoms
were scattered in spendthrift abundance. Whatever I babbled was intended to ward off what I feared I'd say if I weren't careful. The words
stood on tiptoes in my throat and screamed to jump out. In an attempt
to beat them back I told Styron how much I admired his books. But
mention of his writing made it all the harder not to cave in to temptation
and tell him that I wrote too. The abrupt boiling up of infantile ego and
irrational need, the all-compelling urge—I simply couldn't resist it. We
hadn't reached Charlottesville's city limits before I cut loose: "Would
you read my novel?"

For a published author no request from a stranger carries such a freight
of dread. I know this now. I must have sensed it then. But I was power-
less in the grasp of my compulsion and in the presence of a famous writer.
Styron would have been within his rights to order me to turn around
and take him back to the airport. Judging by the pained expression on
his slightly asymmetrical face, I thought he might shoulder open the door
and roll out onto the highway. Instead, in a quiet voice that retained faint
vestiges of a Tidewater accent, he said, "I can't do it now, Mike. Not
while I'm finishing *Nat Turner*. Maybe later."

That was good enough for me. Willing to wait, glad to, I sped on
through April sunshine, relieved to have gotten past the hardest part of
the journey and now ready to enjoy the rest of it. Once we were on the
Grounds, approaching the red brick arcades of the West Ranges, I remarked that after reading *Lie Down in Darkness* I could never view the
university again except through the jeweled prism of his prose. I quoted
sentences verbatim—evocations of autumn, the apple-scented afternoons, the sad light, the drunken crowds at Scott Stadium, the student
body staggering back to Rugby Road, the poignancy of Mr. Loftis lost
in an alcoholic fog, searching for Peyton at a fraternity party.

"Is it still hard to get laid around here?" Styron interrupted my literary
maundering. "I mean, it used to be pretty grim. I remember visiting

friends at UVA. I'd drive up from Duke and they'd say we had to drive
two more hours just to see a girl. Then it was anybody's guess how far
you'd get with her."

"Things have changed," I said with bogus worldliness. But I feared
the day was about to take a terrible turn and Styron was going to ask me
to set him up with a woman.

As we pulled into the parking lot behind the Colonnade Club, he
breathed deeply, maybe inhaling the scent of boxwood hedges or perhaps
screwing up the courage to spill some obsession he had in mind. "Can I
ask you a favor, Mike?"

"Sure," I said, feeling anything but certain.

"Would you drive me to Monticello? I know you're busy and want
to get back to your friends, but I'd like to revisit Jefferson's place."

"I'd be glad to." I exhaled in relief.

We dropped his suitcase in his room and headed for the hills east of
town. Styron stressed that he appreciated every opportunity to glean
firsthand information about Nat Turner's world. To be sure, he said, the
rebellion had occurred in an environment and a topography altogether
different from Albemarle County. Few slaves had had a master like
Thomas Jefferson or a mock-Palladian villa like Monticello to call home.
Still, there was always something for a novelist to learn. He grinned a
lopsided grin. "And it's always easier to do research than get down to
writing."

Styron once admitted in an interview, "I've never written anything
yet that I didn't write so slowly that it drove me half mad." He liked to
stay up late, and that rarely left much time in the morning. He worked
in the afternoon and kept at it until he produced one handwritten page
on yellow legal paper. Emending and editing as he went along, he was
never satisfied with a sentence until he got it precisely right. But he seldom needed to rewrite the first draft. There were sprinters who raced
through a manuscript, then revised it in a dozen drafts. And there were
bleeders who dribbled out a book drop by drop, word by word. Styron
was a bleeder.

At Monticello a chatty docent generally escorted visitors through the
main house, around the gardens, and into the outbuildings. But the
woman who tagged along with us did little talking as soon as she realized
that Styron knew far more than she did. Not that he was overbearing
about it. He simply pointed out things that interested him—Jefferson's

bed with its built-in lapboard for late-night reading, the milled wooden floor planks with wooden nails, the nearly subterranean slaves' quarters.

On the return trip to Charlottesville, Styron asked, "Do you have a little more time you could spare me? There's a family in the county that I haven't seen in a long while, and I'd like to look them up."

By the '80s, Albemarle County would become a haven for Wall Street magnates, Hollywood stars, and wealthy Europeans seeking rural prop-erty and privacy. Among the millionaires who moved in, there were said to be several billionaires, but they were drab, shadowy specters compared to Sissy Spacek, Jessica Lange, Sam Shepard, and John Grisham, who also owned farms in the countryside. Already in the '60s, however, the county had its share of well-heeled residents, and given Styron's reputa-tion as a spoiled rich boy, I assumed his friends might be members of the landed gentry with links to the literary community. William Faulkner's widow and his daughter, Jill, lived there, as did Walter Barratt, a noted bibliophile and collector who had started donating rare manuscripts and first editions to the university's Alderman Library.

But when Styron directed me to follow the winding, tar-crowned road to Crozet, I quickly concluded that our destination wasn't going to be some baronial manse. Back then, that corner of the county wasn't just unfashionable. It was the butt of jokes about rednecks and hill apes and inbred hollers crowded with trailer camps, wheelless cars raised up on cinderblocks, and moonshiners with twitchy fingers on shotgun triggers. You could smell Crozet before you saw it. The site of Morton's chicken-rendering and meat-packing plant, it moldered in noisome juices and blowing feathers.

We parked in front of a small, asbestos-shingled bungalow surrounded by a chain-link fence. A barking dog charged out of the house, followed by an old woman in slippers and a floral housecoat. I thought the dog and the woman meant to chase us away. But Styron brushed past the yapping mutt and stepped into the woman's embracing arms.

"Sty!" she crooned. "Sty, I can't believe it's you."

When they finished hugging and shouting how happy they were to see one another, Styron waved me over. "Mike, I want you to meet an old, old friend, Mrs. Peyton. Her boy, Tommy, and I were at school to-gether. If it wasn't for him, I'd never have passed trigonometry. Many's

the time he and I came here from Christchurch for a good meal and
some TLC."

"Oh, Sty! Sty!" Mrs. Peyton still couldn't believe it.

The small white-haired woman and the tall novelist in his rumpled
suit walked arm in arm into the house. Mrs. Peyton offered iced tea, then
caught herself and said she knew Sty would prefer bourbon. We settled
in the kitchen, a bright space with afternoon sunlight slanting through an
open window and refracting off empty Mason jars and jelly glasses on the
drainboard. I took a bit of bourbon and nursed it while they reminisced.
Styron, who I already recognized could be laconic and sunk deep into
himself, was at ease and outgoing in this setting. He and Mrs. Peyton
exchanged information—ages and names and dates and diseases and
deaths—about family and friends. She asked after Rose and each of Styron's children, and joshed that he should have more kids.

"Four's enough," he said. "I'm forty-one, too old to change any more
diapers."

She praised his books and said how proud she was that he had done
well. It impressed her that he was speaking that night at the university.
Styron seemed pleased and mentioned that he had recently been made a
member of the American Academy of Arts and Letters. Though this
meant less to her than his reading at UVA, she congratulated him and
said she'd pass the news along to Tommy.

As afternoon advanced toward evening, it occurred to me that Styron
had yet to put in an official appearance at the university. Nobody outside
the Colonnade Club knew he had arrived. If we didn't get back soon,
he'd be late for the faculty cocktail and dinner party, and I'd be in
trouble.

With a great laying on of hands and last-minute messages of love to
Rose and the kids, Mrs. Peyton walked us to the car and waved good-
bye. Immediately, a palpable miasma of gloom descended upon Styron.
It isn't mere hindsight and his public history of depression that have persuaded me that from the first moment I saw him he teetered on the brink
of sadness. Dealing with my mother had alerted me to mood swings. The
most Styron admitted to me, though, was that he didn't relish the next
few hours. He said he hated academics.

Not one to take a hint, I promptly turned the ground under my feet
into quicksand by asking whether he had named Peyton Loftis in *Lie
Down in Darkness* after Mrs. Peyton.

He fixed his eyes on the two-lane blacktop. After an agonizing interval during which the only sound was the adhesive rip of rubber on asphalt, he drawled, "I guess I did."

I feared I had lost him and fallen into the untouchable caste of bookworms and library rats. But once we reached the university, he put a hand on my shoulder and said, "I'll see you at the reading, won't I? Don't let me down, Mike. Don't leave me there alone with a lot of people I don't know."

I promised I'd show up and bring along Slim. That's what I called Linda back then. On one of our first dates, we had watched a scratchy print of *To Have and Have Not* at a student film society. Among the movie's many pleasures—Faulkner did the screenplay of Hemingway's novel for Howard Hawkes—it featured a willowy Lauren Bacall, whom Humphrey Bogart referred to as Slim. I had pinned the nickname on Linda. Now no one calls her that except William Styron.

While he was off at the Boar's Head or Farmington or some professor's house, Linda and I supped on cheeseburgers, french fries, and chocolate milkshakes at the College Inn on the Corner. After the draining day, I needed to refuel as I recounted in detail my time with Styron. I saved the best news for last. "He said he'll read my novel. Not now, but after Nat Turner is off his desk."

"That's wonderful," Linda agreed.

And in the truest sense, it did seem a wonder that Styron would do it. Almost four decades later, it still strikes me as a miraculous rite of passage in which I advanced from a captive audience of kind teachers and close friends to a discerning reader who had better things to do than bolster the morale of a fledgling novelist. The thought that Styron might detest the book didn't deter me. People had already expressed reservations about it, and I had no inflated notions of my ability. But I wanted my life to change, and I believed that regardless of his reaction, things for me would never be the same if he read the manuscript.

The leather-upholstered room in the Alderman Library was smaller and more sedate than the amphitheater where James Dickey had done his star turn, and Styron's performance had none of the prating and preening of that occasion. Yet there was a sizable crowd, and Styron read in a subdued voice appropriate to the passage he had chosen—a scene of Nat Turner in his cell ruminating on past events while awaiting execution. If not in style, then certainly in tone and metaphysical speculation, the passage called to mind Albert Camus's *The Stranger* and the concluding pages of Arthur Koestler's *Darkness at Noon*.

Though the crowd was clearly caught up in what it heard, Styron seemed distracted or displeased. He seldom raised his eyes from the manuscript, and as he turned the pages, his hand shook, and this shaking passed into the paper. It came to me with the jolt of a genuine discovery that not every writer easily assumed the role of public figure. After years of solitude, the transition from artist to performer, from author to entertainer, exacted a price, particularly for someone sensitive and/or shy.

Afterward, during the question-and-answer session, Styron grew more restive. When A. K. Davis, a professor a few years short of retirement, posed not so much an inquiry about slavery, Virginia, and the Civil War as an impenetrable conundrum, the sort that a student might confront during a Ph.D. oral exam, Styron gave him short shrift. Then he dismissed half a dozen more questions with monosyllables, and his brusqueness increased when somebody brought up Norman Mailer. Styron said he didn't intend to talk about the deterioration of his friendship with Mailer.

"My question is textual," the man said, "not personal. In *Set This House on Fire,* there's a character named Mason Flagg. You present him as an artistic poseur, a rapist who experiments with drugs and orgies. The narrator refers to him as 'the Apostle of the Groin.' Is he modeled after Norman Mailer?"

"No. He's based on Leroi Jones." Cutting off any chance of a follow-up question, Styron swung around to someone on the far side of the room, hurried through another curt reply, and decided he had had enough.

The moderator, Joseph Blotner, Faulkner's biographer, thanked him, thanked the audience, and announced that there would be drinks and an opportunity for people to speak to tonight's guest. Styron stationed himself near the bar, an aloof presence obviously in no mood to suffer fools or make small talk. I hesitated a moment, then with misgivings shepherded Linda over and introduced her as Slim.

Immediately his expression brightened. He slipped an arm around her waist and clutched my coat sleeve. "Stay right here. Soon as I finish this drink, I'll say my polite good-byes and we'll go back to my room for some good bourbon."

It didn't escape me that we were running interference for Styron, that he was using us as a picket fence between him and people he didn't care to deal with. Yet regardless of his other reasons for keeping us close to him, I believed he also recognized Linda and me as kindred spirits, literary soulmates. When he decided he had done his duty to the Alderman Library, we marched out three abreast, swaying slightly from alcohol and high spirits. Our jubilant voices violated the green hush of the Lawn, and our steps rang out on the scalloped wooden stairs of the Colonnade Club.

At the door to his room I paused, ready to call it a night, wary of pressing our luck. But Bill—by now we were on a first name basis—insisted we come in and have a nightcap. As we drank Jim Beam from toothbrush glasses, he spat out the sour dregs of the evening. "God save me from academics," he moaned. Rounding on the man who had raised the question about Mailer, he wisecracked, "In bed I bet he and his wife jerk each other off. Give me the company of writers any day."

He started to tell us about his friends James Jones, the expat novelist in Paris, James Baldwin, who had lived in Styron's studio in Roxbury early in the writing of Nat Turner, and Carlos Fuentes, with whom he had traveled in Mexico. "I went down there to tour the ruins of Yucatán and damn near killed myself," Styron said. "A defectively wired lamp zapped me with enough volts to put me down for the count."

"Slim and I are going there this summer," I told him. I had never made it to Europe, but I had been to Mexico half a dozen times, driving, riding rickety buses, even hitchhiking around the country. As I saw it, every aspiring author needed to visit such places, experience life in the raw, eat on the cheap, and take risks (mostly to the alimentary tract).

"The three of us should go together," Styron said. "You'd love Fuentes."

Linda seconded the motion. At that hour, after the improbable day and the quantities we had drunk, the idea seemed wildly appealing and plausible. I envisioned us riding on the roof of a bus, drinking wine from a bota, like Jake Barnes, Bill Gorton, and Lady Brett in The Sun Also Rises. Why shouldn't we do it? What was to stop us?

As Bill poured more bourbon, my brain acquired the false clarity that comes in the late stages of inebriation and exhaustion. Mention of Mexico had brought to mind Spain and Hemingway, and that led circuitously to Styron's writing, which led me, in turn, in my boozy exhilaration, to brag that I knew his books better than he did. I remembered passages, whole paragraphs, and proved it by reciting them. I catalogued patterns of imagery amplified from one novel to the next, allusions to composers and pieces of music, descriptions of Papageno and Papagena dancing together on "some far and fantastic lawn." I finished by pointing out his repeated references to the sea, to tides and undertows, to characters unhelmed and unmoored.

Styron's lips thinned, his eyes narrowed. The slight asymmetry of his face—one ear looked lower than the other—was magnified by the bourbon I had swilled. Judging by his expression, he might have been pensive or pissed off. I couldn't guess which and feared he might categorize me as the sort of dimwitted academic he detested.

Instead, he picked up the box that contained the typescript of *The Confessions of Nat Turner,* lifted out the first chapter, and started reading aloud. Nat was dreaming in his cell, imagining himself afloat in the bottom of a rowboat, bobbing on river currents out into the choppier waters of the Chesapeake Bay, then through oceanic waves that tilt toward Africa. That was Bill's response to my remarks. He didn't have to say anything. I believed we were, at least for that instant, on the same aesthetic wave-length.

By the time Linda and I left, it was 4 a.m. We had made plans to meet Styron in the morning and drive him to the airport. So little more than five hours later we stumbled back to the Colonnade Club, squinty-eyed and stricken with thunderous headaches. The door to Styron's room was open, as was the one to the bathroom, and we heard him in there, hacking and gagging. Alarmed, Linda and I exchanged a glance. We didn't know whether to withdraw discreetly or to rush in and administer CPR.

Bill emerged ashen-faced, his tie thrown back over one shoulder. Though not as lively as last night, he was no less friendly, and as we sped up Route 29 in the Oldsmobile, he scribbled down his phone numbers and addresses in Roxbury and on Martha's Vineyard. He wanted us to keep in touch. He wanted us to travel to Mexico together and meet Carlos Fuentes. And there was another thing he wanted, a great favor. The United States Information Service had him scheduled to fly to Russia to deliver a series of lectures. He didn't feel up to that. He said he intended to catch a plane to LaGuardia, rent a car, and drive straight home to Roxbury. Better to get back to *Nat Turner* than travel to Russia and yack about writing, he said. Would Slim please call the State Department—he gave her the number and the name of his contact—and inform the USIS that Mr. Styron couldn't make it? Sorry. Maybe another time.

At the terminal, we tarried in harsh sunlight, blinking and unsteady as troopers just back from battle, half giddy, half guilty that we had survived.

"Bye-bye, Slim." After kissing her on both cheeks, he shook my hand. "Write," he said.

I took that to mean write fiction, work on my novel. I did that, but I also wrote him a letter as meticulously crafted as a Metaphysical poem. For long hours I labored over its diction, grammar, spelling, and punctuation. Then I dropped it into a mailbox with the same soaring desperation as a shipwrecked sailor stuffs a message into a bottle and tosses it into the sea. I doubted I would ever receive an answer. But weeks later, Styron wrote back.

May 30, 1966

Dear Mike,

Never feel self-conscious—which you seem to worry about being. That was a good letter you wrote me and I'm grateful for it. Aside from Slim, whose beauty takes precedence over almost anything mortal, your presence was the most cheering thing that happened to me during my somewhat rushed visit to the University and I do want to thank you for your attention—even if somewhat belatedly. The entire trip was made golden by your company (also by Slim's; forgive me if I seem not to be able to get her out of my mind) and you took the curse off a lot of those academics—so much so that I can even forgive you your having used me as a subject for scholarly study.

I was quite serious about your letting me see your novel when it gets to the end or toward the end. Early fall would be a good time to let me read it. God willing, I will have gotten to the end of my own by then and will have a nice big free open generous mind which, however, will retain enough critical objectivity so that you will be subjected to the most earnest critical scrutiny. Then we shall go to Mexico (with Slim, of course) and wallow in those pleasures and depravities while Random House gets the presses cranking and turns you, overnight, into a Capote-style billionaire.

My most profound thanks again for your hospitality. Keep in touch and never give up the faith.

Ever Yours,

Bill (*not* Mr.) Styron

As a conscientious deconstructor of texts, I should have had no trouble taking a few selected aspects of this letter at face value and discounting the rest as exaggeration. But I yearned to see it all as biblical truth. Though I suppose I knew it was unlikely I would become a Capote-style billionaire, perhaps Random House would one day publish me. And if I granted that possibility, it didn't seem out of the question that Styron and I might travel to Mexico. Whether I'd feel comfortable bringing Linda along was another question. Quite sensibly, I wanted to keep her to myself. But I went ahead and mailed Bill the manuscript on the understanding that he wouldn't get around to it until autumn. Then I started crossing days off the calendar, anxiously awaiting word from him.

Of all the difficulties that confront a writer, the subject of patience, of putting one foot in front of another, one word after another, seldom rises for discussion. Yet nothing poses a greater danger than the temptation to rush, to push a story or character in an unwelcome direction, or to force a response from a reader who isn't ready to offer it. When in a moment of madness I couldn't abide the wait any longer and phoned William Styron that summer on Martha's Vineyard, he sounded out of sorts.

"Am I getting you at a bad time?" I asked.

"Yeah. You caught me disciplining a dog."

Disciplining a dog? Nobody, I concluded, could miss his meaning. In my slobbering and bumbling impertinence, I had behaved like a puppy that wasn't housebroken.

"Sorry," I said. "Just wanted to touch base and check whether you're still up for a trip to Mexico."

"Not now." His terseness gradually loosened into gentler Tidewater rhythms. "You and Slim better go on ahead without me. Send me a postcard."

We did as advised. We set out in a battered Saab whose two-cycle engine sounded like a sewing machine. Every time we filled the tank, we had to top off the gasoline with a pint of oil—a practice that strained the credulity of service-station attendants in Texas and provoked nervous snickers once we crossed the border. Everybody, including Linda, expected us to be incinerated. Nobody believed we'd make it to Mexico City, or to Acapulco, then up the Pacific coast over a rutted unpaved road to Zihuatanejo.

Though I sometimes suffered grave doubts myself about the wisdom of what we were doing, a gauntlet had been dropped. I told Linda this was a test, not a mere vacation. Much as we loved one another, I needed to know before we married whether she could live with a penniless writer. So we slept rough in irrigated fields and arid *barrancas* beside the road. We ate slumgullion at bus stations and cantinas. We saved our money for bullfight tickets and a splurge in Zihuatanejo, where we rented a room for three dollars a day, a price that included fresh-baked bread at breakfast and freshly caught red snapper for dinner.

Linda passed with high marks in every category. She loved the food, the bullfights, the tequila, and the transparent lizards that skittered across the ceiling of our room. She didn't mind the mosquitoes and spiders, and since she was fluent in Spanish, she felt at home among Mexicans.

I, on the other hand, came down with chronic diarrhea, couldn't stomach anything except warm beer, and lay awake at night, my sleep spoiled by creatures that scuttled, hooted, hissed, and stung. In a last stab at impressing Linda with my *savoir faire* and masculine competence, I hired a village fisherman who owned a rubber dinghy and some odds and ends of skin diving equipment. For ten dollars he agreed to ferry us to an island a mile offshore where we could snorkel and spear fish amid gleaming coral beds. It was the perfect opportunity to demonstrate what I had learned last summer on Tortola.

Perched at the bow of the rubber boat, Linda faced into the wind, beautiful and sleek as the polished figurehead on a sailing ship, her hair fluttering about her bare shoulders. She shouted and pointed to a palm-fringed green speck on the horizon. It looked a lot more than a mile away. She didn't mind, but I was beginning to. Beyond the placid waters of the bay, we banged into the mountainous Pacific, and each steep wave tipped us into a deep trough, then shot us to the crest of the next roller. Within minutes, to my shame, I was seasick and retching over the side.

The fisherman laughed. Linda offered to turn back, but I said it was nothing, just a touch of indigestion, and we ploughed on. Once on the island, I scrambled up the stony beach, bent double with dry heaves. Was there, I wondered, some way to be helicoptered back to Zihuatanejo?

Linda said we didn't need to snorkel today, we'd try it another time, but I insisted and gathered up the flippers and masks. The smirking fisherman asked whether I had the strength to handle a spear gun. Ignoring him, I grabbed it and led Linda into the ocean. Soothed by cool water, my quaking belly settled, my nausea ebbed. When a fat, slow-moving fish hove into view, I saw it as a can't-miss target and a chance to rehabilitate my worth in Linda's eyes.

Sure enough, the spear zinged it just behind the gills. But as I hauled it in, the fish suddenly mutated from a finned creature into a spiked cannonball. It was all I could do to prevent what I now recognized as a blowfish, a snorkeler's nightmare, from towing me to the bottom. Kicking and splashing, I wrestled it out of the waves and onto the sand, where the fisherman beat it to death with an oar.

On the return boat trip, as I cradled my belly and gagged up bile, it came to me that I had better marry Linda right away, if she would still have me. We were perfectly matched—she a hearty Hemingway, I a tender, sensitive bud in the Zelda Fitzgerald mode. We honeymooned in Haiti, in the dry-rotted, disintegrating Grand Hotel Oloffson, where Graham Greene had set *The Comedians*. If that weren't enough to make me imagine we were living in a novel, what was described as an attempted coup struck Port-au-Prince during our stay, and hotel guests huddled indoors while the Tonton Macoute patrolled the streets. As it turned out, the coup was actually a domestic squabble within the Duvalier family. When Papa Doc's wife locked him in the toilet, he pressed an emergency alarm that summoned guards and flooded the city with confused troops.

By the time we returned from Haiti, a letter from William Styron awaited me. More than a year after our memorable meeting in Charlottesville, he had read my novel.

July 22, 1967

Dear Mike:

I have just gotten back your manuscript from my friend, whose opinion lit.-wise I respect, and indeed I am sorry to have taken so long—my reasons being that the ms. arrived while I was in Europe and languished there for a full month before I returned, the other—more important—being that I have until only the past few weeks been unable to disentangle myself from the final details attendant upon the publication of *Nat Turner*, proof-reading, changes, additional proof-reading for the long section that is going to appear in the Sept. *Harper's,* etc. So now, in the clear, I have finished the ms., and my friend too, and we seem to agree on all major points.

The first and best point is that you are quite obviously a *writer,* that is, you know how to write, and for you words are not lumpish things to fling on the paper but units of the thought-process to be used meticulously, imaginatively, and with care. You are excellent at rendering mood, have a really fine eye and instinct for nature and the weather, and I was continually impressed, really impressed, by your uncanny gift for dialogue. Your ear here is really magnificent; all that tough idiomatic 20th century speech comes through perfectly, without a single hitch—not just the speech itself, either, but speech in connection with other speech, the dramatic inter-relationship of people talking—as on a stage. All that is truly first-rate.

I wish I could say that with all my admiration for your quite obvious gifts I felt that this novel succeeds as a book, but I have too many reservations about it to say that I think it does. For one thing, I think there is something about the *theme* (in other words, what the writer is trying to say) that bugs me. Your story is about a young man named Chris who, fleeing a rather unhappy relationship with a girl in the U.S., takes off and sets up housekeeping with four or five oddly-assorted fellow-Americans of both sexes on a West Indian island. The story alternates between flashbacks about his connection with the very pregnant girl, whom he loves, and his present situation with Ted and Gerald and Marty and Simone. What frankly troubles and perplexes me about your story, however, is that very little really *happens*; there is very little development either in terms of plot (I hate to use that old-fashioned word) or character. There is a lot of drinking, a lot of talk (quite good and accurate, as I've said) about screwing and booze, some action on the water, but I'm never really certain just where the story is leading us. To be quite blunt, I honestly don't understand what the *significance* of all this is. None of the characters change, that is, nothing in the process of the story happens to change them or to allow the reader to perceive new insights as to what makes people

tick. Ted is noisy and raucous in the beginning, loudly entangled
in his complicated relationships with Marty and Simone, and he
remains that to the very end. Chris himself undergoes no development either, so far as I can see; he rather listlessly observes the she-
nanigans of his fellow housemates, screws Marty, has a spell in jail,
broods about his knocked-up girl, gets the mild hots for Karen,
but nothing else really happens to him; neither he nor we—the
readers—are in any way changed. There seems to be little dramatic
tension in the story. Nothing really *happens* as I say; I hate to be
repetitious and abuse that word, but it is the only phrase I know
how to use to describe my feeling that you had not so much constructed a novel with shifting moods, new insight into character,
and a schema of dramatic tensions as a long and I'm afraid too-
often monotonous record of loud and drunken conversations between or among, rather, a group of not very interesting people. In
short, I honestly can't figure out what the novel is all about.

It especially makes me unhappy to say all this when, as I've already stated, you have so obviously a writer's real gifts: Keen ear
for talk, skill at description, and a gutsy sense of the way people
yammer at and exacerbate each other when they are confined together as these people are. But honestly, and to repeat, I just don't
think you have in this book discovered a *theme*: which is to say that
possibly you have not thought out that striking and original thing
in yourself that it is absolutely imperative to have as a writer if you
are to arrest the attention of 20th-century Americans already so
distracted by the Vietnam war, television, pot, LSD, pornography
and 10,000 other delights.

I hate to be in the magisterial position of telling a young writer
what I think is wrong with his work; after all, it is all too clear that
I may be wrong too. But you asked for my opinion and I gave it,
and I hope it won't create too wrong an effect. The important
thing to me is that you are a writer, with all the fine potential that
that simple word implies. Just as important is the fact that you are
still very young, and have so much opportunity to do the big thing
in the fullness of time. I frankly don't think that you have found
yourself—your true voice—in this book, but I have no doubt that
you will before very long. I would not have gone on at such length

about your work if I did not have faith in what will come from you in the future.

In case that it is any comfort to you, I might report that (although at your age [24] I had not produced a novel) I had an equivalent amount of pages of short stories that now I am glad I put away upon the shelf.

Best of luck always. I have no doubt that you will overcome.

> Yours ever,
>
> Bill Styron

Disappointed as I was that he didn't like the novel, and although I questioned how much encouragement to draw from his comments, I realized something remarkable had occurred. It wasn't just that Styron believed I was "quite obviously a writer" and would "do the big thing in the fullness of time." It was that he had done more than skim the manuscript and respond with polite evasions and tepid good wishes. He identified its flaws as well as its few strengths, and took the time to discuss what I could do to grow as a writer. What moved me most—and does so every time I reread the letter—was Styron's generosity of spirit, his collegiality and readiness to assume an obligation to a neophyte for no better reason than that we both, though vastly different in talent and temperament and age, were committed to writing.

The letter reveals volumes about William Styron—the seriousness and integrity he has always brought to his fiction, the kindness and concern he has shown lost souls, no matter whether they languished in jail, on death row, or in the Laocoön coils of their own unrealized ambitions. It also proves, if such proof is required, that he wasn't the spoiled rich boy and literary networker his critics accused him of being.

Bill and I never have gotten around to making a trip to Mexico. But we have kept in touch, and over the past thirty-five years we have renewed our acquaintance in Paris and Rome and in Austin, when I taught at the University of Texas and he visited in the mid-70s to read from *Sophie's Choice*. With typical magnanimity, he brought Willie Morris along with him and shared his honorarium.

Afterward, we gathered for a party whose guest list, I would like to believe, has never been equaled in that town. Molly Ivins, Ronnie Dugger, William Broyles, James Fallows, William Wittliff, Bud Shrake, Lieutenant Governor William Hobby, and Zulfikar Ghose were all there, as was a loquacious fellow with a guitar who exasperated Styron to the point where he barked, "Look, man, sing or talk. Don't try to do both." The guitarist, Jerry Jeff Walker, did as he usually did under duress. He sang his signature song, "Mr. Bojangles."

In the '80s, when Bill slid into a terrible depression, I was living in Rome and had to glean what I could of his prognosis from mutual friends. I read his book *Darkness Visible* as a kind of primer, and when I subsided into the slough of despond myself, I derived hope from the thought that since he bounced back, I could too. Even in my deepest misery, I remembered what he had done for me. He opened the door to a different world, escorted me through it, and introduced me to the other side.

JAMES JONES

Paris

P UTTING aside the manuscript Styron had read, I embarked on another novel. The new one, *Man in Motion,* was a comedy based on my
travels and travails in Mexico. For the first and only time in my career, I
didn't start at the beginning and write the chapters in sequence until I
had a complete book. I worked on scenes in whatever order they presented themselves, and at the end of six months I had a midden of manuscript pages that needed to be organized.

By a curious quirk of logic, Linda believed that France was the perfect
place for an American to finish a novel about Mexico. She had spent her
junior year in Paris and longed to live there again. With her encouragement, I postponed my doctoral dissertation and applied for a Fulbright
fellowship in creative writing. Proficiency in French was just the initial
hurdle. I needed a recommendation from a writer in a position to pass
judgment on my project. Since George Garrett had resigned from UVA
and departed from Charlottesville, I turned to his replacement, Peter
Taylor.

A celebrated author of short stories, Taylor struck me as an elusive
figure. Unlike other English department faculty, he didn't then have an

office in Cabell Hall. He holed up in a wood frame house across the street and kept such irregular hours that colleagues and students rarely knew where to find him. In fact, for years to come, regardless of the official university calendar, he set his own agenda and flew off to Key West when the weather got cold. He dealt with student manuscripts by mail and didn't return to the classroom until spring.

Lanky and thin, a soft-spoken southerner with cowlicked hair, he looked like an easy touch, a pushover. So it surprised people to learn that he had definite ideas about almost everything pertaining to teaching, publishing, literary prizes, and reputations. One might have been tempted to brand him as rigidly opinionated had he not expressed his ideas so amiably, had his loose-limbed languor not suggested such flexibility.

The day I met Peter Taylor, he leaned far back in the chair at his desk like a first-class airline passenger reclining in drowsy anticipation of a drink, dinner, and the in-flight film. When I asked to audit his course, he drawled that that didn't make sense. "The class is for writers," he said, "not listeners." He tugged at his fleshy earlobe, miming what "audit" meant.

Promising that I was eager to write and anxious for criticism, I explained that I had already taken Garrett's graduate seminar. Officially I couldn't enroll again, but if he would let me sit in on the class, I would be happy to fulfill all the requirements.

"Afraid I can't let you do that," Taylor said. "If I gave you permission, I'd have to give it to everybody. I'd end up teaching two or three times the normal load of students."

"I hate to make work for you, but if I could persuade you to read something of mine at your convenience, on an informal basis—"

"Can't do it," he said. "I have to concentrate on the stories my students turn in. Now I know George Garrett is different. He'd read anything. He encourages everybody. But that's what's wrong with creative writing programs."

"What's wrong with them?" I asked.

"People expect to be encouraged. They expect to get published and make a living as writers. I've been fortunate. I never had to support myself by writing, and that's freed me to write what I want."

Taylor's distinction between writing for a living and teaching writing for a living while working on his own writing wasn't entirely clear to me. But there was no opportunity to ask for clarification. In his unemphatic manner, Taylor plowed on to enumerate his objections to literary politicking, to careerism, to the pursuit of meaningless prizes—"I wouldn't accept one if I won it"—and to what he regarded as the meretricious craving to break into high-paying magazines like *Esquire* and *Playboy.* "I wouldn't let my fiction appear beside a beer ad on one page and a naked lady on the next."

He preferred *The New Yorker,* where in those days nudity was unknown and the ads were tasteful. If Mr. Shawn didn't accept his stories, Taylor said, there were always respectable little magazines and literary journals that would.

Fervently praying that a Fulbright wasn't one of the empty prizes he despised, I plunged ahead and confessed I wanted to spend a year in France and needed a recommendation.

"Why, that's wonderful!" he exclaimed and straightened in the chair. "I had a Fulbright to Paris. I didn't get much work done, but it was a terrific experience. You'll love it there."

When I reminded him that I would never get to Paris unless I got a fellowship, and that I wouldn't get a fellowship unless I got a recommendation, he sagged back like a wave subsiding. "I suppose I could read one of your stories, and if I like it, I'll write a letter."

"I've been doing novels," I said. "I've finished one and I'm halfway through the second."

"I don't read novels."

"You mean novels by students?"

"I mean novels by anybody, but especially not students. The novel is an epic. Very few writers are competent to produce an epic. I don't write them myself. But a short story, that's like a lyric poem. Plenty of people are capable of achieving a lyric. Why don't you show me a chapter of your novel and I'll read it as a short story."

Though this made little sense, I didn't see that I had a choice. I selected a ten-page section from the manuscript I had brought along and passed it to Peter Taylor. Rather than do the expected and say he'd contact me once he had had a chance to look it over, he read the batch of pages on the spot. Pursing his lips, he let his pale eyes slide from sentence to sentence. He sniffed once or twice through the roseate flanges of his nostrils. He turned back to an early passage, then skipped ahead. Finally, he sighed. "Well, this sure isn't a short story. Without a beginning, a middle, or an end, it's tough for me to tell what you're up to."

"Sorry. Thanks for your time." I reached over to retrieve the pages.

"Look, I can tell by talking to you that you're serious about writing. And if you've finished a novel, I know you're not afraid of work."

"No, I'm not. And I admit I have a lot of it ahead of me."

"Yeah, you do. But hard work's a big part of writing, and if you're willing to keep at it, maybe you'll make it. I guess I could write something for you to the Fulbright Commission."

I thanked him again and left, resigned to getting, at best, a lukewarm letter. But as Peter Taylor would prove in his career, he was capable of surprises and abrupt about-faces. After decades of writing short stories and disdaining commercial success and literary prizes, he turned from the lyric late in life and took up the epic. He published a number of novels, including *The Old Forest,* which won the Pulitzer Prize and a $50,000 jackpot from the Ritz in Paris. So maybe he gave me a rave recommendation after all. That spring, I was awarded a Fulbright to France.

As soon as he heard the news, William Styron sent congratulations.

April 6, 1968

Dear Mike:

I've been abominably busy of late, having had to go to Hollywood to "consult," whatever that means, on the film version of *The Confessions of Nat Turner* (that is some scene) and then, recently to Milwaukee to look in on McCarthy at the Wisconsin primaries (I'm a delegate with Arthur Miller to the Conn. convention, both of us for McCarthy).

I'm delighted you got the Fulbright and I'm sure that you will swing in Paris; it still is one of my favorite places, and I've never found it anti-American, really, at all; the French are just a bit individualistically chilly and aloof (though by no means all of them) and Americans want people to slobber all over them like dogs. I've made a note to write to Jim Jones about you and to make the proper introduction; I think you'll like him and Gloria a lot. But since you aren't leaving for France until next fall it may be best for you to refresh my memory on this matter later on this summer;

certainly it'll be fresher in his memory if I write to him about you
more or less around the time you plan to arrive in Paris.

Nat has just passed 150,000 copies, which of course pleases me.
I never thought it would do that good. I envy you and the Va.
weather, but it'll be here soon too. My best to old Slim.

Yours ever,

Bill

With a breathless, slightly dazed sense that events were accelerating and
might, if we weren't careful, spin out of control, Linda and I began laying
track for our departure. We were leaving friends, leaving the snug confines of Charlottesville, the town where we had met and spent the first
year of our marriage. And what made the leave-taking more daunting
was how little money we had. One serious miscalculation or a couple of
banal mistakes could wipe us out.

In addition to transatlantic transportation for me, the Fulbright provided a minuscule stipend of $2,700. Our expenses for the year figured
to be far greater than that. Out of personal savings we had to cover Linda's passage on the SS *France* and the cost of shipping our belongings.
Then there was the matter of where to live. The Fulbright Commission
made no provisions for married couples beyond supplying the names and
addresses of pensions in the Latin Quarter that offered cheap room and
board. It was up to individual Fellows who wanted apartments to find
and pay for their own digs.

Luckily—at least it seemed so at the time—we became acquainted
with a French woman who owned a studio in Paris that she welcomed
us to rent. "But, please," she said, "it's a modest *pied-à-terre* and maybe
not up to your American standards."

Lean and chic, her throat swaddled in foulards, her hair pinned up in
a complicated chignon, the lady had a charming accent and an insinuat-
ing way of talking that seemed syncopated to her sinuous walk. With her
every flavorful inflection, she left me feeling vaguely inferior, like the sort
of vulgarian who can't survive without a color TV, shag carpets, and a
Barcalounger. To show how far off base she was, I stressed that I would
be finishing a novel in Paris and that Linda and I hoped to have an authentic French experience.

In that case, she promised, her apartment was *parfait*. It had *grand
standing, jolies vues* and *poutres apparentes*—a phrase Linda translated for

me as "exposed beams." Located close to Place de la Contrescarpe, the neighborhood dripped literary cachet. Hemingway had lived nearby, in rooms above a sawmill. In either direction—on Rue Mouffetard or down on Place Maubert—there were street markets, cheese and wine shops, and intimate bistros. There were even a few old-fashioned *pissoirs*.

"It would give me deep satisfaction," she said, "to imagine you at my desk, surrounded by my *bibelots,* completing your *roman.* Who knows? Perhaps one day they will put a plaque with your name on the façade."

As for the price, since this was an agreement *entre amis,* with no agent, no question of "key money" to run up costs, she quoted what she called an "interesting arrangement"—$150 a month, with six months rent in advance. Though that whacked a third off my stipend before I even set foot in France, it was less than we paid in Charlottesville. So we took the place sight unseen and signed a contract to move in on October first. Meanwhile, over the summer, the woman would prepare for our arrival. Although she wouldn't be there to greet us, she promised to leave a letter of instructions about the studio and its appliances.

Over that same summer I pieced together the fragments of *Man in Motion* and produced a rough draft that I decided to risk submitting to publishers. George Garrett sent me a list of editors in New York, and I started at the top and mailed the manuscript to each one in turn. After several rejections, I received from Albert Erskine at Random House a letter that, while it didn't accept the novel, didn't turn it down either. I mentioned in a return letter that I was leaving for France in late September, and Erskine proposed that I stop by his office the night before I sailed. In closing he added, "Needless to say, I think you're very good."

According to Chairman Mao, the longest journey commences with a single step. Ours started with a Greyhound bus trip to Washington, D.C. There, we transferred to a bus to Port Authority, New York City. Nine numbing hours on the road afforded me ample time to spin my wheels and ratchet up the level of tension. Between worrying about the move to Paris and fretting over the meeting with Albert Erskine, I managed to afflict myself with miserable apprehension. Although I was afraid to admit it, I was . . . I was afraid. Afraid I would fail as a writer and wind up in France unable to put a single word on a page. Afraid I'd make a fool of myself on the ship and a worse fool in Paris. What if I fell as wretchedly seasick on the SS *France* as I had in the rubber dinghy in Mexico? What if acute culture shock sent me scrambling back to the States like a whipped cur?

In Manhattan, while Linda registered us at a hotel across from Macy's, I rushed off to Random House. Located in those days in a landmark brownstone on Madison Avenue—now part of the Helmsley Palace Hotel—the building had about it the musty hermetic atmosphere of a scholar's retreat. There was the smell of binding glue, aging paper, and pipe tobacco. Albert Erskine's secretary, Suzanne Bevis, fixed me a glass of iced tea and said she had read *Man in Motion,* as she did many unsolicited manuscripts that sailed in over the transom. Having liked it, she handed it on to Albert. Before I could properly thank her—I had in mind dropping to my knees and kissing her feet—she showed me into his office.

Tall and gaunt, with high cheekbones and pronounced hollows beneath them, Albert Erskine bore a striking resemblance to the debonair movie actor Franchot Tone. His desk was littered with books, galleys, page proofs, erasers, rubber bands, pencils, pens, and copy-editor's notes. As I approached, he was preoccupied with the task of straightening a manuscript on his knee, tapping one end, then the other, so that each page was in place and all the edges were flush. A wistful smile passed over his face as he mused, "I wonder how many times in my life I've repeated this gesture. And how often will I do it again?"

I didn't know whether to assure him that his trials would soon be over or beg him to stay on the job until my book was published.

Erskine, it turned out, was a southerner. Like Peter Taylor, he hailed from Memphis, Tennessee. "I heard Peter bought Faulkner's house in Charlottesville," he said. "I mean the one on Rugby Road, not the country place."

When I confessed that I was unfamiliar with either place, Erskine said he wouldn't have known them if he hadn't edited Faulkner and had occasion to . . .

My auditory faculties failed. The din of blood drumming at my ears deafened me. What was I doing here? What chance did I have with an editor who had worked with William Faulkner? An imbecile, I should have found out whom Erskine edited before dumping a first novel in his lap.

Yet when I asked about his current list, I concluded it was best that I hadn't known. Otherwise, I wouldn't have had the nerve to keep this appointment. In addition to Ralph Ellison, John O'Hara, Robert Penn Warren, James A. Michener, and Eudora Welty, he had recently rounded out his stable with a young novelist named Cormac McCarthy. As Vice President and Editorial Director of Random House, Erskine had his hands full. While he claimed to admire *Man in Motion*—by the way, he asked, was I aware that a critical study of Faulkner had the same title?— the most he could promise was to try to farm the book out to a young editor. Several had read it, but none was ready to commit to it. Still, he was confident that if the novel didn't catch on at Random House, some other publisher would accept it.

Far from sharing Erskine's confidence, I did my best to prolong the interview and persuade him of my seriousness and literary acumen. I asked how he came to be an editor. And what was the most difficult part of the job?

"Dealing with egotistical writers," he said. He referred to Norman Mailer as "an absolute shit. The world wouldn't be a worse place if he had never written a word."

Though I liked Mailer's novels, I kept my mouth shut and vowed I would never add to an editor's woes. At the age of twenty-five, I viewed publication as a salvation to be yearned for with all the irrational zeal of a religious fanatic. After Albert Erskine took my Paris address and promised to stay in touch, it seemed to me perfectly sensible to walk around the corner from Random House to St. Patrick's Cathedral. Convinced that nothing short of divine intervention could get my fiction into print, I prayed that *Man in Motion* would be accepted. Then I whispered a prayer that I would like Paris and wouldn't perish of seasickness aboard the SS *France*.

The Atlantic crossing ended without incident, but our arrival at the rented apartment wasn't just disappointing. It was deeply baffling. As promised, the place offered *grand standing,* on the sixth floor. In the absence of an elevator, we reached it by climbing a hundred and twenty steps up a tightly spiraling staircase that funneled the aromas of garlic, oregano, and olive oil from a ground-level Italian restaurant into the flats above. As for *jolies vues,* the kitchen opened onto an air shaft. From the front window, one had to lay his life on the line, lean far over a low railing, and crane his head to the left to get a glimpse of Notre-Dame's spires.

The landlady's letter of instructions proved to be a masterpiece of brevity. "Make yourselves at home," it read in its entirety. Yet this was a tall order since the tiny studio was stacked to the rafters with its owner's belongings. Before we unpacked, we had to clear her clothes and a dozen pairs of down-at-the-heels shoes out of the armoire. Then we dried the stockings she had left soaking in sudsy water in the bidet and stuffed them into a medicine chest, along with the douche bag that swung from a hook on the bathroom door.

Beside the bed stood a mysterious polished metal device. Linda guessed it was a duck press. I opined that it was a medieval thumbscrew. When we finally fell into bed exhausted, the bed itself felt like an instrument of torture. Tilted at an angle, the mattress slanted steeply toward the headboard. That first night, with blood streaming to our heads, we both had lurid nightmares and neck aches. The next night, we switched the mattress around and woke with swollen ankles. Then I improvised a solution, propping up the low end of the bed with the landlady's books.

As Linda and I labored to create some physical and psychic space for ourselves, we spent hours sifting through the refuse of a stranger's life. The woman had saved everything except her fingernail parings. There were her class notes from college, lycée, and primary school. There were hotel and restaurant receipts, matchbooks and swizzle sticks from nightclubs. There were canceled Métro tickets, old theater programs, travel brochures, and prescriptions for migraine pills.

In a cold rage, I cursed her for leaving the apartment in such disorder and cursed myself for renting it. But gradually my fury gave way to fascination, and I found myself swept up as if by an engrossing narrative. It came to me that it might not be haste or slovenliness that I was dealing with, but rather the relics, the fossilized remains, of a woman's life. Maybe on an unconscious level, she wanted us to grope through her personal effects in the hope that we would give shape to them and come to understand her.

Consumed by a compulsion in which intellectual curiosity and outright voyeurism played reciprocal roles, I anthropologically unpacked and examined every object in the apartment. I drew inferences from her clothes, her furniture, her library. She appeared to be vain about her hands and indifferent to her feet; she wore expensive gloves and cheap shoes. Judging by the holy cards tucked as bookmarks into volumes of

Baudelaire, Rimbaud, and Genet, I pegged her as a conflicted cradle Catholic.

As I analyzed the jagged contours of one Frenchwoman's character, I believed I was gaining a better purchase on France, burrowing deeper into the national identity. But once Linda and I had put the apartment into order and started to explore the city, I was disabused of the notion that I would soon feel at home in Paris. It was different in those days— different from the United States, different from what it is now. Street sweepers still wielded brooms of twigs tied to long sticks. Quais along the Seine had yet to be transformed into Formula One racetracks, and the boulevards of the Latin Quarter hadn't been paved over to prevent students from hurling cobblestones at police. On the alert and on edge after the previous spring's riots—*les événements de mai, '68*—the gendarmes were in no mood to be merciful. One evening as Linda and I emerged from a movie theater on Place St. Michel, we stepped straight into a student demonstration, and when we didn't move on fast enough, we got walloped with rubber truncheons.

Struggling to take the measure of the French, I confronted all those notorious idiosyncrasies that require accommodation, or, I should say, capitulation. You did things the French way or not at all. No point asking why it was impossible to buy lined loose-leaf paper, only graph paper. And why weren't you allowed to touch the fruit and vegetables in the market? Why were the parks like maximum-security prisons, with the grass strictly off limits and little kids parading back and forth like cons in an exercise pen? Why was there no place to sit except in penitentially uncomfortable wire harp chairs? And why did you have to pay some whiskery old witch for that privilege? More than anything, why did women have dominion over the men's room, bustling around while a guy unbuttoned or unzipped?

Then there was the unfathomable mystery of the language. Because in high school and college I had studied it as though it were as dead as Latin—a tongue to be haltingly translated, never spoken—my French remained rudimentary. Whenever possible, I let Linda speak for me. But she badgered me to experiment and put myself in situations where, sink or swim, I had to speak for myself. When I went to open a checking account, she accompanied me to the Banque Nationale de Paris, but insisted I go in alone.

"Remember," she said, "if you're at a loss for words, talk around the subject. Try different grammatical constructions."

Resigned to sounding like a cretin, I lined up at a window attended by a girl in her teens. One of those gamine creatures whose looks were arresting rather than conventionally pretty, this teller, I thought, was too young to be judgmental. When it came my turn, she breathed a single word. "Monsieur?"

I blurted the sentence I had memorized. "Je voudrais ouvrir un con."

Birdlike, she cocked her head. "Comment?"

Thinking I had committed an error in pronunciation, I repeated that I would like to open an account, changing only a couple of stresses.

She smiled. "Encore, s'il vous plaît."

Supposing my mistake must be grammatical, I reformulated the sentence. "Est-ce que c'est possible d'ouvrir un con?"

She laughed into her fist to keep from laughing in my face. People in line behind me began to titter. I had been warned that the French could be cruel to foreigners who foul up their language, but this seemed sadistic. Tellers from nearby windows moved over to listen to me butcher *la belle langue.*

Blushing and babbling, I tried to talk around the subject. Let them have their little joke, I thought.

Someone tugged my sleeve. Tired of waiting outside Linda had come to check on me. But as soon as she heard my strangled attempt to *ouvrir un con,* she fled. I followed her into the street, where she was bent double with laughter.

"Okay, I screwed up," I said. "My grammar's bad, my pronunciation is awful, my accent is terrible—"

"No, you were perfect. Everybody understood you. It's just you kept repeating that you wanted to open a cunt."

I let Linda go back in and arrange the account. It would be days before I uttered another word in French.

The prospect of contacting James Jones intimidated me less than it might have because he spoke English. Although he answered the phone with a rasping *Allô, oui?* his voice, its volume and midwestern vowels, was unmistakably American. This pleased me, as did the news that Bill and Rose Styron were in town, staying with the Joneses. He invited us over to his apartment to have a drink, then go out to lunch with them.

The Joneses lived on Ile St. Louis. You didn't need to be a member of the literati to know that. A recent National Geographic article about Paris carried a brooding photograph of the novelist in his living room overlooking the Seine.

Linda and I headed downhill along Rue de la Montagne Ste. Gene-vieve, past a Vietnamese bistro that had replaced the zinc bar where, in *The Sun Also Rises,* Jake Barnes dances with Lady Brett. It was a cool, bright October day, with a gusty wind that fluttered the newspapers clipped to the kiosks. Headlines shrilled the story of Jackie Kennedy's shocking marriage to Aristotle Onassis.

Beyond Boulevard St. Germain, we entered a jigsaw puzzle of alleys that brought us to a footbridge to Notre-Dame. In those days, before it was sandblasted clean, the cathedral was soot-darkened, its stained glass windows obscured by grime. It looked as if the cathedral had survived a fire that had burnt its gargoyles to charred stumps.

Jones's building had a turreted corner and an impressive entrance. A lovely little blond girl, Kaylie, opened the door, then scurried back to the television where she and her adopted brother, Jamie, were eating po-tato chips out of a bowl and watching a western dubbed into French. An Indian in war paint trotted his pony up to a cavalry officer, raised his palm, and said, "Ça va?"

Jim and Gloria Jones greeted us with no more ceremony than Kaylie had. The family was accustomed to—perhaps it's fairer to say surfeited by—company. Every year a fresh crop of writers, film makers, professors, publishers, and college kids pitched up in Paris and gravitated to this apartment as if an American passport guaranteed them automatic access. Although that first meeting was a vivid event for me, I wonder what, if anything, the Joneses made of Linda and me. We must have seemed aw-fully callow—just twenty-four and twenty-five—nervous and trying not to show it, eager to impress and not quite knowing how to go about it. Linda, I remember, wore a checked Evan-Picone pants suit, the only dress-up outfit she owned.

The other two women, both in early middle age, had been out to the races at Longchamps. The fresh air and sunshine seemed to have revived Rose Styron's tan from the previous summer on Martha's Vineyard. Small and dark, she couldn't have looked more different from Gloria Jones. Once a movie stand-in for Marilyn Monroe, Gloria was a zaftig blonde in a Chanel suit that showed off her figure.

The two men were subdued, pale, perhaps hung over. Like Styron, Jones, had on a suit coat and tie. *Esquire* once rated the latter among the world's worst dressed men and published a snapshot of Jim in Levis, beaded Indian moccasins, and a belt spangled with silver and turquoise. Now that everybody wore jeans, beads, headbands, and other Indian paraphernalia, Jones dressed like a banker or businessman. Short and wiry with a pugnacious jaw, bushy sideburns, and a bantam rooster's comb of hair, he rattled the change in his pocket and asked what we wanted to drink.

It was easy to see why so many people had observed that he didn't seem at home in Paris. He didn't even look entirely comfortable in his own clothes. And his house and its furnishing reminded me of the beautiful, elaborate shell a scruffy hermit crab might brashly claim for itself. His material was Middle America and those on its margins, especially those ready to take desperate risks to win a foothold on a slightly higher rung. Now the greatest risk for Jones was to live as an outsider in a city that would never accept him for reasons his critics never understood.

While he fetched the liquor from a bar that had been fashioned from an antique church pulpit, Styron said he had just returned from a lecture tour of Russia. This was the USIS-sponsored trip he had had Linda postpone two years ago in Charlottesville. From Moscow, he and Rose had flown to the central Asian republic of Uzbekistan, where they visited Samarkand and Bukhara. Those fabled cities didn't exist on my mental map. Not even in the realms of imagination could I envision them. But Styron led me over to a globe and located them in the lost heart of the continent, wakening in me a hunger to see the Silk Road that would take twenty-five years to satisfy.

When Jones came back with the drinks, he brought Styron a Scotch on the rocks.

"I've switched from bourbon," Bill said. "Scotch has fewer calories, and my doctor says it's healthier."

We joined Rose and Gloria at a floor-to-ceiling window and gazed out at the barges and *bateaux mouches* floating past on the Seine. The women were discussing Jackie Kennedy. They simply couldn't believe that the lovely national icon had married the troll-like Greek shipping magnate.

"Shit," Jim said, "all the millions he's got, I'd marry him."

"Watch what you say," Gloria razzed him. "Next thing you know it'll be in the newspapers."

They told us about a journalist who had spent days hanging around the apartment, cadging drinks and dinner, never acknowledging that the article he was in Paris to write was about them. He depicted the Joneses as American Gothic caricatures who spoke rotten French, had no appreciation of culture or fine cuisine, and spiked every sentence with "fuck," employing it as noun, verb, adjective, adverb, and punctuation mark.

"I haven't heard you say 'fuck' a single time," I said.

"Oh, fuck!" Jim exclaimed. "I forgot to say 'fuck.'"

We finished our drinks, and Gloria telephoned for two taxis. Bill, Gloria, and Linda piled into one, and Jim, Rose, and I followed them in the other to La Coupole. Though I needed no reminder that it had been one of Hemingway's haunts, Jones gave me a capsule summary of the brasserie's literary significance. Paris and its history were much on his mind, for he was doing a novel, *The Merry Month of May*, set against a backdrop of the previous spring's student protests.

"They barricaded the Sorbonne and the streets around it with tree trunks and burning cars," he said. "They damn near brought down the government. The whole country came to a standstill. But soon as De Gaulle realized he had the army behind him, it was over. You don't stop tanks with cobblestones and slogans."

This sounded more like the Jones I had expected—terse, tough-talking, obsessed by military tactics, one-on-one confrontation, and tests of courage. Born into middle-class circumstances, he had joined the army as a teenager and chosen to live like a bottom dog, a character from a 1930s social realist novel, a working stiff with calluses on his palms and dirt under his fingernails. During World War II, he fought in the Pacific, in bloody campaigns that left him with a love-hate relationship with authority, violence, and American notions of masculinity. Reputed to be a mean boozer and brawler, he had drawn flak from reviewers almost as often for his presumed bad temper as for his prose.

Yet even as they mocked his barbarous style, surprising numbers of critics and fellow novelists admired him. He was a writer who could break your heart in *From Here to Eternity* with the scene of Maggio playing taps for his dead friend Prewett—then turn around and break your jaw for looking at him wrong. Mailer called him "the worst writer of prose ever to give intimations of greatness," and compared *The Thin Red Line,* not unflatteringly, to Stephen Crane's *The Red Badge of Courage.*

Jones's estimation of Mailer was less favorable. He recounted to me a belly-bumping and head-butting contest he had had with Mailer at a *Paris Review* party in New York. "Norman's not tough. He's never given me a bit of trouble. He knows what I'd do to him."

Then he asked, "Have you ever been in a fight? I mean one where people got their teeth knocked out?"

When I confessed that I hadn't had a fistfight since college, he seemed disappointed. But Jones had a soft side that only somebody willfully blind would miss. As we arrived at La Coupole, a scabby-faced beggar sat at the entrance with a beret in his lap and a scattering of copper coins in the beret. Lagging a step behind Rose Styron and me, Jim tried to hide what he was doing, but I caught him slipping the clochard fifty francs.

"Just one of my superstitions," he muttered. "Never step on a crack."

La Coupole has undergone numerous reincarnations over the past thirty years. The décor has changed, the quality of the food has waxed and waned, prices have soared, and finally the grand old establishment was bought up by a chain of brasseries. But whenever I eat there, a vivid sense of that first occasion and of my ingenuous younger self is still etched on my mind's eye with the exactitude of an art deco motif incised in glass.

On Styron's recommendation, I ordered a dozen snails, then had no idea how to eat them. Bill demonstrated how to winkle the shriveled grey blobs out of their shells, dunk them in garlic sauce, and pop them into my mouth. Snails tasted, I decided, like delicious rubber bands.

As we polished off several bottles of Beaujolais, talk turned to *Deep Throat,* the first American porn film to cross over and become a cultural reference point. Styron had screened it for a group of friends at his studio in Roxbury. But their kids kept sneaking into take a peek, and he had to shut off the projector while Rose chased them out again and again.

At the end of the meal, Jim and Bill lit up contraband Cuban cigars, and the conversation segued to *The Confessions of Nat Turner* and the controversy that had embroiled it. Hard on the heels of critical raves and pensive editorials praising him, Styron had come under attack from members of the black community who questioned his scholarship and his presumptuousness for writing from a black man's point of view. When he spoke on campuses, students shouted him down and accused him of racism. In Hollywood, black actors threatened a boycott to prevent a movie of the novel from being made. Ten black academics published a book that claimed Bill had slandered Nat Turner as a weak, sexually thwarted man in the throes of hopeless passion for a white woman. This misrepresented the historical record, they argued, and reduced Nat to the cliché figure of a black lusting for white flesh.

With every effort to defend himself, Bill said, he felt he inflamed matters and sank deeper into a debate that was unwinnable. He wanted to get back to his work. There was a book about the Marine Corps he was writing and some autobiographical sketches from his postwar days in New York that he thought might coalesce into a novel. But he also believed it was important to defend the principle that an artist was free to follow his imagination.

"I adhered to the existing historical evidence," he said. "There isn't much. The rest I had to invent. As for Nat's frustrated love for a white woman, that doesn't strike me as implausible motivation."

"Of course it's not." Jones flicked the ashes from his cigar. "Just think how many spades have a yen for white women."

A decade later, during a eulogy for Jones, Bill would refer to Jim as the kind of naïf who could use the term nigger and mean nothing hurtful, nothing pejorative. But that afternoon at La Coupole, Styron appeared to be pained by the word "spade." That wasn't how he would have put it. He observed that sexual desire and even enduring love weren't unknown between owners and slaves. Indeed, it was the necessity to conceal these relationships and to deny the feelings that fed them that heightened the potential for explosive violence.

"Yeah, and there's the whole class thing," Jones added. "If you're poor and black, a white woman represents success. Look at Martin Luther King."

"What about him?" I asked. King had been assassinated just six months earlier, and after Jones's crack about "spades," I was in no mood to listen to him unload on the civil right's leader.

"He was fucking white women left and right," Jones said. "The FBI had it on tape."

I didn't believe it. Truth to tell, I was appalled that anyone would suggest it, and I was prepared to argue with Jones. This sounded like the sort of smear J. Edgar Hoover or George Wallace would spread. But then, to my surprise, Styron confirmed that from his own involvement with the civil rights movement he had learned that Martin Luther King had indeed had white lovers. Years would pass and Martin Luther King's biography would appear before I accepted that Jones and Styron had been right.

Jones made another remark that I had difficulty dealing with. When Hemingway's name came up, he proclaimed that, "The problem with Papa was he always wanted to suck a cock. But when he found one that fit, it had a double barrel."

Hideously coarse as this comment was, I could understand, and almost forgive, Jones's cruelty once I read Hemingway's collected letters. At the start of Jones's career, when *From Here to Eternity* was in galleys, his editor sent a copy to Ernest Hemingway, hoping for a blurb to promote the young novelist. Hemingway replied: "To me he is an enormously skillful fuck-up and his book will do great damage to our country. Probably I should re-read it again to give you a truer answer. But I do not have to eat an entire bowl of scabs to know they are scabs; nor suck a boil to know it is a boil; nor swim through a river of snot to know it is snot. I hope he kills himself as soon as it does not damage his or your sales. If you give him a literary tea you might ask him to drain a bucket of snot and then suck the puss out of a dead nigger's ear. . . . He has the psycho's urge to kill himself and he will do it."

That day in Paris, when I longed to join what I regarded as the community of writers, I was aware that I might be rejected. Or that I might be published and have my work greeted by indifference or hostility. But the idea that my literary elders might wish me ill or do me harm had never occurred to me. To the contrary, I wanted to believe that this was how Linda and I would live from now on—having lunch and spirited talks with the likes of William Styron and James Jones. At the end of the meal, it pleased me when Jim invited me to drop by his office next week. Despite some of his opinions and his crudity in stating them, it mattered to me to be accepted by him.

Afterward, in the radiant light of an autumn afternoon, we walked the Joneses and the Styrons to Boulevard Raspail, where they hailed a taxi. Since the Styrons were leaving the next day for the States, we shook hands and kissed them good-bye. Then, as Linda and I set off toward our apartment, Rose stopped us and warned, "Crosswalks don't mean anything in Europe. I got knocked down by a motor scooter in Italy. You kids be careful."

With that motherly touch, she climbed into the cab, and we strolled up Boulevard Montparnasse. At Closerie des Lilas, we turned left under an *allée* of chestnut trees that had started to shed their leaves. In the Luxembourg Gardens, slate-gray pigeons with jeweled necks slanted against a sky of enameled blue. With evening coming on, kids began to pull their sailboats from the fountain, and carp submarined around in the shallows as if they planned to leave the water too. The crone in charge of the chairs was collecting her last centimes of the day. At that moment, I couldn't imagine why I had ever had misgivings about moving to Paris. I could envision staying on here indefinitely, just like James Jones.

Jones's severest critics may have contended that he settled there for the wrong reasons— to enjoy France's sybaritic pleasures, to swan around with his social and literary betters. But it's possible, I've come to believe, that we both responded less to what was palpably present in the place than to what was absent. With its crowded centuries of history, Europe reminded me of nothing in my own past, and its intensity of smells, tastes, and colors called to mind nothing of the circumstances in which I grew up. It's strange that while the United States represents the essence of opportunity, of second chances and reinventing the past, so many American artists and writers have felt the need to go abroad to start over.

In that simpler and safer age, when terrorism, or the threat of it, hadn't reduced every diplomatic mission to an armed camp surrounded by electrified fences, metal detectors, heat sensors, and surveillance cameras, Sargent Shriver, the American ambassador, urged Fulbright Fellows to avail themselves of the facilities of the U.S. Embassy. If we felt homesick, we were free to drop by the commissary for a cheeseburger and to watch the weekly broadcast of National Football League films.

The day of my visit to James Jones's office, I left the apartment planning to catch the football highlights, then join Jim on Ile St. Louis. But the quai at Métro Place Maubert was crowded, and as I rushed for a car, its doors started sliding shut. I thought if I stuck out my arm, the doors would spring open, like American elevator doors do. I thought wrong. They clanked like a guillotine against a chopping block. Luckily my hand wasn't between them. It hit a window, and I thought I would come away with nothing worse that bruised knuckles. Wrong again. The window didn't have safety glass. My left fist shattered it.

At first I felt nothing. Then a shock of pain sizzled from my wrist to my armpit. The purple, crescent-shaped gash on my wrist resembled the scar on a suicide survivor. Miraculously, there was no blood. My system needed a second to process the insult to it. Then suddenly the wound gushed bright red, and an American tourist groaned, "God, are you cut!"

Pinching the flaps of skin between the fingers of my right hand, I sprinted for an exit. A *poinçonneuse,* one of the women who, before the advent of automation, manually cancelled Métro tickets, blocked my path. I assumed she was offering first aid. One more mistake on my part. She screeched, "Les américains sont tous des grands enfants," and demanded that I sign a paper relieving her of responsibility. I brushed past her so abruptly she twirled like a turnstile.

On Place Maubert, pedestrians gaped at the blood and kept their distance. Maybe they feared I would fall dead at their feet with God knows what bureaucratic consequences for them. I stumbled into a pharmacy where a kindly clerk swaddled my hand in gauze. Although he soothed me, "C'est pas grave," he recommended that I hurry to the closest hospital, Hôtel-Dieu. It sounded like a funeral parlor, one with the motto, Check in at the Hotel of God and come out in Heaven or Hell. Given how badly I had botched opening a bank account, I wasn't about to trust a French doctor to understand as I explained how I had slit my wrist.

Reeling over to a taxi stand, I asked the cabby to drive me to the American Hospital. I knew it was in Neuilly, but had no idea that that was at the opposite end of Paris. I slumped into the back seat and surrendered my fate to the mercies of morning rush hour. Before we reached the Right Bank, blood had soaked through the boxing glove of gauze on my fist, and the cabby complained that I was ruining his upholstery. He ordered me to hold my arm out the window.

Now blood flew off the bandage and spattered passing cars. Their drivers eyed me in alarm. In the rearview mirror, the cabby also looked worried. But I felt curiously serene. The city, its splendid bronze statues, the colonnades of plane trees and wrought-iron fences constructed of spears dipped in gold—everything had acquired a lovely shimmer, and it pleased me to think that I would have quite a story for James Jones this afternoon.

At the American Hospital the doctor on duty was English and languidly unimpressed by my problem. While he clowned around with a couple of nurses, he dispatched me to an examining room with instructions to clean my cut. He'd be along momentarily.

As I peeled away the sopping gauze and let it fall into a gory coil on the floor, I went weak at the knees. Though the bleeding had stopped, the flaps of skin yawned like a thirsty mouth. At a sink, I knelt down and turned on the faucet. When the thirsty mouth opened wider, I closed my eyes. There came a sound of lips lapping at a stream and a sensation of pins and needles—no, it was screws and nails—piercing my wrist.

The doctor sauntered in, gave the cut a cursory glance, and praised my cleaning job. He had me stretch out on an examining table while he stitched me up, counting aloud each suture. When he reached twenty-six, he knotted the thread and pumped an ampule of anti-tetanus serum into my shoulder with what felt like a soldering iron. I'd have an interesting scar, he said; *un souvenir de votre visite à Paris,* he called it. He recommended waiting a couple of weeks before having the stitches removed. Meanwhile, I'd better stay in bed for the rest of the day. Some patients suffered a reaction to tetanus shots.

I had no intention of heeding his advice. Nor once I was home would I listen to Linda, who begged me to lie down. Changing out of my bloody clothes, I charged off to the rendezvous with Jones. A guy like Jim, someone who had survived the invasion of Guadalcanal, would never let a paltry twenty-six stitches slow him down.

At his turreted building, I rang the bell and waited what seemed in my gate-legged state a good long time. A swarthy, mustachioed woman, a domestic, opened the door, and in French as deeply flawed as mine, asked what I wanted.

"I have an appointment with Mr. Jones," I said.

"Pas ici."

"No, not here. In his office."

She spat out something in Spanish and stepped into the street and pointed to another door in the building. Sure enough, there was his name on a typewritten card, beside an intercom button. I pressed it, and the lock unlatched. As I climbed the stairs, a man every bit as swarthy and mustachioed as the woman appeared on a landing above me.

"I'm looking for Mr. Jones," I managed in French.

"Pas ici." Although superior to the maid's, his accent also had a Spanish lilt. I assumed he was a fellow domestic, perhaps her husband.

"Where is he?" I asked.

"At the racetrack. Do you want to leave a message?"

Wobbling a little, I clung to the stair railing as if to a lifeline. My emotions stewed just beneath the surface, and I was tempted to erupt and let them out. How the hell could Jim do this to me after all I had gone through to get here?

I departed in petulant grief, like a schoolboy who had been stood up for the prom. Padding across Pont de la Tournelle, blinded by the foil glint of the Seine and sunlight splintering on the finials of Notre-Dame, I was preternaturally conscious of the pulse in my wrist, the thud in my heart and head. Apart from fury and disappointment and wooziness from the shot, the feeling that seethed through me was what a fool I had been to believe Jones would become my friend and Paris my home. I hated the place and these appalling people who, when they weren't pretending not to understand you, mangled your hand on the Métro, demanded that you sign away your rights and hang your bleeding arm out the window on your way to the hospital. Then they neglected to show up for appointments.

As I trudged up the spiral staircase to our studio, the steps were gummy under my feet and smelled like garlic and oregano. I might have been walking on wedges of pizza.

"We're leaving," I announced to Linda and plunged headlong onto the bed. Before I blacked out, I said that if Jones called, I didn't care to speak to him.

By morning my head had cleared and my mood improved marginally. Still, I insisted we leave Paris. Although nominally attached to the Sorbonne, I was free to live anywhere in France. Soon the weather here would be cold and wet. Unable to keep the windows open, we'd die of asphyxiation from the stench of the Italian restaurant. Why stay? Why not follow the sun and settle in the south, on the Riviera, like Gerald and Sara Murphy? What I didn't admit to Linda or myself was that I felt overwhelmed in Paris. Reversing the theme of the traditional French novel, I wanted to escape the city and hurry to the provinces where the slower pace and reduced scale were more manageable.

Linda's readiness to move more than matched mine. She was eager to see the rest of France. We were formulating plans to sublet the apartment, buy a car, and bug out at the end of the month when the phone rang. It was James Jones. Despite my vow, I didn't refuse to speak to him. He had an excuse and an apology; I remember that much. And he invited me to come over as soon as possible—right then, if I liked.

Jim met me at the front door and apologized again. "I hate to be one of those assholes that makes a promise, then breaks it. I said I'd be here, and I should have been. But our schedule, Gloria's and mine, sometimes gets screwed up. Hey, what happened to your hand?"

When I told him, he whistled. "Twenty-six stitches! That's not a scratch. Come in, sit down."

Leading the way to the living room, he wore a blue shirt with billowing sleeves and a broad open collar that gave him a slightly elfin appearance. Before we sat down, someone let himself into the apartment. It was the swarthy, mustachioed handyman I had encountered the day before on the landing outside Jim's office. Now the handyman was nicely dressed in a beige wide-wale corduroy suit. I guessed he'd have to change before he got down to his chores.

"Gringo!" he bellowed at Jones and threw his arms wide.

"Spic!" Jim shouted back, and the two men exchanged a big, back-slapping *abrazo*. Even for Jones, this struck me as excessive—hollering racial slurs, then hugging a servant. He motioned to me. "Mike, meet Carlos Fuentes. He's about to become the Mexican ambassador to France. But like most novelists he's so fucking poor, he's crashing in my office until his rooms at the embassy are ready."

"I'm going out for lunch," Fuentes said. "I give you back your office. Write well."

"Are you really the new ambassador?" I asked.

"Yes. In my country—throughout Latin America—it's a traditional post for writers. It means little."

After Fuentes left, we moved next door to the studio apartment that Jones had fitted out as an office, with bookshelves, a desk, and an upright manual typewriter. Framed reviews, photographs, and magazine articles about Jim festooned the walls, along with copies of *New York Times* best-seller lists showing various Jones titles on lofty rungs of the ladder. A few items not normally associated with the novelist's craft also caught my eye. There was an extensive collection of pistols and knives, including a bayonet with a brass-knuckles handle. A tall, pink-ribbed vibrator, a device as decorative as it was provocative, perched atop a bedside table. I wondered whether it belonged to Jones or Fuentes, but I restricted myself to questions about Jim's work habits and his strategy for getting started each day.

He told me he composed on a typewriter, rarely by hand, and followed the example of Hemingway, who claimed that the key to starting in the morning was to stop the day before at a point where you knew what came next. When Jones felt he was writing well, he read and revised the previous day's pages before beginning a new passage. Otherwise, he pushed on without looking back. Since he believed he had a knack for dialogue, he sometimes jump-started himself with a patch of it. "If nothing else," he said, "dialogue fills up space and gives you a feeling you're getting somewhere."

"Getting somewhere" meant a great deal to Jones, and so did getting better. It galled him that reviewers considered his first novel his best and compared later books unfavorably to *From Here to Eternity*. "That's bullshit," he fumed. "It stands to reason that as you get older, you're bound to improve. I know a lot more about life, about writing, than when I took on *Eternity*."

Took on Eternity. The words had a ring that suggested a religious quest. In another novelist's mouth, they might have smacked of pretension or hubris. But when Jones said them, they sounded like the assessment of an honest laborer girding himself for a huge job. He built his books the way a man in his hometown of Robinson, Illinois, might go about building a house—board by roughhewn, hand-sawed board. When he was in his mid-twenties this plain, earnest carpentry had produced a splendid, unexpected cathedral, and for the rest of his life, it hovered over him, just as Notre-Dame hovered behind his Paris apartment. The sheer weight of *From Here to Eternity,* its imposing shape and long shadows, must have been almost overwhelming. Yet that didn't stop him. Jim kept hammering away, taking on Eternity over and over again.

In my opinion, he never equaled the achievement of his first novel. While there's no shame in that, there's sadness and, for aspiring writers, it's a scary precedent. Everybody prefers to believe he's getting better; nobody wants to go backward. In the troubling instance of any artist who has fallen, the tendency is to search for reasons. Drink? Drugs? Bad marriages? Careless living? But often it has seemed to me that the true mystery, the miracle, resides in the singular success, not the subsequent falling off. Most of us fail. A few, like Jones, create something that lasts, and then, if they're brave enough, they don't quit, they don't complain, they keep working.

Later that fall, Linda and I did leave Paris, but we returned from time to time and met Jim for coffee at neighborhood cafés or meals in small, smoky brasseries and hole-in-the-wall Vietnamese restaurants. Since he never tired of roaming the city and sharing his favorite sites with visitors, we joined him on many a long ramble. During one of them I screwed up my courage and asked a question that had nagged me since the day Styron introduced us. How had he managed to remain friends with Bill after that article in *Esquire,* the one where Norman Mailer accused Styron of reading aloud and ridiculing passages from *Some Came Running* at dinner parties?

"Never mattered a damn bit to me," Jim said.

"Why? You think Mailer was lying?"

"Nah. It could have happened. We're all like that. Writers, I mean. We can be real bastards. But that doesn't stop us from being friends."

That was the way Jones was—or one of the ways. He took life and people with a pinch of salt, and seldom complained or expected apologies. He had that peculiar American penchant for putting all relationships on a first-name basis and never standing on ceremony. Accosted on one occasion by a man who introduced himself as the film producer Sam Spiegel, Jim said, "Hiya, Sam." A minute later, when the man claimed he had been joking, he was actually Sol Segal, Jim said, "Hiya, Sol."

"You really don't remember me, do you?" the man asked. "You don't know who I am?"

"Nope," Jim said, "and I don't give a shit."

In the early seventies, when I showed up at his apartment with my first published novel, I confess I found Jones's offhand attitude deflating. He said the cover looked great. Then he deposited the book on a coffee table and started mixing drinks. Disappointed that he hadn't— Hadn't what? Set off fireworks? Read my immortal prose on the spot?—I was crestfallen until a woman made the sort of entrance that did deserve thunderous applause. Tall, slender, and tawny-haired, Lauren Bacall glided into the room. Barely acknowledging her presence, Jim muttered over his shoulder as he grappled with an ice tray, "Betty, this is Mike. He just brought me a copy of his first novel."

Betty, the original Slim, picked up the book and riffled its pages.

Glancing at the author bio, she declaimed in a theatrical voice, "Born in 1943! Honey, do you have any idea what I was doing in 1943?"

I conceded that I couldn't guess.

"Well, I'm not going to tell you. You're far too young to hear about it."

James Jones's identity was so inextricably linked to Paris and had for so long been defined by his ferocious independence, it stunned me in 1973 to receive an express letter saying that he planned to give up France and hoped to land a teaching job in the States. That he should ask for my help added to the shock. Surely, I thought, a novelist of his stature could simply bestow himself on one of the best creative writing programs. Vance Bourjailly, his old friend, ran the show at the University of Iowa, and his cronies at the *Paris Review* had connections at Harvard, Yale, Duke, Berkeley, and Columbia.

But I did as Jim urged and spread word of his availability. When nothing worked out at universities in the West, where Jones preferred to live, I canvassed colleges in the East, then the South. Harry Antrim, a former professor of mine at UVA and then the chairman of English at Florida International University in Miami, was interested, but admitted some bewilderment and posed the same questions that had passed through my mind. Why would Jones want to teach? And why at a state university that had been slapped down on the heat-warped runways of the former Tamiami Airport for a student body of commuters, Hispanics, and blacks? Did Jones, reputed to be rich, understand how little academics got paid? Before he hired the man, Antrim asked me to put these matters to Jones as discreetly as possible.

With gruff candor, Jim conceded that he was returning to the States because of worry about his physical and financial health. While he had made a lot of money, he had also spent a lot. The apartment in Paris was his primary asset. He intended to sell it, but was having trouble finding a buyer. Now over fifty, he was anxious to provide security for his family. The salary, not to mention the medical benefits, of a teaching job would take up the slack in his writing income, and once he was in the States, he thought he'd be in a position to earn a few bucks lecturing and riding the literary conference circuit. Could I arrange a reading tour for him? What should he charge per appearance?

Because he hadn't been to college, Jones had no frame of reference and asked me to act as intermediary with Harry Antrim. In the early stages, he expected me to negotiate everything from his salary to his course schedule. Eventually, I confessed that at the age of thirty, with two virtually unknown novels to my name, I wasn't ideally placed to advise him or to bring much muscle to the bargaining table. Weren't there friends, publishers, an agent, who could do better on his behalf?

Though the question had the potential to embarrass him, Jones didn't duck it. Nor did he spare me. He acknowledged that I wasn't his first choice. He had let a lot of people know what he needed. Most, he said, hadn't bothered to reply. Others begged off with the excuse that they couldn't help him. He was on his own, and the clearest proof of this was that FIU was his only job prospect and I was the lynchpin to it. "I actually think I'll fit in better there," he said, "than at some fancy school."

According to all reports, Jim did more than merely fit in at FIU. He stood out. Popular with students and colleagues, he played a prominent role in the Miami community, appearing in TV advertisements to promote the city's diversity and commitment to the arts. Harry Antrim remembers him fondly and says his hiring caused just one problem. When a shipment of Jones's belongings reached the States, there came a concerned call from immigration authorities to the English department. They demanded to know why the new faculty member was importing a crate of guns and knives. Once Antrim cleared Jim's collection of weapons through customs, things went smoothly.

At the end of the spring semester, however, Jones sold his apartment on Ile St. Louis, and sensing that time was short, he decided to make a sustained push to finish *Whistle*. He and Gloria and the kids relocated to Sagaponack, Long Island, where he died of congestive heart failure two years later, his last novel uncompleted. For a quarter of a century, few serious American writers had received such rotten press. Now that Jim wasn't around to enjoy them, the tributes, the touching eulogies and reminiscences, rolled in. But all of them eliminated from his life that year of teaching at Florida International, and it's easy to understand why. It jars; it doesn't suit his image or the interests of those who claim to have always been on his side. James Jones's repatriation, the casual rebuffs of academia, the fickleness of friends, the roller coaster of literary reputation, his premature death, they all alerted me to facts of life I wouldn't otherwise have learned so early. A writer, any artist, must play many roles—living in the moment, dwelling on the past, anticipating the future, nurturing his sensitivity, toughening his hide, and in the end, praying to last long enough to finish what he has in mind.

On Gloria's recommendation, a publisher asked me to write Jim's biography. Though touched that she thought of me, I knew I was wrong for the job. So George Garrett, my original mentor at the University of Virginia, produced the first major biography of Jones. Nothing is ever lost, as George always said.

I still go back to Paris and often see Jim. His picture, along with those of a pléiade of other writers—Baudelaire, Rimbaud, Camus, Sartre, Hemingway, T. S. Eliot—is available on postcards at Latin Quarter bookstores. It's an uncanny likeness of him smoking a cigar, his eyes fixed on the middle distance, a half smile on his lips. But on the back of the snapshot, there's a heartbreaking error. It dates the photo from Key Biscayne, Florida, 1985—seven years after his death.

Not that Jim endures only on a postcard. He lives on in his novels and in the memories of people who loved him. I recall one of our rambles through Paris that ended at Les Arènes de Lutèce. The ruins of an ancient Roman amphitheater on the Left Bank, a miniature Coliseum, the arena is now the setting for spirited soccer matches, desultory games of boules, and torrid adolescent trysts.

The day Jim and I went there, we saw a little girl with a pet guinea pig. She was determined to hold the fidgeting fluff ball on her lap. When it persisted in squirming, she dealt it a hard whack to the head.

"Mais non," Jim protested. "Ne fais pas ça. Sois gentille." Don't do that. Be nice.

The phrase remains with me, the plea he never would have made for himself, "Sois gentille." James Jones was.

HAROLD ROBBINS

The Riviera

I N early November we bought a Volkswagen Beetle, stuffed it to the gunnels with our belongings, and headed for the Mediterranean. Wet, blustery weather dogged us all during the drive. My left wrist, the one I had mangled on the Métro, was still cuffed in bandages and smarted from the damp and itched to distraction. Shaking the fist I couldn't scratch, I believed it was better to be moving south than to hibernate in Paris. For weeks I had been unable to work. In addition to the itching, an agony of anticipation consumed me, and I couldn't concentrate on a new novel without obsessing over the manuscript that I imagined floating through the halls of Random House. Life revolved around the mail delivery, and after the rising anxiety of morning, I subsided into desolation for the rest of the day when no word arrived from Albert Erskine.

When we reached the Riviera, the rain stopped, but a cold, steel-gray sky glowered just above the palm trees. Despite the evidence of my senses, I refused to allow for the unpleasant reality that beaches called Tahiti and Baie des Anges experienced winter. The instant this freakish polar spell ended, I was convinced that summer would return, and the sand would be carpeted with suntanned bodies bared to the legal limit.

At American Express in Cannes we collected our mail—still nothing from Random House—and got the name of a doctor. My bandage needed changing. With luck, the stitches could be removed and I'd scratch the scar to my heart's content.

Linda accompanied me to an address at a waterfront high-rise on La Croisette. Since the debacle at Banque National de Paris, she was at pains not to leave me alone with French speakers. In asking the doctor to tend my cut, there was always a chance I'd invite him to indulge in deviant sex.

A well-barbered gentleman in a tweed coat with leather elbow patches let us into a penthouse that would never be mistaken for an American waiting room. It looked more like the Playboy Pad of the Month.

"You have money?" the doctor asked in English. "I will not lie. I am very expensive."

I assured him that as a Fulbright Fellow I enjoyed medical coverage through the U.S. government.

"You deal with the government," he said. "I deal in cash."

"That's fine. As long as I get a receipt to file an insurance claim."

"An informal receipt, yes. Not something the French *fisc* should see."

He beckoned me near a liquor trolley, next to a window with a sea view, where the light was better. "Who made this bandage?"

"The American Hospital in Paris."

"Ridiculous." He gave it a tentative tug, then a savage yank that ripped off the adhesive and released a yelp from me.

"Your husband," he told Linda, "is a cow-hard. Perhaps he would like cognac to calm him."

I insisted I was okay. He just caught me off guard.

The doctor lifted my wrist close to his face, like an astigmatic fellow squinting at a watch. He frowned. I frowned too at the black centipede of stitches that puckered my now hairless pink arm.

"This is boolshit," he said. "The stitches should be tied outside. These are inside, under the scab. What I must do—"

He went ahead and did it. He knocked off the scab and started prying out the stitches with what appeared to be a pronged dental instrument. Already accused of cowardice, I winced but remained silent as slivers of glass popped out.

"This is boolshit," he repeated. "Who cleaned your cut?"

I told him I had.

"So you are a doctor?" he asked. "Is that what you make with your Bullbright—medical studies?"

Through clenched teeth I said I was a novelist, not bothering to add "unpublished."

"How bizarre! What a coincidence! I have for another patient the most famous American novelist. The most famous writer in the world."

Did Updike, Bellow, or the aging John Steinbeck live in Cannes? I wondered. Or was there the literary equivalent of Jerry Lewis? Some writer regarded as a nincompoop in the States, but a genius in France?

"You must know him," the doctor declared. "Airald Rowbeans."

"Who?"

"Airald Rowbeans. Surely you have read his big best-seller *The Car Pet Beggars.*"

Ah, Harold Robbins! Author of *The Adventurers, The Carpetbaggers, Stiletto,* and *Lucky Lady.* Though the doctor offered to arrange an introduction, this was one literary encounter I decided to do without.

For a dreary, drenching week our search for a place to live carried us away from the Côte d'Azur, into the hill country a dozen miles inland where a necklace of tiny jeweled villages swagged from the Italian border to St. Tropez. There we looked at villas, vacation flats, renovated farms, and a converted granary, all far beyond our budget. Then we stumbled upon a stone cottage that we could afford on the fringes of Auribeau sur Siagne, a then undeveloped hill town that in watery winter light resembled a toy castle in an aquarium. Surrounding it was a miniature forest comprised of knee-high trees—actually a vineyard picked clean of grapes but aflutter with flaming orange leaves.

The cottage was of recent vintage, and reputedly designed by a renowned architect. The real estate agent let drop an ambiguous reference to Le Corbusier. The owner was a friend or former student of the master, and this house was a sublime example of something or other. Linda, whose expertise in these areas I deferred to, concurred that the place had many of Le Corbusier's hallmarks—molded concrete walls, skylights, an enclosed courtyard, and an intricate ensemble of rooms constructed as "a machine for living."

One basic amenity was missing, however. The house lacked a central heating system. The real estate agent swore that as soon as the current cold front passed, the living room fireplace would be more than sufficient to warm us on the odd chilly morning or evening. But although the rain did stop once we moved in, the temperature plummeted. During December, several hard freezes printed ferns of frost on the skylights, and two dustings of snow transformed the "machine for living" into a frigid crypt for dying.

Amid the futile consolations of symmetrical lines, Linda and I burrowed deep into that jumble of concrete boxes. Closing off one refrigerator of a room after another, we draped blankets over the windows, destroying views of a landscape worthy of Cézanne, and restricted ourselves to a semicircle directly in front of the fireplace. Writing was off the agenda. I had my hands full chopping wood and feeding it into the blaze. But if as W. H. Auden wrote of Rimbaud, "The cold had made a poet," then I hoped those arctic days would improve my prose.

In addition to foraging in the fields for wind-fallen trees, I dragged dead vines from the vineyard and filched sheets of cork oak that had been left to dry beside paths in the hills. I quickly learned the burning properties of all combustible materials—the transient warmth of newspaper; the medicinal-scented uselessness of eucalyptus; the snapping, spitting blue fizz of fresh pine; the dense, iron-hard grain of gnarled olive branches that took a long time to start, but burned for hours; and the beautiful snaking flames released from vine roots.

In the end, survival dictated that I install an oil-burning stove in the fireplace and run a metal flue up the chimney. This smudged the whitewashed walls and fouled the air, yet warmed the cottage enough to allow us to live indoors without coats and gloves. As we reduced this marvelous landmark of modern architecture to a slum, it came to me that no matter what else you might say about a work of art, it wasn't comfortable to live in one.

Nor was it comfortable to live on constant alert for a letter from Random House. When one finally arrived, I steeled myself against disappointment with the thought that at least the waiting was over. Again I was wrong. Albert Erskine said that the manuscript I had submitted six months ago might be more appealing to a young editor if I revised it. Did I care to give it a polish? Or would I rather have the book back?

Erskine offered no guarantees nor any advice about what needed to be changed. But since he seemed as reluctant to reject it as I was to withdraw it, I decided to rewrite *Man in Motion*. While my youthful ignorance back then is readily apparent, I cannot emphasize too much the force of my yearning. To say I longed to become a published writer is a pallid way of putting it. I wanted to do great things, lasting things. I wanted to move people's emotions and move myself far from the place I came from and the person I used to be.

So I wrote every morning. Then in the afternoon Linda and I retreated to the VW, our only reliable source of heat, and drove aimlessly around the Riviera. Untroubled by the traffic that turned these roads to purgatory during the summer, we explored the peninsulas of Cap d'Antibes, Cap Ferrat and Cap Martin, cruising through acid yellow forests of mimosas and pink almond orchards, where blizzards of blossoms drifted in our wake. We toured perfume factories in Grasse, ceramic kilns in Vallauris, the spiny botanical gardens of Eze, and the old fishing port of Villefranche, where fishermen had long ago been elbowed out by the Seventh Fleet. We walked the ramparts of medieval villages, we ate in a restaurant where Zelda Fitzgerald once flung herself down a flight of stairs in a fit of jealousy over Scott, and we visited the Matisse Chapel, whose tile walls reminded me of a men's room that had been runed over with the Magic Markings of a talented graffiti artist.

When there was nothing else to see, and I had sent the revised manuscript off to New York, I confronted once more the slow march of days, the withering life of winter in a remote French town, the agonizing wait for mail. Quite apart from the expense, I would never have taken it upon myself to telephone Albert Erskine. In that era, publishing depended in every respect on the written word.

To keep from climbing the walls, I told Linda to contact the doctor who had tweezed the stitches and glass out of my wrist. If he was still willing, I was ready to swallow my pride and welcome an introduction to Harold Robbins.

The doctor replied that Monsieur Rowbeans would be pleased to meet us at the bar of the Carlton Hotel in Cannes. Did I know the place? Of course I did. Not that I felt comfortable going there.

Hiding the Beetle back near the Gare, in a neighborhood of slummy pensions and impoverished North Africans who hawked counterfeit jewelry and handbags, Linda and I skulked into the chic part of town like a couple of cat burglars. The window displays appeared to have been laid out for aesthetic, rather than commercial, purposes. Passing in front of an unbroken tapestry of couturier gowns, designer suits, silk scarves, and

luxurious leather goods, I wondered, in the same way a child might puzzle over babies, where money came from. The wrinkly old folks in
wheelchairs pushed by nurses, the posh couples at sidewalk cafés warmed
by portable heaters, the swank, smirking owners of Mercedes and Masar-
atis seemed to have sprung full blown from the brow of Mammon. Did
this mean that if you weren't born to it you'd never have it?

With shifty-eyed uncertainty, we sidled up to the Carlton Hotel,
headquarters of the annual spring film festival. A candy-apple-red Jensen
Interceptor sparkled beneath the porte cochère. To add to its preening
arrogance, the car sported California license plates in a silver Beverly
Hills frame.

Feeling obliged to account for our threadbare existence, I stopped at
the front desk and explained that we had an appointment with Harold
Robbins.

"He's in the bar," the concierge said.

"Would you point him out to us?"

"You'll have no trouble recognizing him."

Enthroned at a corner table, Robbins wore a safari suit and an Austra-
lian bush hat with a leopard-skin band and one side of the brim bent up
at a jaunty angel. Puffing a slender cigarillo in an ivory holder, he had
slung one leg over the arm of his chair, and metronomically swinging his
chukka boot back and forth, he beguiled a young blonde. He didn't stand
up when I introduced myself. He did, however, doff his bush hat as he
shook Linda's hand. Though bald, he had luxuriant sideburns, gristled
with hairs as white as dental floss. He looked to be about sixty, a good
thirty years older than the blonde. I don't recall that he gave her name,
but he mentioned that she was a computer programmer from the IBM
plant in Nice who sometimes assisted him in "a technical capacity." His
wife, he said, was in Beverly Hills with their newborn baby. Harold
planned to join them soon. The Jensen needed servicing, and he intended to fly it to LA with him.

Conversation with some writers can be as difficult as extracting teeth.
With Robbins it was easier than lifting fruit from a Jello mold. Comfortable in the role of master of ceremonies, he ordered a round of drinks,
asked a perfunctory question—"So you're here on a Fulbright?"—then
with no prologue launched into his life story. Bits of this narrative I had
gleaned from his first novel, A Stone for Danny Fisher, an autobiographical, coming-of-age story set in Hell's Kitchen. Utterly unlike his other

books, it had gritty touches that I honestly admired, but he wasn't interested in hearing that. Waving off compliments with the cigarette holder, he clearly had a lot of ground to cover before he hit the literary phase of his career.

The computer programmer listened with rapt attention. Linda and I did our level best to emulate her, but Harold's flaws as a raconteur were the same ones that his fiction suffered—anemic motivation, sketchy transitions, and characters, including his swashbuckling younger self, who careened from cliché to cliché. After making and losing several fortunes in his early twenties, he claimed he became a sugar importer. When prices plunged, he went bankrupt again, but realized his life had all the ingredients of a major best-seller and a major major movie. Success and international celebrity followed. Still, he never forgot the lessons he learned selling sugar. Once he discovered there was big money to be made in books, he wrote with businesslike diligence and brought in best-sellers by the boatload.

Writing, like any enterprise, he told me, demanded knowledge of the marketplace and a knack for getting your money up front. "It comes down to the initial pitch. That's what Faulkner never got through his head. Bill believed in finishing a book, hoping a publisher would pick it up, reviewers would love it, and readers would buy it. What he forgot was everything he learned in Hollywood. That's where I perfected my pitch."

Unprompted, Robbins demonstrated the pitch for his next project. Not exactly E. M. Forster's classic definition of fiction's cause and effect—the king died and then the queen died of sadness—this was more along the lines of the well-hung business baron, having been abandoned at birth, devotes his every waking hour, when not making love or money, to the search for his mother. Little does he suspect that she's a starlet employed by the studio he's just bought. Still beautiful and strongly sexed, svelte of waist and firm of breast, her nipples the color of ripe plums, she meets her son and falls madly . . .

"When I walk into my editor's office," Robbins said, "that's all I'll have—a concept. When I walk out, I'll have a check for a million dollars."

In those days, that figure was much aspired to, a million bucks. According to all reports, Philip Roth had topped it with *Portnoy's Complaint*. Did Robbins, I asked a leading question, believe Roth's publisher had ponied up the money on the basis of a pitch about "the Raskolnikov of jerking off," the boy who put "id back into yid?"

Harold readjusted his wide-spread honcho posture, removing his right leg from the arm of the chair, throwing his left over the other arm. "I doubt Phil's made a million. He's never earned a fraction of that on his previous properties. If he did this time, more power to him. All I'm saying, Mike, is you'll never make a million bucks unless they print a million books, and they'll never do that unless you get a million-dollar advance."

My head swam—and not simply from the absurd numbers and circular logic. The waiter had served another round of drinks, and the alcohol contributed to the general ambiance of over-stimulation. After months of isolation and the shortage of heat and light in our house, the Carlton seemed sinfully profligate with its electricity, liquor, and bowls of peanuts and olives. Trying to make a joke of our misery, I mentioned that we had nearly died this winter of the cold weather.

"But winter's the best time to be here," Robbins said. "Seeing the Riviera in summer and saying you love it is like looking at a woman with her clothes on and thinking you love her. You never know until you get down to the bare truth."

"C'est vrai," the blonde agreed.

I wasn't sure I followed. Getting down to the bare truth in our cottage was an invitation to chilblains and pneumonia. Still, I couldn't deny that I appreciated the prodigality of the Carlton, and I was tempted to lie back and surrender to opulence. But another part of me believed I had better put this seductive Satan in his bush hat and safari suit behind me. Bracing myself, I thanked Harold Robbins for his wise counsel and said we had to leave.

"Hey, no. You just got here."

"It's Linda's birthday. I'm taking her out to dinner." The first statement was the truth, the second a lie. We would celebrate at home, where the tile floors were as cold as an ice skating rink.

"How old are you, honey?" Robbins asked.

"Twenty-five," Linda told him.

"That's a great age. You deserve a great birthday. What's your favorite dish?"

"Roast rack of lamb."

"That's what my cook's fixing tonight. Have dinner at my house. There's champagne. There may even be some kind of cake."

As he garnished the menu of attractions, I didn't ask whether his house had heat. That went without saying. And I didn't wonder whether I could justify accepting his hospitality. I needed to quit thinking of myself. This was Linda's day, and only a churl would deny her a chance to enjoy it. Retrieving the Beetle from the Gare, I sped back to the Carlton and followed the swerving rear end of the red Jensen up to Le Cannet, to an exclusive community called La Californie.

Harold Robbins's villa looked as though it had been conveyed intact from Beverly Hills to the barbered hills above Cannes. Formidably gated, fenced in by stucco walls, the property was further screened from prying eyes by rows of cypress trees. An aggressive gardener had trimmed their natural flame-tipped shapes into Doric columns. From the front terrace, Robbins gestured to houses on lower slopes and identified their owners by name and title—Count this and Begum that, Infanta this and former dictator of that. "It's a great place, France—even if the French do have peculiar habits like fighting with their feet and fucking with their faces."

He showed us the swimming pool, a rectangle of cobalt gleaming under evening mist.

"It's the first heated pool on the Côte d'Azur," he said. "And the villa's fully air-conditioned. That's another first."

"Very nice," I said.

"Yeah, it's fun. That's my yacht." He directed our attention to a marina where dozens of ocean-going vessels all looked equally ostentatious from that distance.

"Nice."

"Not that one. The one next to it," he said. "The biggest one."

"How long is it?" Linda asked.

"I have no idea. I never use it except for parties during the film festival. The rest of the time my wife runs around in it. She likes to skin dive."

"Don't you?"

"It's not I don't like it. My health won't permit it." After lighting a cigar, he held the dead match to either side of his head as if to singe his sideburns. "I've got punctured eardrums."

"What a shame," Linda said.

"Nah, I had it done by a doctor so when I'm eating a chick I can breathe through them."

He delivered the line in such a deadpan voice that it barely caused a hiccough in the conversation. I glanced at the blonde. No reaction. Maybe Harold had exceeded her grasp of demotic English. Then again, perhaps she knew he was telling the truth—or restating a larger truth from his fiction.

Inside the villa, Robbins disappeared into the kitchen after delegating the blonde to give us a tour. Adjacent to a master bedroom decorated in high bawdy-house style, there was the Holy of Holies, a windowless cubicle as austere as a monk's cell. With no books, papers, or pens to distract him from his duty, Harold worked here in Zen-like simplicity with only a chair, a desk, and a Dictaphone into which he emptied himself, body, mind, and soul. This was one occasion when I thought I could do without asking an author about his writing habits.

At dinner, Robbins picked up where he had left off at the Carlton, eschewing bookish conversation in favor of a disquisition about his personal theories and preferences. He discussed wines, their years and labels, and the proper serving temperature for red, white, and rosé. He described the difficulties he had had convincing his cook to try his hand at *la cuisine américaine*. He praised California produce, Florida orange juice, and Skippy Peanut Butter. Still, our meal that night was resolutely French. The lamb was delicious, the wine, despite the capsule history that preceded its pouring, excellent. Then there was a chocolate gâteau, complete with candles for Linda to blow out. Finally, Robbins produced a prettily wrapped package. Unless he kept a supply of birthday gifts on hand, I couldn't imagine where he came up with the necklace inside it.

Linda exclaimed that he shouldn't have. She protested that she couldn't possibly accept it. He didn't listen and continued lowering it over her head. The necklace didn't fit past her brow. Beads dotted her forehead like an Indian princess's dowry.

"Looks terrific," Robbins said. But he removed it, unhooked the clasp and refastened the necklace around her throat. "Now it's perfect, and so are you."

At the end of the evening he strolled us out to the VW and asked, "Anything you want from the States?"

Seized by a piercing sense of all that I wanted at that moment, especially a positive response from Random House, I must have radiated a neediness that Robbins couldn't help noticing. "Hey, would you kids like to fly back with me? My treat."

It sounded like a line from his fiction, the turning point in the plot where a couple of poor waifs morph into jet-setters, then molder into corruption. These course-changing coincidences and life-altering encounters had never rung true in Robbins's novels. But I think he believed in them and would have flown us to Los Angeles if only to prove that his world view was valid.

"Thanks a lot," I told him. "But I have to stay here and write."

"I understand." He clapped a hand to my shoulder, coach to callow junior varsity scrub. "Keep at it. I'll call when I get back, and we'll do this again."

It never happened. Harold Robbins never called, and neither did I. Some experiences are unrepeatable, I decided. Yet I've always been grateful for his hospitality, and I haven't forgotten his counsel; you can't sell a million books unless you get a million-dollar advance. That none of my publishers has recognized this self-evident wisdom doesn't render it untrue. And just because Linda noticed the next time we parked near the Gare that the North Africans were selling necklaces like hers for ten francs doesn't mean she wasn't grateful for her birthday gift.

Robert Penn Warren
and Eleanor Clark

Westport, Grenoble, and the south of France

"TALENT is extremely common," Kurt Vonnegut once remarked. "What is extremely rare is the willingness to endure the life of a writer. The problems are physiological among other things. Sitting still is something the body was never meant to do for any length of time. Enduring solitude is something the human mind was never intended to put up with for very long. . . . The work itself is exceedingly tedious. It's like making wallpaper by hand for the Sistine Chapel."

And that, as Vonnegut didn't get around to saying, is the easy and pleasurable part—the creative act that, for all its difficulties, is the one thing a writer can control. Everything else is in the hands of editors, publishers, reviewers, and readers who, like the ancient Greek gods, pull off our wings for their sport. Pull off our wings and make us wait.

Seven months after I first sent *Man in Motion* to Albert Erskine and he began passing it around Random House, I received a letter from a young editor who had read the original and revised manuscripts. He liked the novel enormously and thought it publishable. Once the powers-that-be decreed whether to permit him to take it on, he promised to be back in touch. If he got the go-ahead, this would be the first novel on his list, so he shared my eagerness.

Two agonizingly silent months passed before my resolve cracked and I shot off a telegram: "Yes or no on *Man in Motion*?" When there was no immediate reply, I figured I had overplayed a weak hand and lost; I had been a fool and fumbled away my last best chance. But days later, in its own good time, an answering telegram arrived: "Hope terms acceptable. Letter follows."

Convinced that he had accepted the book, I said we should celebrate. But Linda believed that after so many delays and disappointments it would be rank arrogance to assume anything. And she was right. The editor's laggardly letter was a letdown rather than a call to uncork the champagne. It offered a $1,500 advance, which he claimed was "standard" for first novels. What was worse, he said the manuscript needed substantial rewriting that would postpone its publication by eighteen months.

Although the advance seemed rock bottom, I didn't have the nerve to demand better terms. Accepting what struck me as a lousy deal, I promised to do whatever I could to improve *Man in Motion*. (Parenthetically, I should admit that while I thought the money was far from "standard," I lacked any basis for comparison. None of the handful of novelists I knew ever disclosed the details of his contract. Even now that I've met hundreds of writers and we have discussed everything from our marriages to the frightening filigree of our psyches and the more frightening condition of our prostates, I have yet to hear anybody admit what he got for a first novel. Out of shame that they have been mercilessly screwed, authors tend to remain silent on the subject.)

Eventually the young editor sent longer, chattier letters, and once my signature was on a contract, he resumed praising *Man in Motion* for its energy and irreverence, its galloping pace and coruscating humor. In his opinion, it was a contemporary gloss on the classic road novel, a comic variation on *Easy Rider,* and he couldn't wait to go over it with a blue pencil. First, however, he planned to take a vacation to "someplace warm and healing."

That was the last I heard from him. The "warm and healing" resort turned out to be Chicago, where he signed on as an editor at *Playboy.* This I learned from Albert Erskine, who, after another long silence, informed me that the fellow had resigned from Random House, leaving my manuscript in limbo. Since Erskine felt I had been treated shabbily, he volunteered to make room for me on his list. But I would need to be patient. Warren, O'Hara, Welty, and Michener had novels scheduled for the same season as mine.

Erskine added that when an editor left Random House, he customarily drafted a report on pending projects. For months, Erskine had been mulling over the memo that my editor had dumped in his lap. Because it was "shrill and largely negative," Erskine had debated whether to show it to me, but finally decided I should see it.

The young editor's parting words packed the wallop of a sucker punch that almost floored me. For days I couldn't bring myself to reread the memo. For years, its memory tormented me. With no mention of his previous zeal or the novel's "energy" or "irreverence," he excoriated *Man in Motion's* flaws—the flatness of its style, the immaturity of its conception, the embarrassment of its execution. Far from needing mere revision, he declared that the book required major surgery, a plot transplant, a new author. Apologizing to Erskine, not me, he confessed that he had accepted it only out of ambition to start his own list. But now he had to be blunt—as if he had been shadow boxing with kid gloves up to this point. The novel was unsalvageable, and the solution simple: "Pay Mewshaw his small advance and let him go."

To Erskine's credit and my enduring gratitude, he said this was sadistically unfair. He had no intention of cutting me loose. Still, he recommended that I review the manuscript in light of the memo and make changes where necessary. As for his own editorial suggestions, he would reserve them until we spoke face to face.

Returning to *Man in Motion* under these circumstances reminded me of the previous fall, when the doctor at the American Hospital had ordered me to clean my own cut. Sick to my stomach and weak at the knees, I wanted to shut my eyes, switch on the water, and pray that all the impurities washed away. But open-eyed and painfully alert, I forced myself to comb through the manuscript line by line, and naturally I noticed countless ways that it could be improved. I changed the first person narration to third person limited, ironed out the unnecessarily kinked chronology, rearranged chapters, added several scenes, and to complete the radical surgery, renamed all the characters.

Though I didn't realize it at the time, my experience wasn't unusual. Many writers find the birth of a book a rough process involving a detached publisher with a lousy bedside manner and a physician/editor whose forceps delivery leaves scars. With repetition things don't necessarily get better. Whether it's a first novel or the fifteenth, an author has to forget what he went through last time and accept that it's going to hurt again.

If I had had the brains or the balls, I might have asked for a new contract for my new novel. But I was too drained to dare do that. After the punishing gauntlet I had gone through, I simply mailed the revised manuscript to Erskine and was too numb to react when he replied with equivocating brevity. The new version of *Man in Motion,* he wrote, had its pluses and minuses. He would save specific editorial comments until I came back to the States. When would that be?

In December 1969, trading in our tickets on the SS *France,* I booked flights for Linda and me on Icelandic Airlines, the only reliable discount carrier that crossed the Atlantic in those days. Although faster than an ocean liner, this required traveling to Paris, then to Luxembourg by bus, followed by a three-hour hop to Reykjavik, a couple of hours on the glacial ground, and an eight-hour Calvary on a turbo prop. The day after we landed, Linda and I caught a train to Westport, Connecticut, to spend the weekend at Albert Erskine's.

I didn't regard the visit as a social occasion. The prospect of our long-delayed editorial session filled me with dread. Although Random House's accounting department had at last spat out a check for $1,500, it didn't seem impossible that they might demand their money back if I didn't satisfactorily answer Albert's queries.

As it transpired, we spent a total of forty-five minutes in his office. We changed a word here and there, deleted several paragraphs and inserted a few sentences for clarity. Why this couldn't have been done months before and by mail, I never asked, and Albert never explained. That was simply the way he liked to work—at home, with the author at his elbow and his wife, Marisa, an Italian countess, downstairs preparing gourmet meals. He detested New York City, the current publishing ethos, any mention of publicity and book promotion, and many of his prominent colleagues at Random House. It was often observed that Erskine was of the old school. While he continued working well into the eighties, he conducted himself as if the business hadn't grown from a cottage industry into a multinational conglomerate. It isn't difficult to conceive of the contempt he would have expressed at voice mail, e-mail, laptop computers, and the Internet.

While Albert could be a professional scold, he proved to be a sterling editor, a thoughtful friend, and a gracious host. A loyal man himself, he inspired loyalty in others and stayed connected all his life to the writers he had met at Vanderbilt and later at LSU's *Southern Review*. When literary polemicist Richard Kostelanetz accused him in *The End of Intelligent Writing* of being the Godfather of the Southern Mafia, Erskine pled guilty. But for a man born, raised, and educated in Tennessee, he didn't carry much regional baggage. While it's true that his list was top-heavy with white males, he also worked with Ralph Ellison and Eudora Welty, and although it was his association with the best-seller James A. Michener that made him invulnerable at Random House—Michener's contract specified that he had the right to leave when and if Albert did—he had also edited avant-garde authors such as Malcolm Lowry and Paul Bowles.

After I finished my Ph.D., I took a job teaching at the University of Massachusetts at Amherst, and that fall *Man in Motion* finally came out. But the process had been so long, I felt a bit as I imagine a female elephant does when giving birth after a twenty-two-month gestation period. I couldn't quite relate to the emotions surrounding the conception and suddenly had difficulty coping with a new set of problems. No longer struggling to get published, I now worried about how to get reviewed, read, publicized, and distributed. The book received a few nice notices, especially Larry McMurtry's in the *Washington Post,* but in vast stretches of the country it fell into a void and overall managed to sell no more than two thousand copies. Fortunately there was a modest paperback deal, which pleased Random House and persuaded Albert Erskine to buy my next novel. Still, far from convincing me that I was a full-fledged writer, the book's reception made me feel I was clinging to a sheer cliff by my fingernails.

Since we lived little more than two hours north of Westport, Linda and I were frequently invited for weekends at the Erskines'. Sometimes Donald Klopfer, the co-founder of Random House, showed up with his wife, Pat, or John Hersey drove down from New Haven or Peter de Vries swung by from his home farther along the Post Road. Before dinner Albert decanted the wine to let it breathe, and Marisa busied herself in the kitchen, making every dish from scratch. She wouldn't have dreamed of serving store-bought pasta or dessert. She even whipped up her own mayonnaise. Then Albert called the guests to the table, urging them to take second and third helpings, repeating what had been the mantra of his boyhood home in Memphis: "There's a lot more in the kitchen."

After the other guests were gone and the dishes were done, Albert and I would walk his dog, a black lab called Alex, down the leafy tunnel of Cavalry Road and return to the house for a nightcap. This was my favorite time, when Albert was most likely to be talkative. With luck, I could coax him to tell stories about William Faulkner.

When it suited him, Albert said, Faulkner fell silent and remained mute for hours, sometimes for days. In the company of strangers, he pretended to be deaf, or he got blind drunk, which gave him another excuse to go quiet. He never read reviews, shrugged off questions about his work, never replied to fan letters, and ignored importuning scholars and autograph hounds. When people sent him self-addressed envelopes hoping for his signature on a scrap of paper, Faulkner crossed out their addresses and used the envelopes for his own correspondence. Some fans, Albert said, sent checks, thinking Faulkner would endorse them, and they'd get his autograph that way. But he tore the checks up and tossed them in the trash. Though not generally given to levity, Albert cracked up laughing whenever he recounted these anecdotes.

One evening Anatole Broyard, then the *New York Times* daily book reviewer, came to dinner at the Erskines'. A legendary man about town during the forties and fifties in Greenwich Village, Broyard now lived in Westport with his wife and family and commuted into the city with scores of other suburbanites. Still, he gave the impression of a guy who knew the streets and knew the score. A hipster, a holdover from the bebop era, he was an elegant, epigrammatic stylist in his writing and an indefatigable charmer in his relationships.

Since Cleanth Brooks was among the guests, the conversation inevitably turned to the South. Anatole mentioned that he was from New Orleans. Then, in a tangent, we started talking about race, and Anatole announced that he was black. "It's right there on my birth certificate," he said. "One-sixteenth black."

I took a closer look. He had blue eyes and crinkly hair. It appeared to me conceivable that he might be part black. But his admission had no impact on the conversation, and we went on to different topics.

Over the next couple of decades, I met Broyard periodically in New York and spoke to him frequently by telephone when he switched from daily reviewing to an editorial position on the *Sunday Book Review.* Many of his colleagues at the *Times* knew he was black and that he had served during World War II in a colored Army unit. Nobody cared, least of all Anatole himself, who would have objected to any attempt to categorize him.

So it was puzzling after his death when Broyard became the subject of an article in *The New Yorker,* by Henry Louis Gates Jr., who alleged that Anatole had led a "secret" life. According to Gates, he shunned relatives in New Orleans and concealed his racial identity, never acknowledging even to his children that he was black. A few years after this article, Philip Roth published a novel, *The Human Stain,* whose black protagonist passed for white. Reviews of the book routinely claimed that the character was based on Broyard. But before the image of Anatole as a racial obfuscator becomes scriven in stone, it strikes me as worth stressing that someone who admits at a Westport dinner party that he's black cannot be terribly worried about passing for white.

At a Sunday lunch, Albert introduced an old man as Harold Loeb. He didn't need to say more. The name and, on second glance, the man were recognizable. Though he carried a cane and hobbled painfully, he was broad-shouldered and broken-nosed—the very image, fifty years after the fact, of Robert Cohn in *The Sun Also Rises.* Here was the source for Hemingway's college boxer who had been overmatched at Princeton and got his nose flattened, the romantic who read *The Purple Land* as if it were a self-help book, the sap who slept with Lady Brett Ashley and mistook sex for love, the man who talked too much and didn't drink enough, the bully who beat up a bullfighter and had no comprehension of the Hemingway Code.

Because Harold Loeb came from a family of wealthy Jewish financiers, Hemingway's fictional depiction of him had an ugly undertone of anti-Semitism, not to mention jealousy. At the time he was writing *The Sun Also Rises* and vilifying the rich, Papa was about to trade in a first wife with a modest independent income for a second wife with extravagant resources. So as much as I admired Hemingway's work, I was sympathetic to Loeb and interested in hearing his side of the story. The problem was how to broach the subject without embarrassing him.

But then Loeb brought it up himself. With puppy-like ingenuousness, he announced, as I would wager he had hundreds of times, "I knew Hemingway. He based Robert Cohn on me."

That this might impress some people as a dubious pedigree, not a boasting point, didn't seem to have penetrated his self-regard. Where another man might have exaggerated the differences between himself and his slanderous portrait in a novel, Loeb appeared pleased to remain trapped in amber. He even dressed as Hemingway had described Robert Cohn—like a preppy undergrad in slacks and a polo shirt with an unbuttoned collar. Though his weathered face suggested that experience should have taught him hard lessons in caution, he charged out of his corner with the ungainly exuberance of a club fighter. No matter how badly he got knocked silly by subtler blows, he kept swinging from the heels and ending up on his keister.

"Hem was never any good at boxing," Loeb said. "He was too slow and heavy, and he had that bum leg from the war. I wasn't afraid of him. I'd have fought him. After what he wrote, I got mad, and he sent word that I better not show my ugly Jew face. But I bumped into him in a bar. I stood right behind him. He spotted me in the mirror. That was his chance if he wanted to take a poke at me. He just blushed. The back of his neck turned bright red, and he didn't say a word."

A novelist and publisher of *Broom,* one of the many short-lived little magazines in the Latin Quarter, Loeb abandoned Paris after the '29 crash and became a businessman in the States. Yet that earlier era still exerted a powerful, if peculiar, hold on him. Others might praise France's beauty, history, and culture, the creative foment that pervaded it after World War I, the splendid concentration of artists, writers, composers, philosophers, philanderers, and poseurs. Loeb might have mentioned the famous figures he had met—Picasso, Gertrude Stein, James Joyce, Man Ray—but he didn't. Instead, like a college boy just home from a junior year abroad, he blurted, "I went to Paris for the women and the wine. A lot of us did. America was a pretty puritanical place back then. There was the Volstead Act, you know, so you couldn't drink. But in France you could buy alcohol, and it was no trouble meeting women. Forget about the artistic side. French girls would go to bed with you."

"Oh, Harold," sighed the woman he was paired with at lunch, "that's silly."

"No, it's not. Hemingway and Fitzgerald, I bet they were both virgins when they got married. I sure was."

"Oh, Harold."

He craned around to Albert Erskine. For an instant I feared he would ask when Albert lost his virginity and then proceed around the table and put the same question to the rest of us. But he did something worse, bringing up a name that was never to be uttered in the Erskine household.

"Hey, do I remember right? Weren't you married to Katherine Anne Porter?"

A pall of silence, an appalled silence, settled over the table. The grimace on Albert's face was one I recognized. He might have been irritated at a printer's error, an idiotic copy-editing mistake, a line dropped from a finished book. These niggling foul-ups gave him dyspepsia. He dabbed a napkin at his lips. "Yes," he said, "for a very short and unhappy time." Then he excused himself, left the room, and never returned.

It took twenty minutes for his absence to register on Harold Loeb. "Is something wrong with Albert?" he asked.

Nobody answered. Why bother? Just as a rose is a rose is a rose, here was a man who was what he was and would forever be. Hemingway had nailed him dead five decades ago. Guileless, tactless, constantly inserting his foot between his teeth, he had lost the capacity and perhaps the will to wriggle free from his literary chrysalis.

The next year, when Loeb died during a visit to Morocco, Erskine said, "Harold would have been a happier man all his life if he had known he'd be buried in Marrakech. That's the perfect resting spot for a romantic sophomore."

Despite his jaundiced view of publishing, Albert proposed that I go into it. He needed an assistant and pressed me to take the job. While he may have considered this high praise, I saw a red flag. Didn't he have faith in me as a writer?

"You Irish and your thin skin!" he protested. "You remind me of John O'Hara. When somebody told him, 'I read your new book a second time and liked it even more,' O'Hara said, 'What was wrong with it the first time?'"

"Sorry, it's just that I'd rather be a novelist than an editor." Eager to work full time on fiction, I told him I intended to jump off the tenure track at UMass and return to Europe. With Rome as our temporary base, we thought we could live cheaply. When our savings ran out, maybe I'd find a part-time teaching job in Italy.

At this, Albert perked up. Because of Marisa, he was an irrepressible Italophile and a font of information about the country. He urged to me to talk to his old friend Robert Penn Warren and his wife, Eleanor Clark. They had both spent years at the American Academy in Rome. Had I read Eleanor's *Rome and a Villa*? No, well, then I should do so immediately. Meanwhile he would invite the Warrens to dinner.

I did as instructed and agreed that *Rome and a Villa* was a superb book. As for Robert Penn Warren, I had been reading him since college—the poetry, the novels, and his textbooks *Understanding Poetry* and *Understanding Fiction*. While completing my second book, *Waking Slow,* I had reread *All the King's Men.* There was a chapter in it about Jack Stanton's divorce, the collapse of his academic career, and a dreamlike drive to California that I wanted to remember and I wanted to forget. Since my novel was set in Los Angeles, I hoped to evoke some of the same resonances as Warren had without slavishly imitating his depiction of a man emotionally beached at land's end. Because my fiction continued to draw heavily on autobiographical events, I also hoped to learn from Warren's successful reimagination of Louisiana politics and Huey Long's career. Increasingly it had become clear that for all my admiration for experimental novels and the Modernist tradition, I was a realist and needed to master the conventions of the genre while at the same time developing a distinctive voice.

It was cold that spring night, with a threat of frost to the newly bloomed irises. The Warrens arrived at the Erskines' house ruddy-cheeked and slightly breathless, as though they had jogged over from their home in Fairfield. At once I made the mistake of referring to them as the Penn Warrens.

"The last name is Warren," Eleanor corrected me. "No Penn."

"That's what happens," Albert said, "when you use your middle name on books. You're lucky people don't insert a hyphen."

Robert Penn Warren told Linda and me to call him Red. But his age—going on sixty-seven—and his eminence made the nickname catch in my throat. Then, too, although he had the high, freckled coloring of a redhead, his hair, what little he had left, was white. William Styron had commented on Warren's resemblance to a sailor—"that seamed and craggy face which has gazed, like Melville, into the briny abyss, that weather-wise expression and salty presence which have made him physically the very model of a sea-dog." But it was of Popeye, not Melville, that he reminded me. Compact and muscular, he bristled with energy, punctuating his remarks with abrupt gestures of his chunky arms, speaking in such a rush that he fell to spluttering and stuttering. There was also something about his eyes, a squint that called to mind the cartoon character.

As a teenager Warren had qualified for an appointment to the U.S. Naval Academy. But when his younger brother tossed a lump of coal and accidentally hit him in the left eye, that ended his plans for Annapolis and set him on course to become a writer. Eventually, the eye had to be removed and replaced by a glass one.

If Red resembled Popeye, Eleanor Clark bore no comparison at all to Olive Oyle. She and her sister Eunice had gone to Vassar during Mary McCarthy's era, and while Eunice wound up cruelly caricatured in *The Group,* Eleanor possessed the glamor, gray matter, and ambition to compete with McCarthy. In her fifties, she was a handsome woman, well-dressed and with well-coiffed ash-blond hair. But like her husband, she had a facial imperfection. Her upper lip looked slightly askew, as though she had been born with a harelip and had undergone cosmetic surgery. Her mouth pulled to one side, giving her a disapproving air or, in her least attractive moments, a supercilious smirk.

When Albert told the Warrens that Linda and I had spent a year in France, Eleanor smoothly switched gears from mid-Atlantic English to fluent French. Linda found the transition easy to make. I, of course, flubbed it, and with every word I mispronounced, Eleanor said, "Read my lips." (This was long before President Bush's notorious tax pledge.) "Now repeat after me."

Perhaps she regarded these attentions as a favor. While plenty of people fell short of her linguistic standards—she dismissed Mary McCarthy's Italian as "atrocious"—at least she tried to improve me.

The language lesson might have lasted throughout the cocktail hour had Red not rescued me. "I remember my first trip to Paris," he said. "I was just out of college and visiting Allen Tate. At dinner one night, he introduced me to F. Scott Fitzgerald. I couldn't think of anything to say except how much I loved *The Great Gatsby*. Fitzgerald turned on me like a snake and shouted that he was sick of college kids talking nonsense about his book. He never wanted to hear its title again. He wished he had never written it."

"What did you do?" I asked.

Red laughed. "I left the restaurant. I was crushed."

As I would come to appreciate, Red often defused tense situations with self-deprecating humor. In my presence, he never confronted his wife. Instead, he tried to pacify her when she turned dogmatic and stepped between her and her target when she lost her temper.

Red went on to ask who had directed my dissertation on William Styron. When I told him Douglas Day, both he and Albert knew that Day was writing the authorized biography of Malcolm Lowry.

"Have you read *Under the Volcano*?" Eleanor broke in. Before I could answer, she set about disparaging Lowry's best novel and by implication Day's biography. "I lived in Mexico," she said. "I'm familiar with the sort of expatriate riffraff Lowry wrote about. He was just another self-congratulatory drunk—Cuernavaca was full of them—passing off his incoherence as genius."

Since Albert had edited *Under the Volcano*, I expected him to speak up in its defense. He didn't. Neither did Red or he react when Eleanor found fault with another of Albert's authors, Paul Bowles. She characterized The Sheltering Sky as "childish nihilism about depressing, worthless people."

To change the subject, I asked Warren whether living in Connecticut and teaching at Yale made it difficult as he continued writing about the South.

"I don't need to live there to remember it," he said. "No matter where I am, I'll always be a southerner. As for Fairfield and New Haven, I regard them as luxury hotels I check into and out of whenever I want."

Though I didn't say so, I wasn't sure I agreed that writing about a South that you remembered was the same as writing about the South that actually existed. And wouldn't Warren, like many other relocated southern authors, have been wise to address the issue directly in his fiction? As for spending your life in a luxury hotel, wasn't there a high price to be paid for that?

When Marisa called us to dinner, I hadn't finished my drink, and as I carried it into the dining room, Eleanor looked askance. "Surely, Mike, you're not going to be so rude as to bring a cocktail to the table."

In the sideward tug of her upper lip there was the intimation of a smile. Taking her remark as a joke, I replied with one of my own. "Surely, Eleanor, you're not going to be so rude as to point out my faux pas."

She didn't laugh, and I assumed this was the last time we would see the Warrens. But as Albert poured the wine and Marisa ladled out the *fatto a mano* pasta, the conversation turned to Italy, and Eleanor was pleased that I had liked *Rome and a Villa* and thrilled that Linda and I would be in Rome the coming fall. The Warrens' daughter, Rosanna, was there studying art, and Eleanor hoped we'd look her up. Rosanna was going through an awkward stage, she said. Having an American couple to call on would be a great solace not only to Rosanna but to her parents.

Eleanor recommended that we stay at the American Academy in Rome. Why didn't I apply to the director, Bartlett Hayes, or her old friend Frank Brown, a classicist at the Academy? When I mentioned that I might set my next novel in the Middle East, she immediately suggested I contact Doris Shoukri at the American University in Cairo. Red had lectured there one winter when the Warrens traveled to Egypt with the Styrons for a sailing trip up the Nile. Then she added that she and Red planned to spend the coming year in Grenoble with their son Gabriel. We were welcome to visit whenever we passed through France.

Although I nodded and smiled and murmured the appropriate noises, I didn't know what to make of this woman who, after needling me one moment, offered helpful advice and hospitality the next. Once the Warrens left and Albert and I were out walking the dog, I asked about Eleanor Clark, and Albert conceded she could be prickly and opinionated and, at times, a pain in the ass. She wanted him to be her editor, but he had ducked that honor and passed her on to Pantheon, another Random House imprint. Still, she was awfully good to Red, whose first wife, Albert said, had been "a real bitch and crazy to boot. With Eleanor you just have to let her speak her piece and keep in mind that she doesn't mean to be as insulting as she sometimes sounds."

That September, carrying all we owned in four suitcases, Linda and I caught a cheap flight to Copenhagen and started the long trek to Italy by train. In Paris, at American Express, we picked up a letter from Eleanor, who repeated that she and Red counted on us stopping in Grenoble. They had rented a villa that was reputed to have belonged to Stendhal. It had plenty of room, she promised, "even if it is haphazardly arranged."

Robert Penn Warren's new novel, *Meet Me in the Green Glen,* had just appeared to "mixed reviews," as publishers euphemistically put it. Months before, Albert had been blunt with me about the book. Referring to it as "a tired novel," he was of the opinion that at his age Red should stick to poetry. People, including authors themselves, Albert said, forgot how much stamina a sustained narrative of several hundred pages demanded.

In Grenoble, the air was sharp and clear, and by early October snow already capped the mountains. The Warrens collected us at the train station in a brand-new beige Mercedes. "We call it *Meet Me in the Green Glen,*" Red said. "It cost almost the whole damn advance."

Eleanor drove while Red manned the navigator's seat for the ride out of town to Villa Stendhal. A gabled structure, it was gray and unprepossessing compared to its vivid setting in the foothills of the Alps. The Warrens occupied the back half of the building. The owners lived in a separate apartment around front. Our room was behind glass double doors gauzily draped with transparent curtains. The doors opened onto the dining room, and on the other side of the table was the room where Red and Eleanor slept. Gabriel, off at school for the day, had settled in what must have been a maid's room. To my surprise, the Warrens, not unlike us, appeared content to travel light and camp out in improvised quarters as long as they had adequate light to read by and space to work in.

While Linda and Eleanor shopped for dinner, Red and I walked the family dog. No relaxed afternoon stroll, this hike up into the steep hills had about it the strenuous urgency of a forced march. For an hour we climbed. The dog strained at its leash, and as Red reined him in, he never looked likely to lose his grip or his breath. Thick through the chest, he ambled along, his arms jutting out at angles from their sockets. Red told me he had a bad shoulder and exercised with barbells.

"Have you heard from Albert?" I asked.

"Just a note with a batch of reviews—the bad along with the good. Some of them were truly vicious," he conceded.

"You two have been friends so long, I assumed you stayed in close contact. I suppose that was another of my misconceptions about publishing—that editors and authors were forever firing off letters to each other. I was beginning to feel shortchanged."

Red laughed and paraphrased Conrad's *Heart of Darkness*: "'Mister Perkins, he dead.' Editors don't have time to correspond with writers. They're too busy hunting for best-sellers and having lunch with agents and publicity people. Not," he added, "that Albert has ever been very communicative. You should have seen him with Faulkner. The two of them could sit for hours sucking on their pipes and saying not word one."

As young men, Albert and Red had moved from Vanderbilt to Baton Rouge, where Red taught at LSU and Albert went to grad school. They both worked on *The Southern Review*. "Back then he was a fun-loving guy," Red said. "He liked to dance and go down to New Orleans for parties. Then he met Katherine Anne Porter and shocked everybody by marrying her. She was one tough woman and a good bit older than him. He was in his twenties; she must have been over forty. It didn't last long—just long enough to knock the starch out of Albert. He married a second time, and that didn't last either. Then he had terrible trouble with his teeth and almost went broke getting them fixed. Things didn't turn around until he got together with Marisa and began investing in the market. He's a sharp cookie with money."

This I had surmised. In addition to badgering me to take care of my teeth—"You only have one set. You need to floss after every meal"—Albert urged me to begin buying a portfolio of stocks and bonds. He offered to help pick them. He handled investments for a few of his authors, James Michener and the Warrens among them, and was happy to do the same for me. But since he had paid a meager $3,700 advance for my second novel, I wondered where he imagined I would get any spare money to invest.

Barring the unexpected, I was resigned to teaching again, and from my year at UMass, I was aware that academia and writing weren't always compatible. I marveled that Red managed to be so prolific while holding down a full-time position at Yale. But he admitted, "I do as little as I can get away with. I teach my classes. I read the students' stories. But I don't waste my breath on those that are hopeless, and I don't attend departmental meetings or serve on committees."

"That's fine for you. You're Robert Penn Warren. I couldn't get away with that."

"When I started out, I wasn't Robert Penn Warren either," he said. "But a writer's got to be ruthless with himself and whatever or whoever steals time from him."

He tugged the leash, and the dog turned and led us back to the house, where Linda was setting the table and Eleanor was gutting an immense fish. A *colin* of five or six pounds, it barely fit into the poaching pan. As she lugged it from the sink to the stove and sliced onions and potatoes atop it, she was admonishing Gabe, who had ridden his moped home from the *lycée* without a hat. "Do you realize how much body heat you lose through your bare head? You'll catch your death of pneumonia."

Gabe argued that he had plenty of hair to keep him warm. But his mother ordered him to wear a hat from now until the weather changed next spring. Then, while the *colin* cooked, she asked to speak to me alone. We crossed to a converted barn that she had commandeered as her office. Seated at a desk, she parked me on a stool, like a dunce, and said, "I'm worried about Gabe. I'd be grateful if you'd speak to him."

I hoped that she didn't expect me to persuade him to wear a hat. My mother never had any success with me. But Eleanor wanted me to talk to Gabe about college. An avid skier, he headed for the Alps every weekend. She didn't object to that this year. He spoke excellent French and had had little trouble acclimating to classes at the *lycée*. But she feared his passion for skiing would interfere with next year's college plans.

"He's threatening to apply to Amherst." Eleanor shuddered, as if her son were about to throw his life away on drugs, demon rum, and dirty-legged women.

"Amherst is a fine school," I said.

"But it's not Yale or Harvard. Talk to him, Mike. You're closer to his age. He'll listen to you."

I doubted that. Why would he listen to someone he had just met?

"Because you write," she said. "Albert sent Red the galleys of your new novel. Gabe's seen them lying around. And you've taught college. He'll respect your opinion."

"From everything I hear, Amherst really is a good college."

"Not good enough for him to fulfill his potential. If he goes there, he'll take off at every chance and ski in Vermont. He might as well go the University of Colorado. Please, help me, Mike."

Her voice sounded peremptory rather than pleading. It took iron in the blood to resist giving in. "What if he asks where I went to college?"

"Albert said you went to the University of Virginia."

"That was for graduate school. I was an undergraduate at the University of Maryland."

Her mouth twisted an extra millimeter, and she seemed to reassess me. "The fish must be ready by now."

In the dark, on the return trip to the house, our breath formed trumpets of frost in the mountain air.

As we ate the potage Eleanor had prepared, the silence was as thick as the soup. But gradually the wine loosened our tongues, and we discussed books—Eleanor was reading *I Promessi Sposi* in Italian—and Gabe's day at school. Red and Gabe had an affectionate, teasing relationship, and as father quizzed and joshed his son, the gibes bounced back and forth between them. When Red stumbled over his words, stuttering as he sometimes did, Gabe accused him of talking gibberish, and Red didn't object.

After clearing the table, Gabe went to his room to do his homework, and the four of us washed the dishes. Then we continued talking over a second bottle of wine. Linda said what a nice boy Gabe was and how eager we were to meet Rosanna. Since we had delayed having children, it interested her that Eleanor hadn't had kids until she was in her late thirties, and Red in his forties. What had it been like, she asked, for Rosanna and Gabe to be raised by writers, and moreover, famous ones?

The Warrens explained that they had discouraged the kids from reading their books. This must have made Gabe and Rosanna two of the few American high-school or college students who hadn't read Robert Penn Warren. Red and Eleanor were also careful not to push them into writing. After allowing Bennett Cerf to publish a short collection of Rosanna's juvenilia, they decided that had been a mistake and stressed that writing was for personal satisfaction, not fame or fortune. (Apparently this had the right effect. Rosanna went on to become an accomplished poet.)

At eleven o'clock, Eleanor set out cups and saucers for breakfast, declared that Red had had enough to drink, and disappeared into the bedroom. Red stayed with us, chatting and sipping wine. Half an hour later, Eleanor stormed back into the kitchen in a loose-fitting flannel nightgown. "It's late," she shouted. "You're so loud I can't sleep. Put away the bottle and come to bed."

Sheepishly, Red corked the wine and bade us goodnight. Just as sheepishly, Linda and I tiptoed into our room.

In the morning the postman delivered a letter from Rosanna, and Eleanor read parts of it aloud. Rosanna reported that on a visit to St. Peter's she had felt like a character from Hawthorne's *The Marble Faun,* a New England Protestant repelled by the mumbo jumbo of Mediterranean Catholicism. I thought it best not to mention that I'm Catholic.

As the Warrens chauffeured us to the train station, the talk was of when we would get together again. Perhaps when they visited Rosanna. Eleanor reiterated that we should stay at the American Academy. But once in Italy our plans evolved in unexpected ways. After an exploratory trip to Israel, I decided to set my next novel in Morocco, not the Middle East. Still, before we moved there, we invited Rosanna to dinner several times, and she gave no indication of the awkward stage her mother believed she was going through. A lovely combination of Eleanor's good looks, Red's warmth and charm, and both of their brains, she was proof, Linda and I thought, of the splendid job they had done raising their children.

We got a chance to tell the Warrens this in person that winter when we picked up a new car in Munich, then passed through Grenoble en route to North Africa. As we left, Red handed me a carbon copy of a letter he had sent Albert about *Waking Slow.* "Mewshaw has inventiveness," he wrote, "real narrative pace and feel for story, variety of effects, strong visual sense and style. Once you start reading, you keep on."

I was deeply touched. There was no one whose approval I would rather have had.

That summer, we returned to the south of France, to the village of Auribeau sur Siagne, where we had lived during my Fulbright year and where a friend from our previous stay let us housesit his villa while he and his family vacationed in Ireland. The son of a German Jew who had emigrated to England, cornered the market on nonferrous metals, and been knighted, Philip Mayer was a wealthy man who disdained luxury and safety. A free-lance journalist, he had taught himself Russian, Czech, and Hebrew, and filed articles for the *Irish Times* from Israel, from Prague during the spring of '69, and from Saigon and Phnom Penh shortly before they fell. Even at home, he found it difficult to sit still. Depending on the season, he drove up to the Alps to ski or down to La Bocca to swim. He taught me to play tennis so that he would have a partner. Once a week he manned the phones for the Samaritans, an organization that counseled suicidal callers around the clock.

He claimed to be delighted that I made use of his house. For my part, there was nowhere else I ever worked as well. In the coming years, I would write five novels in Auribeau living as Philip's guest. While I tried to express my gratitude and dedicated a book to him, I felt that nothing I ever did or said was adequate. Then it was too late. A diabetic, Philip died alone in 1983 in a Dublin hotel of insulin shock.

During that summer of 1972, Robert Penn Warren fell critically ill and was flown to the States, to Yale Hospital. When I telephoned Albert Erskine, he sounded more furious than frightened. Somehow rumor had spread that Red was an alcoholic at the end of his rope, dying of cirrhosis. The truth was a French doctor had misdiagnosed his symptoms and didn't recognize that one of Red's medications had clashed with another drug he'd been prescribed. He was out of danger now, Albert said, and on the road to recovery.

Meanwhile, Eleanor had gone back to Grenoble to pack their belongings and close up the house. Since Rosanna and Gabe were off on a bicycle trip, she had to cope alone, then drive the Mercedes down to Nice for shipment to New York. Albert asked whether I minded that he had urged her to call us in Auribeau if she needed a hand.

I didn't wait for Eleanor to call. I rang and invited her to stay at Philip's house when she came to Nice. Although in her systematic fashion she had every detail of the car's shipment and her return flight nailed down, she said she would appreciate some free time before she joined Red.

Those days in Auribeau, Eleanor swam, she hiked, she sat under a *théoule* tree and read. Linda and she shopped at the morning market in the village. One night Eleanor fixed a dinner of Provençal specialties; another night she cooked dishes that she had learned in Brittany while writing *The Oysters of Locmariaquer*. Every afternoon, once the heat diminished, she challenged me to a tennis match and made it clear she wasn't in the mood for hit-and-giggle games. She meant to win. Yet so long as I took the struggle seriously, she had no problem with losing.

That's my lasting memory of Eleanor Clark—perspiring at the far end of the tennis court, limned against the blue-green Alpes Maritimes, surrounded by a mandala of sunlight. For a woman of such refinement, such stylish elegance in so many endeavors, she had surprisingly poor form and ragged tennis strokes. When I timidly observed that she might want to change her backhand grip, she rejected the suggestion and continued through sheer doggedness to chase down shots, shovel balls back, and win points that any other player would have given up as lost. A ferocious competitor, she flung herself into those matches with the same abandon she showed in literary debate.

It occurred to me then that writing might not have come to her any more naturally than tennis, and that each of her books must have been achieved by virtue of the same headlong effort that she expended on court. It couldn't have been easy to negotiate the conflicting demands of her roles as wife, mother, homemaker, and author married to a far more famous author. No matter what other emotions I felt, I did admire Eleanor's determination, her commitment to Red and their children, and her willingness to win ugly if she had to.

Still, it was wearing when she brooked no disagreement and defended her views with the snarling combativeness of a dog guarding a bone. One evening, years later in Rome, the Warrens joined us for dinner, and as an homage to our days in France, Linda fixed *boeuf bourguignonne* rather than pasta. To round out the table, we invited Jack and Corda Zajac, a couple of artists that Red and Eleanor knew from the American Academy, and Donald Stewart and his Italian wife, Luisa.

The Stewarts had settled in Rome in the early sixties, with Don working as a writer and magazine editor, and Luisa as a fashion model, then a photographer. Gore Vidal referred to them as "the most beautiful couple in Italy." Don's father, Donald Ogden Stewart, had been a celebrated humorist, playwright, and screenwriter who won an Academy Award for *The Philadelphia Story*. But his career took a surprising tangent. Known as a high-society *bon vivant,* a member of the Smart Set and boon companion to Dorothy Parker, John Dos Passos, and Ernest Hemingway—Bill Gorton in *The Sun Also Rises* is based on him—Donald Ogden Stewart married Ella Winter, a radical activist and former wife of the muckraker Lincoln Steffens. Then he joined the Communist party and came under the sharp scrutiny of the FBI. In the early fifties as other leftists in Hollywood were hauled in front of the House Un-American Activities Committee and bullied to name names, Donald Ogden Stewart chose to leave the country rather than testify. Exiling himself to London, he lived there, black-listed and marginalized, until his death in 1980.

Eleanor Clark herself had gone through a phase as a Trotskyite, and nothing better demonstrated her commitment to the cause than the fact that she married Trotsky's secretary to give him American citizenship. Ever Eleanor's nemesis, Mary McCarthy dismissed this *mariage blanc* as "pretentious." But maybe it would be more accurate to observe that Eleanor, for all her feistiness, was a romantic. When Albert Camus came to the United States, she courted him by sending a bouquet of flowers.

Although her politics, like her marital status, had long since undergone a sea change, Eleanor was curious about Donald Ogden Stewart, whom she called "an old Trot," and about his son, who had experienced a minor chord of the major upheavals that had altered the course of his father's life. From the time he was a teenager, Don was under FBI surveillance. After Harvard, he worked at *The New Yorker,* wrote short stories and poems for the magazine, and published a novel, *Crow,* all before he turned thirty. Then he married Luisa Ghilardenghi, and they moved to Italy for a year. As that one year grew into decades—they still live there today—and the couple had children, Don signed on as a consultant for *Playboy*'s international editions.

To Eleanor this was unfathomable, unforgivable, and paradigmatic of everything wrong with the world. How could anybody who had been associated with William Shawn bear to be employed by Hugh Hefner? There had to be something else, something better, Don could have done, and by extension there had to be some deeper, some worse, explanation for what he did.

Though I hoped she had got this off her chest before the Stewarts arrived, a strong whiff of contempt remained to curdle the air. All during dinner Eleanor was dead set not just on being right, but on reaching every conclusion via the high road. Whenever Don spoke, she brought him up short, disputed his opinions about Rome and the Italians, and took vehement exception to anything he said about publishing. When he observed that a corporate mentality appeared to have gained ascendancy—Random House, for instance, had been bought by RCA—and that, as Truman Capote put it, every writer now had to peddle his books, Eleanor exploded.

"That's an excuse for untalented writers to become publicity hounds and television whores. Red and I don't *peddle* our books. We don't lick the boots of critics or chase after readers."

Don quietly asked whether they delivered guest lectures, gave readings at universities, and signed books at stores.

"That's different," she snapped.

"I disagree. Where do you stand on this?" Don asked Red.

To all appearances, Red stood on quicksand and wished he could sink out of sight. But when Don pressed him about speaking tours and TV interviews, he conceded that he had done them and been paid for it.

"But that wasn't to peddle your books," Eleanor objected. "You were discussing literature, history, politics, civil rights."

"Well, it was usually linked to the release of a novel," Red said, "or a book of poems or a movie. The publicity people at Random House organize those things."

"I'm not suggesting you're a self-promoter," Don said. "Just that the days are over when an author could count on a publisher to stay loyal and let his books find their audience. Now a writer can't even count on getting reviewed."

"Is that how you justify working for *Playboy*?" Eleanor demanded.

Don didn't answer. He moved to the opposite end of the table to talk to Jack Zajac.

Much as Eleanor diminished the pleasure of Red's company, I stayed in touch with him, and later, as Director of Creative Writing at the University of Texas, I arranged an honorarium for Red to visit us in Austin and speak to the student body. Then, in 1977, Albert sent word that Eleanor had been stricken with an eye malady that was blinding her. As her vision failed, she was forcing herself to complete a final book, *Eyes, Etc.: A Memoir*.

The news prompted in me a turbulent stew of emotions—sorrow for her, sympathy for Red, shame at the anger I had harbored toward Eleanor over the years. Distressed not to be in a position where an offer of help amounted to more than lip service, I tried to imagine what it must mean for her to be going blind. At sixty-four, she was still an enthusiastic hiker and skier and the same relentless retriever of tennis balls I remembered from our matches. Equally at home in foreign cities and the rural countryside, an astute judge of art as well as literature, she was about to lose touch with much of what she lived for. Soon Red, Rosanna, and Gabe would vanish from her field of vision, and she would never see her grandchildren.

More than anything, however, it was the idea of a writer losing the use of her eyes that troubled me. Homer, Milton, and Borges notwithstanding, it was inconceivable that she could continue to create in darkness. Even if the fine mesh of memory held all she would ever need of faces, objects, slants of light, and their spatial relations, there was the unimaginable difficulty of not seeing how words adhered into sentences and how paragraphs filled the page.

Through Albert I got the galleys of *Eyes, Etc.,* and they moved me more than anything Eleanor had ever written. While the memoir fell short of the exacting standards of her best books, it had a passionate, yet pitiless, candor about her attempts to cope. Working with a Magic Marker on a yellow legal pad, she described how she scrawled a word or two per page, in letters big enough to register on her deteriorating retinas. When I read that she still took stabs at tennis, tracking the ball by sound, I thought my heart would break.

As an occasional reviewer for the *New York Times* and *Washington Post,* I never got to choose the books I wrote about. At *Quest,* however, I had some success at suggesting titles, and since the magazine specialized in stories of human endurance, the pursuit of excellence, and triumph over adversity, I believed that a review of Eleanor's memoir would appeal to William Plummer, the book editor. He gave me the go-ahead, and I rushed off a review, ending with an allusion to Dylan Thomas's line about raging against the dying of the light. Since *Quest* had a long lead time, I was anxious for it to run while Eleanor could still read.

To my astonishment, months before the piece was scheduled to appear, I received a typewritten letter from Eleanor, who retained the capacity to handle her correspondence and dole out punishment to anyone who crossed her. It seemed that Plummer, a friend of Red's, had shown him the review "as a courtesy," and Red had passed it, in turn, to Eleanor. Plummer believed the Warrens would be pleased by what I had written.

Lord knows what Red thought of the review. I never heard from him. But Eleanor was irate. She accused me of producing sentimental slop that made her sound like a "sob sister." Why had I emphasized the personal at the expense of the aesthetic? Other readers—she mentioned none by name—had compared her prose to George Orwell's. Why hadn't I called on the scholarly arsenal I had acquired at UVA and placed her memoir in its proper literary context? As for the facile crap about the dying of the light, she maintained that that was flat-out inaccurate. Shapes and colors were fading, not light.

Fortunately, she concluded, there was time for me to rectify my factual and interpretive errors. She insisted that I study her list of editorial comments and revise the review. In the long run, both *Quest* and I would be better off, she said, for her criticism.

In the past after publishing reviews, I had gotten grumpy complaints from aggrieved authors. I had received crank letters accusing me of critical prejudice or personal malice. But Eleanor was the first and last author in my experience to object to a positive review, and she was the only one who ever demanded emendations in a piece that had yet to be published.

William Plummer apologized for putting me in an awkward spot. He was satisfied with the review and intended to run it as it stood. Even Eleanor's cavil about the Dylan Thomas quote seemed to him too literal-minded. Once she calmed down, he was sure she would change her mind.

While it might have been wiser not to reply to Eleanor's letter, I felt that silence would be disrespectful. So I sent a short, measured aerogram, stressing that while I realized her comments sprang from a lifelong devotion to ideas and debate, she had to understand that *Quest* wasn't a literary or intellectual journal. Discussions of Orwell and other influences on *Eyes, Etc.* were of less interest to its audience than the personal virtues her memoir nobly embodied.

Eleanor's response cautioned me to read this letter carefully and "don't get your Irish up." For my own good, she had several hard, unvarnished truths to impart. But before she got to them, she felt compelled to mention my execrable penmanship. My tiny, hen-scratched cursive had almost cost her the little sight she had left. Next time, type, she instructed me.

As for the hard truths, she couldn't comprehend why I would write for a magazine that didn't place the highest premium on intellectual excellence. I should challenge *Quest* and its readers to raise their standards. If Orwell's work wasn't familiar to them, then I needed to educate them, and if they refused to learn, I should find a better venue. It served no purpose, she said, to write down to an audience. That would ruin my prose, which already had its problems.

Just because my review was acceptable to *Quest* didn't mean it was right or worthwhile. She had once been in my position, young, headstrong, and resistant to correction. In a review of Katherine Anne Porter, she had taken a Marxist tack, shortchanging Porter's artistic accomplishment in favor of a political interpretation. But Philip Rahv, editor of *Partisan Review,* had forced her to rewrite, and she had always been grateful for the lesson she learned; only a child or a fool refuses to acknowledge when he's wrong.

Like a little boy woodshedded by a stern schoolmarm, I should have taken my lumps in silence. Eleanor wasn't apt to be swayed by anything I wrote, and as Albert had advised years ago, she probably didn't mean to sound as insulting as she did. But in a return letter, I attempted to broaden the scope of the discussion, as if Eleanor and I were a couple of panelists politely debating the relationship between writers and reviewers. The subject, I stipulated, was freighted with potential for hurt feelings and charges of favoritism. Of the thousands of books published annually, the vast majority never got reviewed. Some had the good fortune to land in sympathetic hands; some fell into the limp clutch of indifference, and others into claws determined to draw blood. The present system was little better than a lottery. Surely it could be improved. But was letting authors see reviews in advance and insist that they be revised really the answer? While I understood why she had accepted Philip Rahv's advice, wouldn't she grant that it was different for an editor, rather than the writer under review, to demand changes? How would she have responded if Rahv had shown her piece to Katherine Anne Porter, and Porter insisted that she rewrite?

The questions went unanswered, as did my letter itself. The break with Eleanor bothered me far less than the lost link with Red. I suppose I expected him to intervene as he often had in the past, acting as a referee or arbiter, easing an impasse with his self-deprecating humor. But years passed. Then decades. Red died. Then Eleanor. I never saw or heard from the Warrens again.

ANTHONY BURGESS

Rome and the Cannes Film Festival

I N the fall of 1971, Rome enjoyed an unbroken skein of bright crisp mornings and balmy afternoons that stretched on into November. During days when a sirocco wind blew out of the south, the air was heavy with African heat and crackled with static electricity. Housewives watered down the cobblestones in front of their houses, flung carpets over their windowsills, and walloped away the sand of the Sahara.

Although the leaves didn't turn gaudy colors as they do in New England, the rich earth tones of the buildings and ruins became a subtle spectrum of pastels. The most dramatic change was visible in the quality of light, the play of shadows on the city's convoluted streets, which were as chambered and complex as a nautilus. After burning without focus all afternoon, the sun in the evening brought to the sky the clarity of *vino bianco*.

The smell of autumn in Italy seemed to me much the same as in America—the smell of melancholy and remembrance, of roasting chestnuts, woodsmoke, and burning leaves. But there was also the aroma of spices, pizza crust, and roasted meat as Romans rushed to eat a last meal alfresco. At an outdoor restaurant on Piazza del Popolo, I once saw a party of eight pass around a truffle the size of a man's fist. Each diner sniffed it, eyes shut in ecstasy, then handed it to the waiter and had him shave microscopic slices onto their pasta.

Smelling, touching, looking, tasting—during that season everybody appeared to be storing up sensations as a defense against the catastrophe they recognized was coming. Finally the weather broke with the abrupt emphasis of a slamming door, and cold rain soaked the city. If, as Eleanor Clark wrote in *Rome and a Villa,* the streets are the real home of Italians, then during those wet winter days the town had the haunted look of a house abandoned. Weeds sprouted in the mortar between bricks, white marble slabs were veined with green moss, and the metal flanges that bolted ancient buildings together bled streaks of rust. As a vast loneliness settled over the piazzas, nothing looked more forlorn than those empty cafés, where tables and chairs were stacked haphazardly like flotsam washed up by high tide.

When the sun reappeared, it was too feeble to provide warmth, too wan to burnish the city's colors. Linda and I had begun packing for a trip to Israel when Albert Erksine forwarded a letter from Anthony Burgess, who had read the galleys of *Waking Slow* and responded enthusiastically: "A poignant piece of invention. . . . It's essentially a true picture of America today, and its talent is very formidable. Such solid construction, such fluency, such totally credible characterization make this a very memorable novel." Since Burgess's return address and phone number in Rome were at the top of the page, Erskine suggested that I thank him in person.

At this remove in time it may be difficult to remember the multifaceted role Anthony Burgess played in the cultural life on both sides of the Atlantic during the seventies and eighties. A tax exile from England, he boomeranged around the globe, touching down for brief stays in the Far East, on the island of Malta, at various American colleges, and in Italy, all the while bringing out novels, biographies, books of criticism, film scripts, plays, and librettos. A natural phenomenon as indefatigable as the weather, he had kickstarted his career, according to legend, when doctors informed him he was dying of a brain tumor. To create a financial cushion for his wife's imminent widowhood, he wrote four novels in the space of a year.

Though predictions of his death proved decades premature, Burgess kept working at the same breakneck pace. He taught, reviewed books, and tossed off lively copy for newspapers; he appeared on TV talk shows as a commentator on a polymathic range of subjects; he played the piano and sang; he wrote musical scores and operas and was reputed to have acquired fluency in a dozen foreign languages. He described his best known novel, *A Clockwork Orange,* published in 1962, as partly a philosophical examination of free will, partly a Russian lesson. Since its cast of delinquent characters spoke an argot loosely derived from Russian, Burgess promised that readers would finish the book having learned, if nothing else, several hundred words of the language. Subsequently, in a film script for *The Search for Fire,* he invented an entire vocabulary of grunts and groans and crude locutions for Neanderthals. Then, after adapting the Bible for a TV miniseries, *The Life of Jesus Christ,* he translated the poetry of Giacomo Belli, rendering the spectacularly obscene Italian dialect into demotic English.

With so many more interesting and profitable ways to occupy himself, Burgess hardly seemed the sort to bother blurbing books. But he had become the Blurb King, and as young novelists charged out of the starting blocks, he read them all and took the time to say something nice about each. Some cynics groused that he was simply promoting himself by attaching his name like a franchise logo to every new book. Yet while it was questionable how many additional sales his endorsement delivered, any author who didn't get a quote from Anthony Burgess had to suspect that he was starting off with two strikes against him.

So I was relieved as much as grateful that he put his imprimatur on my second novel. (Little did I dream that a dozen books later my publisher would still prayerfully collect quotes to attract the attention of reviewers and readers.) When I called Burgess to thank him, his wife answered the phone. Not the wife whose widowhood he had worried about and rushed to provide for. That wife had died long ago, and Anthony remarried an Italian translator named Liana. Speaking flavorful English, Liana asked if I was a friend to Anthony (she pronounced the name Antony). And could I come right over? Some badness had happened, and she needed help.

"I'm not a friend. Mr. Burgess wrote kindly about my new novel, and I wanted him to know I appreciate it."

"But if he read your book, you must be friends. Come quick." Though her voice throbbed with urgency, I had already lived long enough in Rome to realize that I might be mistaken. Many Italians had a histrionic style that charged even commonplace exchanges of information with high drama.

"I don't want to interrupt Mr. Burgess's work," I said.

"Antony is not here. He is in Mini-soda, in Mini-apples making an opera. But he would want you to come today, this minute," she declared. "I have been *sciapatta*—robbed in the street. Two boys on a motorbike stole my handbag. They took my money, my cards, my keys, everything! I am obliged to change the locks on the apartment, but I can't get to the locksmith because I have a baby and the *sciapattori* might break in while I am gone. *Per piacere,* help me."

Why she couldn't call the locksmith to her apartment or leave her baby with a neighbor, Liana didn't say, and I didn't ask. Together Linda and I hurried across the Tiber to Trastevere. Then, as today, guidebooks referred to the area as a worker's quarter, a rough-and-tumble *rione* where authentic Romans lived. But there had cropped up rows of boutiques that specialized in scented candles, handmade jewelry, potpourri, and pirated blue jeans. One barbershop hung out a sign advertising Hippy Hairstyles, and amid the old-fashioned trattorias, blaring discos and a Brazilian supper club had opened for business. Along with Italians who had gravitated to the gentrified neighborhood, ABC correspondent Peter Jennings rented a penthouse overlooking the central piazza, and a well-known CIA agent lived next to the jail.

The Burgess's apartment was regally located on Piazza Santa Cecilia, in a restored building of high-ceilinged rooms. In the front hall, in a position of prominence, stood what appeared to be a marble bust of a Roman emperor. On closer inspection, it proved to be a bust of Anthony Burgess, his Hibernian head crowned by curls as artfully sculpted as acanthus leaves. To my eyes, Anthony's hair in life never looked any realer than those stone tresses. Worn long and combed over a bald spot, his hair sometimes resembled a raccoon, sometimes a carelessly flung Frisbee, sometimes a straw hat on a horse with the brim drooping over its eyes.

By contrast, Liana, although frothing with worry, had not a single strand of her coiffure out of place. Short and shapely, she wore hip-hugging faun-colored slacks and knee-high boots. Fulminating about Rome, its filth, its crime, its corruption, she herded us into the kitchen to meet the "baby," who proved to be a boy of six or seven. Unlike his mother, who spoke English with a Sicilian accent, and his father, who had the plummy voice of a BBC newsreader, Andrea talked in the jaunty tones of a Cockney street urchin.

Barely pausing for introductions, Liana dervished about and promised she wouldn't be gone long. "Just a few minutes. There is food to eat, mineral water for drinking. Andrea is sometimes hungry. You too maybe." She stopped at the door, drew a deep breath, and struggled to get a grip on herself. "This all makes me so fastidious," she shouted as she scurried out.

"Fastidious?" I looked blankly at Linda.

"She means bothered, flustered. Bugged."

It shouldn't have puzzled me that the word's Italian connotation was the opposite of its English meaning. This was, after all, a country where a popular cigarette bore the brand name of Stop, apparently on the assumption that smokers would see it and think Go!

With his mother away, Andrea clowned around the kitchen, climbing up on the table, jumping off chairs, sitting on the drainboard beside the sink, and fooling with the faucets. There was something wired and feral about the boy. Or so it seemed to us. But then that was back before we had children, and other people's kids all seemed peculiar. Linda did her best, telling him stories, asking him his favorite movies, favorite colors and flavors and singers. Mocking her questions, mugging his answers, Andrea kept monkeying around the room until he grew tired of that. "I'm bored," he announced.

So was I. An hour limped by. Then another. Where was that locksmith? Siena? Liana could have had the whole door replaced by now. When Andrea complained that he was hungry, Linda asked what he'd like to eat, and the little guy canted his head and gave her a leer. "How about your bum?"

"That's not nice," I said.

"Oh, isn't it?" he taunted me. "Have you tried it?"

Linda fixed sandwiches of prosciutto and mozzarella. After gobbling his down, Andrea grabbed mine and bit off half. Then he said he was going to his room. For an instant our hearts soared in the hope that he would nap. But minutes later he bounded back into the kitchen dressed in a martial-arts tunic. Flailing his tiny fists, kicking his feet, he accentuated each lunge with an ear-piercing cry. As he ricocheted around the room, bouncing off walls, he appeared to be having an epileptic fit.

Finally he struck a pose, left arm extended, right arm coiled and ready to strike. "It's time for karate."

"We don't know a thing about karate," I said, fearing he intended to use us as punching bags.

"Why don't you go practice in your room?" Linda suggested.

"No, it's time for my class. The *palestra* is across the piazza."

"Your mother will take you when she gets back."

"That'll be too late."

"She'll be home in a few minutes." Linda echoed my own fervent wish.

"No, she won't," Andrea squawked. "You're going to make me miss it. The maestro will be mad." He pogoed around the room, punching the air, screaming and kicking. His battle cries became one long, skirling shriek.

"Take him," I told Linda. "Take him before I start kicking him back. I'll stay and guard the house."

"What if his mother comes?"

"What if she doesn't? That's what worries me."

"If she shows up," Linda said, "come and get me right away."

I swore I would.

"You don't suppose this is what it's like to have kids?" she whispered.

"Of course not. He's upset that his mother had her purse snatched."

But when Linda left with little Kung Fu, I surrendered to suspicions that got worse with the passage of each minute. Maybe this was exactly what it meant to be a parent. It meant being desperate to escape, desperate to the point of parking your kid with anybody gullible enough to buy your story.

No, that was silly, paranoid. Liana must have had good reason to be gone so long. Or there could be a bad reason. Maybe she had had an accident. Maybe the same thugs that had robbed her swung by again and kidnapped her. She could be in the hospital or dead. And without her handbag, she wouldn't have an identity card. How would the police know where to contact us? And how could we get in touch with Burgess in the States? If by some miracle we managed to find him, what if—dread thought—there was nobody except Linda and me to care for Andrea until his father flew back?

By now it was late afternoon, and the December light was failing. More than five hours had passed since Liana left for the locksmith's.

When Linda and Andrea returned from karate practice, Linda looked frazzled, and the boy was cranky and continued to punch and kick and bellow. He was thirsty. He demanded a glass of milk. Linda poured him one, then lost patience when Andrea chugged it down and wiped his mouth on her sweater.

Andrea whined that he was hungry again. I tried not to add to the chorus of complaints and helped fix his dinner. We were due to meet friends at a restaurant. I called and pushed back the reservation. Then I phoned our friends and confessed I couldn't guess when we would get away from the Burgess apartment. At this rate, we might have to spend the night.

Three more hours passed before Liana breezed in. She offered no apology and no explanation beyond a repeated litany of laments about Rome, its inefficiency, the insanity of the narrow streets clotted with cars, the sloth of bureaucrats, the Byzantine closing hours. "It all makes me so fastidious," she moaned. "Now, if you don't mind, I am too tired to entertain tonight. When Antony returns, we will invite you for dinner. I must rest and you must go."

Go we did. We bolted for the door without a good-bye to Andrea or a backward glance at Burgess's imperial bust.

The following spring, we were house-sitting Philip Mayer's villa eight miles from Cannes when the annual film festival took place. Among the movies that year, none generated more controversy than Stanley Kubrick's production of *A Clockwork Orange*. Early reviews raved about its visual excitement, Malcolm McDowell's riveting performance as a music-loving sociopath, and the black comic genius of the choreographed scene of rape and savage assault. But then a second round of articles called the film an incitement to violence and accused Kubrick of exploiting a fine novel for crude commercial purposes.

Burgess chimed in, adding intellectual weight to the argument that his literary meditation on good and evil and free will had been trivialized. What's more, he felt ripped off. Kubrick had bought the film rights years ago, when Burgess had been strapped for cash and accepted a pittance as full payment.

To capitalize on the publicity, Penguin rushed a paperback of *A Clockwork Orange* into print and lined up a series of interviews and TV appearances for the deeply affronted author. During the Cannes Film Festival,

Burgess held a press conference at the Carlton Hotel, a modest adden-
dum to the immense advertising blitz financed by Hollywood. Linda and
I decided to attend, and if the opportunity presented itself, thank Burgess
for his blurb and inquire whether new locks had been installed yet on his
apartment.

Against all odds, the event attracted several hundred reporters and
photographers who abandoned the beach and its rump-and-nipple-scape
of starlets willing to strip for publicity. Despite a disheveled suit and disheveled hair—today it appeared that a pair of lobster claws lay draped
across his forehead—Burgess was eloquent in his defense of the primacy
of fiction, convincing in his Jesuitical discussion of the necessary correla-
tion between free will and salvation, and puckish in his comments about
the absurdity of a multimillion-dollar screen version of his book. Then,
lighting a cigar, he opened the floor for questions.

As at all film festival press conferences, there were professionals on
hand to translate the proceedings. But Burgess, the eminent polyglot, assured them their services wouldn't be required except in the extraordinary circumstance that a Magyar or Mayan wished to speak to him.

To the audience's embarrassment, however, Burgess had trouble with
French and performed no better in Italian and Spanish. Not only did he
misconstrue the questions, he couldn't string together coherent answers.
Perhaps he was nervous, perhaps hard of hearing, but as his famous fluency deserted him, reporters began to grumble.

An obsequious moderator suggested that translators might save time
and allow Anthony to respond to more questions. But Burgess wouldn't
hear of it, not even when his flubbed answers threatened to cause a walk-
out. Several people were already on the way to the door. No longer asking permission, the moderator started to impose a translator when a
woman sprang to her feet, clambered atop a chair, and screamed, "Let
him speak! Let him speak! Why must there be censorship? Why are you
afraid to hear what he has to say?"

Anthony alone appeared unperturbed by this outburst. Puffing the
cigar and patting the lobster-claw curls on his forehead, he stood impas-
sively at the microphone while photographers whirled around and
snapped shots of the distraught woman. Her reaction to the flashbulbs
was to crouch down on the chair and pull her skirt tails up over her head.
But she couldn't hide from Linda and me. We recognized Liana co-
cooned in that linen tent.

Burgess murmured into the mike that if it would expedite matters, he would agree to have a translator. After that, the Q & A proceeded smoothly, and once the press had extracted the quotes it came for, the moderator announced that copies of *A Clockwork Orange* were on sale. Mr. Burgess had graciously agreed to sign books for anybody who cared to line up.

Linda had had enough and left. I suspect she meant to put distance between Liana and herself. But I stayed and got in line, and when it came my turn, I introduced myself to Burgess and told him how much I appreciated his blurb for *Waking Slow*.

At the mention of my name and novel, a dim flicker of recognition focused his close-set eyes. "Why, yes, what a pleasure to meet you." He shook my hand. "Refresh my memory. Do I owe you something? A letter? A recommendation? Money?"

I swore the debt was all mine. Linda and I had spent a delightful eight hours in Rome getting acquainted with his son Andrea.

"Yes, yes, Liana said you were a godsend. And your marvelous novel, is it out yet? Is it doing well?"

I confessed that three months after publication, it was well on its way to being remaindered.

Anthony scowled. "Terrible business, publishing. I'd like to switch to music. Writing songs and musical comedies and operas, that's the way to make money. Here, let me sign that."

On the inside cover of my copy of his novel, he scrawled his name, then sketched a line drawing of a hybrid orange with a clock face with numerals and bolts and springs flying off it. "As soon as I look after these other good people, Michael, why don't you and I go down to the terrace and have a deserved drink."

I stepped aside and waited. The next person in line didn't have a book to be signed, but he had a reporter's spiral notepad. After talking to Burgess for a minute or two, he moved over beside me. Weedy and sun-pinkened, he wore white socks under open-toed sandals. "Are you a friend of Anthony's?" he asked.

"Just met him," I admitted.

"He talked to you for a long time. He must be a very generous man, don't you think?" He had an accent that might have been Scottish or Welsh.

I agreed that Burgess was generous.

ANTHONY BURGESS109

"He promised me an interview. He told me you're a writer too and invited me to have a drink on the terrace with you."

Although disappointed that I wouldn't have Burgess to myself, I smiled and said, "Great."

"I see you and Nigel have become friends," Anthony said once he finished signing paperbacks. "Michael has just published a smashing novel," he told Nigel.

"Brilliant! I'll look for it on the best-seller list."

I might have saved Nigel the trouble.

"I expect you're in Cannes to explore the film possibilities," Burgess said as we made our way onto the terrace. "Your writing is so visual, Michael, your dialogue so spot on, they should let you have a crack at the script."

"I didn't know you had a movie deal," Nigel said, suddenly alert to new possibilities.

"Nothing solid. Just a couple of lukewarm nibbles." Even this was an absolute lie. To date, *Waking Slow* had prompted no enthusiasm, no interest at all, from Hollywood.

"You're too modest," Burgess said. "Michael's novel is set in Los Angeles. That automatically gives it a leg up. Some studio will grab it."

Seated on wire-harp chairs at a table far from the power corners next to the parapet overlooking La Croisette, the three of us must have seemed a sorry lot to the Carlton's haughty waiters. They hurricaned back and forth, ignoring Nigel's "Garçon!" and Burgess's gesticulating cigar. Only after they had served the stars, moguls, and tobacco-brown old men accompanied by prettily painted *poupées* did they get around to us. Since mixed drinks cost as much as I usually paid for a meal, I ordered a *citron pressé*. Nigel and Anthony each had a glass of champagne. Burgess proposed a toast to literature.

"Actually," Nigel announced, "I'm more than just a journalist. I do a bit of creative stuff on the side."

"I had a hunch that might be true." Burgess concentrated on the chains of bubbles in his champagne. "You struck me as the creative sort."

"That's why it's such a thrill to meet you and get a chance to trade ideas. And of course interview you."

Like Burgess, I fixed my eyes on my glass. Queasy with recognition, I knew what was coming, and so did Anthony. Had I sounded this awful in my pursuit of authors? Was I as smarmy and Uriah Heepish as Nigel inching up on the big question—will you read my work? I prayed that I hadn't been and prayed, too, that this moment would pass painlessly. How had I ever put myself—how had I put so many novelists—in this hellish position?

But Anthony was affably relaxed. Signaling for the waiter to pour him a refill, he said, "If you gentlemen will excuse me for a second, I have to find a loo."

At first it didn't hit Nigel. He believed Burgess would come back. All he had to do was wait. But I knew better and viewed his comment about a trip to the water closet as code. As the author of the Enderby novels about a besieged poet who habitually hides in the bathroom, Burgess was undoubtedly an expert at such escapes. We could wait eight hours as Linda and I had for Liana. We could cool our heels until closing time. We could take up permanent residence on the Carlton terrace, and Anthony still wouldn't return. Nigel's was one book the Blurb King wouldn't be reading or praising.

At a different time, I might have resented getting stuck there with Nigel and stiffed for the drinks—one of which, Burgess's second champagne, remained untouched. Instead, I admired the deftness with which he had shifted the burden from his shoulders. Like a jujitsu artist, he had absorbed our energy, our need, and turned it against us. Whatever the extortionate price of three champagnes and a glass of lemon juice, the lesson was worth it.

After half an hour, I told Nigel to finish off Anthony's bubbly before it lost is effervescence. He didn't ask why. By now he knew the score. I picked up the bill, wished him the best of luck, and headed off in a direction where I wasn't apt to cross paths with Burgess.

Years later, at the American Academy in Rome, I ran into Burgess at a dinner party the night he gave a reading from his translations of Giacomo Belli. Again the foxy flicker of recognition brightened his eyes. Again, as if in a recorded announcement, Anthony asked, "Do I owe you something? A letter? A recommendation? Money?"

"Not a thing. You've already given me so much."

PAUL BOWLES

Tangier

I N January 1972, when Linda and I departed from Rome, picked up a new car in Munich, and set off for Morocco, I had a slowly coalescing notion of what I would write next. Using Hemingway's *For Whom the Bell Tolls* as a template, I wanted to do a novel of ideas that was also a novel of action—a story of well-intentioned but woefully ill-equipped people who break a friend out of jail, partly for humanitarian reasons, partly to make a political statement. With the United States then in convulsions over the Vietnam War and Morocco recovering from an attempted coup and the botched assassination of King Hassan by one of his generals, the book was meant as a meditation on revolution and violence.

But for me, the idea of a jailbreak that goes tragically awry had personal resonance. My childhood friend Wayne Dresbach had been in prison for eleven years of a life sentence for shooting his parents when he was fifteen. Since I believed he was unjustly convicted, I had often fantasized about freeing him. While for a writer there may seem no harm in mulling over even the most sociopathic scenario, it must be remembered, as Wallace Stevens observed, that the imagination can kill a man. No sooner had I started taking notes for *The Toll* than George Jackson's brother tried to bust him out of the Marin County Courthouse. The consequences for everybody, including innocent bystanders, were catastrophic.

While a grim novel was gradually unfolding in my mind, the events of my daily life described a gentler trajectory. We drove across France, then through southern Spain, zigzagging from coastal towns to tiny whitewashed villages in the interior. Wherever we traveled that winter, we seemed to follow in the wake of trucks hauling oranges and lemons. Fruit that fell to the pavement was pulped by passing cars, so that we rode along on the sugary, astringent smell of citrus.

To add to the intoxicating sense that we were launched on the sweet life, our car was a fire-engine-red BMW 2002. Although back then a Beamer carried none of the pejorative yuppie connotations that it has now—it cost only $1,000 more than a VW Beetle—it was a powerful, smooth-riding machine that drew admiring glances in rural Spain and figured to provoke awe in Morocco. But it didn't escape me that there was something slightly out of kilter about setting off for North Africa and pondering a bleak, death-haunted narrative at the wheel of a new BMW. As soon as we landed in Tangier, we garaged the car, checked into a ghastly cloacal pension, then went in search of Paul Bowles as if he were the head customs officer, the only one who could certify our arrival.

Until his death in 1999, Bowles and the city he inhabited seemed synonymous, both existing in an ether of hash fumes, hallucinations, and existential angst. Although Tangier had lost its status as an International Zone and many of its brothels and gay bars had closed down, it retained a reputation for political intrigue, sexual tolerance, and weird vibes. It also still attracted artists, writers, and renegade socialites with an appetite for hijinks and low life. Jack Kerouac, William Burroughs, Brion Gysin, Jean Genet, Allen Ginsberg, Tennessee Williams, Truman Capote, the Rolling Stones, and Barbara Hutton, the Woolworth heiress, had all done time there. But Paul Bowles and his wife, Jane, had taken root for the duration.

In his autobiography, *Without Stopping,* Bowles remarked: "I had always been vaguely certain that sometime during my life I should come into a magic place which, in disclosing its secrets, would give me wisdom and ecstasy—perhaps even death." For him, Tangier was the spot that provided all three, and Bowles never looked back. He regarded the past "as one remembers a landscape, an unchanging landscape. That which has finished is finished. I suppose you could say that a man can learn how to avoid making the same actions which he's discovered were errors. I would recommend not thinking about it."

To refer to Bowles as an expatriate was not so much to understate matters as to miss the point. A consummate outsider, he was the very embodiment of alienation and indifference to ambition and fame. His passage through life could be calibrated by the bridges he had burned behind him. He defined himself by what he abandoned—his country, Western culture, one successful career after another.

Starting off as a surrealistic poet, he had published in *Transition* magazine at the age of sixteen. Then he ran off to Europe and befriended Gertrude Stein and Alice B. Toklas in Paris and Christopher Isherwood in Berlin. When he returned to the United States, he studied musical composition under Aaron Copland and wrote the scores for half a dozen Broadway and off-Broadway plays, including *The Glass Menagerie,* and he did a libretto based on Federico García Lorca's *Yerma.* In New York, he knew Orson Welles, William Saroyan, W. H. Auden, Benjamin Britten, Dashiell Hammett. He translated Jean Paul Sartre's *No Exit* into English, and after editing Jane Bowles's *Two Serious Ladies,* he began to write himself.

That Jane was a lesbian and Paul bisexual caused complications in their relationship, but none that an extemporized marriage couldn't surmount. "We played everything by ear," Bowles said. "Each one did what he pleased." And what pleased him in 1947 was to set his course on the basis of a dream and relocate to Tangier. There he wrote *The Sheltering Sky.* Later, in another of his episodic shedding of skins and renunciations of the past, Bowles stopped writing his own fiction and started to record the music of desert and mountain tribes. He also transcribed folk tales and the life stories of illiterate Moroccans.

If anybody could save me from foolish mistakes and serious missteps in this country, I assumed it was Bowles, and I was determined to meet him. Only one thing gave me pause. Although we had hidden the BMW, it was harder to conceal our identity as a conventional straight couple largely ignorant about drugs.

Since I had his address in le Petit Socco, I figured it would be easy to find Bowles. How many middle-aged Americans, after all, lived in the souk? Strolling along Rue Essiaghin—Silversmith's Street—Linda and I looked for a short man with a white cap of hair. Perhaps by then he had

gone native and wore a kaffiyeh or a turban and burnoose. Still we believed we would recognize the face we had seen staring out from the
backs of his novels—the thin, determined line of his mouth, the patrician
nose, and the faraway expression of his washed-out eyes.

There was, however, a great deal to distract us from our search. At
stalls and cavelike shops, vendors hawked freshly butchered meat, aromatic spices and bolts of cloth spangled with sequins and shot through
with metallic thread. Some women wore veils and voluminous djellabas,
with only their henna-dyed hands exposed. But Berber women walked
about barefaced, proud of the enigmatic tattoos on their chins, foreheads,
and cheeks. Rambunctious kids rocketed through the crowd, begging
for dirhams and my Bic pen.

Exotic and edgy, mellow and menacing, Tangier, as Bowles wrote,
had the eerie illumination and distorted distances of a dreamscape: "covered streets like corridors with doors opening into rooms on each side,
hidden terraces high above the sea, streets consisting only of steps, dark
impasses, small squares built on sloping terrain so that they looked like
ballet sets designed in false perspective, with alleys leading in several di-
rections . . . the classical dream equipment of tunnels, ramparts, ruins,
dungeons and cliffs . . . a doll's metropolis."

In this doll's metropolis, we soon discovered that Bowles's Petit
Socco address was a mail drop. He didn't live anywhere near the souk or
the Casbah, but rather in the European quarter on Chemin des Amoureux,
across the street from the U.S. Consulate in a high-rise building that resembled nothing so much as a middle-class American apartment complex.
I pressed the button beside his name on an intercom at the entrance. It
was out of order, so Linda and I took an elevator to the fourth floor and
rang his bell.

A trim, formal gent in his sixties opened the door. Dressed in a tweed
sport coat, a V-neck sweater, and a bow tie, he might have been a character from a Paul Bowles short story, an innocent lamb doomed to plunge
through the bland surface of the world into the savage delirium beneath
it. He called to mind the linguistics professor in *A Distant Episode* who
travels to North Africa to study nomadic tribes and is taken prisoner by
them, has his tongue cut out, and is traded away as a slave.

Bowles had no apparent qualms about inviting two strangers into his
home. Accustomed to pilgrims making their way to his apartment, he

offered hospitality as though we were all wayfarers in the Sahara whose random tracks had intersected.

In contrast to the building's suburban exterior, the room he led us into had the arabesque motifs of an antechamber to a mosque or one of those alcoves where Moroccan men recline on straw mats and drink mint tea. Dimly lit and darkly paneled in wood, it smelled of smoke from the fireplace and, unmistakably, from kif. We sat on the floor, on plush over-lapping carpets. A man came in, carrying a hammered brass tray, and set out glasses and a silver pot. Pouring tea, Bowles lifted the pot high above the glasses, then lowered it and raised it again to aerate it in a ceremoni-ous ritual I would often witness in the Islamic world. In the background, a recording system played the Moroccan music Bowles had taped with financing from the Ford Foundation.

The man who brought the tea sat down with us but said little, and when he did speak, it was in Berber, which Bowles translated. He ex-plained that the fellow was one of his sources for the folk tales he tran-scribed and published. Although critics contended that Bowles must have invented these narratives or, at the very least, greatly embellished the rambling fragments he heard, Bowles swore otherwise. He maintained that he transformed oral anecdotes into written ones in the same straight-forward fashion as he recorded tribal music.

When we asked about Jane, he said she had had to be institutionalized in Spain, across the Straits in Malaga, where she was cared for by nuns. Nothing more could be done for her. She had gone mad, perhaps from poison put into her food by a Moroccan maid, perhaps because of a spell cast by the same maid. He offered these alternate theories with the dispas-sion of an attending physician, but added nothing that might be con-strued as a genuine medical or psychological diagnosis.

Presently a second man showed up. While the first Moroccan wore a baggy brown djellaba, this one had on skin-tight jeans and a black T-shirt with the sleeves rolled up over his muscular biceps. He intro-duced himself as Mohammed Mrabet. The most widely published of Bowles's local "authors"—*Look and Move On* and *Love with a Few Hairs* were his best known titles—he spoke jovially to his translator in English and ignored the other fellow. Sitting apart, on a banquette beside the fireplace, Mrabet regarded the rest of us on the floor with amusement. When Bowles broke out a stash of kif, Mrabet told me, "He smokes too much. He is always getting high. This is not good for an old man."

Bowles didn't respond. He emptied the tobacco from a Marlboro cigarette, replaced it with kif, and tamped it down. I felt compelled to defend him against what sounded like the revenge of the dummy against the ventriloquist. "Dope doesn't appear to affect his writing," I said.

"He is no longer the writer," Mrabet declared. "He only translates. I am the writer."

"You mean you tell him stories."

"Yes, and he types them."

"You're lucky to have such a good typist."

Mrabet laughed. "I am very lucky in life."

Bowles still didn't respond. Although it was unclear how much the other Moroccan understood, he glared contemptuously at Mrabet, who acted oblivious to him. It was a rare example of literary rivalry between illiterates.

After he lit the joint, Bowles passed it to Linda. She took a toke and handed it back to Bowles, who, ever the considerate host, offered it to me. A lifelong nonsmoker, I had never learned to inhale and knew from humiliating experience that the shallowest puff of weed would send me into paroxysms of coughing. When I admitted as much, Bowles fetched a spoon and a Wilkins coffee can that contained what appeared to be coagulated motor oil.

"It's *majoun,*" he said. "A kind of hashish candy. Have a taste. But be careful. It's strong."

I swallowed a spoonful as I would a dose of medicine. It had the consistency of marzipan, with an herbal overlay that stuck to my teeth. When it had no immediate effect, I spooned another dollop into my mouth, remembering too late the character in *Let It Come Down* who eats too much *majoun* and ends up so addled he hammers a nail into an Arab's ear.

"Tell me about the novel you plan to set here," Bowles said.

"Not here." I didn't want him to think I was poaching on his territory. "In southern Morocco."

"Marrakech?" he asked between tokes. In his coat, bow tie, and V-neck, he looked hilariously out of place reclining cross-legged on a carpet blowing a joint. The sight made me smile, and the smile felt stiff as a mask on my face.

"No," I said, "on the other side of the Atlas."

Replying to my strangely tongue-tied efforts to supply a synopsis of the plot, Bowles whispered, "I see," and stared over my shoulder as if visualizing the shape of the book. "A man goes out in search of his life and discovers his death."

That sounded more like one of his books, not mine. I tried to correct him, but discovered another spoonful of *majoun* going into my mouth. Then Mrabet interrupted. "You must tell this story to no one else in Morocco. Just to talk about a jailbreak will make you trouble. To mention it might put you behind bars."

"I'm plotting a book," I said, "not a jailbreak."

"The police here have no idea of literature. They won't see the difference."

I mentioned that I hoped to visit a Moroccan jail. Mrabet chortled. "Kiss your husband goodbye," he told Linda. "You won't see him for a long, long time."

Anesthetized by *majoun,* I considered this alarmist malarkey. But Bowles said, "Better listen to Mrabet. He knows about jails."

"Since I am a child this big I have been in many of them." Mrabet held his hand a foot off the floor. "They locked me up for being always in the streets. Ask me everything and I tell you. Jails are dirty, stinking, and dangerous. Just the food can make you sick."

Warming to the subject of danger and disease, Bowles began to caution me about a host of potential disasters we faced in Morocco. According to accounts of his childhood, his father had tried to kill him as a baby by stripping him naked and putting him outdoors in a basket during a blizzard. Real or imagined, the incident seemed to have left its mark on Bowles's psyche, and he vividly described illnesses he had contracted in the Sahara, in Central America, and Ceylon. Like Port Moresby in *The Sheltering Sky,* he once caught typhoid fever and suffered the same agony his character died from.

"Do you have medical insurance?" he asked.

I told him that we did. Suddenly my teeth felt numb, and judging by the tightness of my cheeks, I was smiling again.

"Good. Be sure to carry your insurance card wherever you go. When you're driving, leave it on the dashboard where people can see it. Otherwise, if you have an accident and are unconscious, doctors won't know whether they'll be paid and you're liable to be left to die."

While the substance of what he said was urgent, his voice, perhaps under the influence of kif, was flat and affectless. Or had my hearing been impaired? He droned on and on, warning me to be vigilant whenever I was at the wheel of a car. Even in the city, Moroccans tended to walk in the middle of the street. At night, in the countryside, they sometimes stretched out on the asphalt for warmth and slept. If I weren't careful, I'd kill somebody, and if that happened, the victim's family and friends would attack us on the spot. At best, we'd have to pay a bribe; at worst, we'd wind up in jail for months awaiting trial. In the event of a serious collision, his advice was to hurry to the nearest airport and flee the country.

From his books, I would have predicted that Bowles would treat such worries as opportunities rather than dangers to be avoided. I expected him to encourage me to take risks, push close to the edge, plunge over it and savor the fall. Instead, he asked where we were staying in Tangier, and when I told him, he exclaimed, "Why there? That's a terrible place. You should move to the Minzah Palace."

Because the apartment windows were draped and, no doubt, because of the *majoun,* my sense of time was warped. Even as I grew ravenously hungry, it didn't occur to me that night had fallen. But despite the joints that Bowles lit one after the other, he never lost track of the conversation or of an inner clock that kept accurate time. Finally, he discontinued his warnings and said he was sorry. He had an appointment and would have to leave. Mrabet and the other man went down in the elevator to get Bowles's car from the garage. He, Linda, and I followed a few minutes later. Though I had surprisingly little trouble standing, my head floated like a helium-filled balloon.

By some inexplicable leap, we started discussing Charlottesville and the University of Virginia. It turned out that Bowles had gone there—in imitation of Edgar Allen Poe, he claimed—and stayed for a semester before leaving for Paris. Had I been aware of this before I ate the hash candy, I might have been astonished. At that moment, however, it didn't strike me as implausible that this nattily dressed gent might be an emeritus prof at UVA who still ordered his wardrobe from Eljo's on the Corner.

Downstairs, on the street, we waited in front of a fruit stall illuminated by kerosene lanterns swarmed over by insects. Moths had crawled inside the lantern globes and frantically fluttered about, desperate to escape. Magnified shadows of their beating wings fell across Linda's and Bowles's faces, and as they spoke about the beauties of Albemarle County in autumn, I had the impression of watching a film whose sound track was wildly out of sync. Then the film flew off the reel as a 1964 Mustang convertible skidded to a halt at the curb. The djellaba-clad Moroccan was at the wheel. Mrabet sat in back. The racy Mustang belonged to Bowles.

It came to me what a fool I was. From the instant we set foot in Tangier I had been mistaken at every turn, misled by my amateurish assumption that in most respects Bowles and the central characters in his novels were the same. Now, more than anything, I regretted that I hadn't offered him a ride in our fire-engine-red BMW. I'm sure he would have enjoyed it.

By the time Linda and I returned to Tangier in 1997 with our younger son, Marc, Bowles was in his mid-eighties, housebound and bedridden. Largely due to Bernardo Bertolucci's screen adaptation of *The Sheltering Sky*, he had changed from a cult figure to a contemporary icon. Still, he lived in the same apartment and refused to have a phone. Assured by a mutual friend, the novelist John Hopkins, that Paul would want to see us (I had corresponded with Bowles during the intervening decades, and he had generously called my third novel, *The Toll*, "the best book I have read about Southern Morocco"), we showed up with John at his door one night and rang the bell.

Minutes passed before Bowles called out that he was coming. More minutes slipped by as we listened to his labored breathing drawing nearer. Then arthritic fingers fumbled at the locks. He opened the door wearing a brown woolen robe as heavy as a military greatcoat. "I had to get out of bed," he said. "It takes a long time."

Leaning on John Hopkins, he took longer yet to retrace his steps through the living room. It still smelled of woodsmoke and kif smoke, and the same carpets covered the floor. But it didn't look as if anybody had lounged there listening to Berber music and eating *majoun* for many, many years. Books, papers, clippings, and correspondence were strewn about on the banquette beside the fireplace, on the hammered brass table, on the sagging seats of leather hassocks, and all over the floor.

The bedroom was just as cluttered, and a black tarp tacked over the window deepened the feeling of claustrophobia. Books and newspapers spilled off shelves and littered the floor, along with a bedlam of pill bottles, broken medicine vials, old Band-Aids and Breathe Rite strips, throat lozenges furred with lint, used Kleenexes, cotton swabs, plastic straws, and tubes of unguents and salves.

As John helped him into bed, Bowles didn't bother removing his robe. It was a balmy night in March, the last hours of Ramadan, when the Islamic world holds its breath waiting for the appearance of the new moon, but the frail old man was cold. As he lay back, propped up by pillows, he resembled a doll, a small, pale citizen of the city he once described as a doll's metropolis.

He pointed to a disfiguring skin graft on his left nostril. "A tumor," he explained. "Malignant. I had it operated on in Paris. 'That'll be nine thousand francs.' That's all the doctor said."

Recently he had been in the United States for more surgery. The hip and femoral arteries in one leg had had to be repaired. He hoped never to go back to America. "I wouldn't have left in the first place," he said, "if I liked it."

He would die in Tangier. That fact hovered behind each breath he drew, every word he uttered, each quavering effort he made to pick up or put down the water glass on his night stand. Shading his eyes from the glare of an overhead halogen lamp, he looked like a disoriented traveler. After surviving the immensity of the Sahara and the vastness of the sea that surrounded the island he had owned off the coast of Ceylon, he was now lost in a single room where the impenetrable tarp over the window prevented him from knowing night from day.

Stricken with sadness and a sense of my own mortality, I longed to say something consoling. The best I managed was to tell Bowles that my sixteen-year-old son was back at the hotel reading *The Sheltering Sky*. As James Salter has put it, if life passes into anything, it passes into pages, and as long as an author's books live, he lives too.

But Bowles wasn't buying it. "That's probably all he'll ever read of mine. That's all anybody reads." Like James Jones lamenting the success of *From Here to Eternity*, like F. Scott Fitzgerald angrily rejecting Robert Penn Warren's praise of *The Great Gatsby*, here was another author who believed that his early work had overwhelmed a life's achievement. This saddened me almost as much as seeing him in his feeble state.

I went off to the bathroom to get away. But it was worse in there—filthy medical equipment, a tumbled refuse of boxes and bottles, the sink with a rusty faucet that leaked what looked to be a bloodstain on the porcelain. To die like this, alone and in squalor, seemed to me worse than Port's death in *The Sheltering Sky*, worse because a man of Bowles's awareness would not allow himself even the scant relief that Port clung to, focusing on "the line made by the joining of the wall and the floor, . . . [fixing] it in his mind, that he might have something to hang on to when his eyes should shut."

That was it, I thought. Bowles had nothing to hang onto. Or maybe it was I who couldn't get a grip. Clinging to the edge of the sink, I found myself wondering whether it was worth it to have Bowles's career, his success, if it meant winding up this way. But then almost at once I recognized the irrelevance of the question. One way or another everybody died, and distressing as it was to see him reduced to this, I knew Paul wouldn't prefer to die in some nursing home in Florida or antiseptic clinic in Switzerland. If ever the cliché applied, it did now. This was truly how he would want to go.

When I returned to the bedroom, a Moroccan of about twenty was there. Muscular and smiling, he might have been a youthful reincarnation of Mohammed Mrabet. Paul's mood brightened as the boy cooked up a bowl of clear broth, which Paul sipped from a cup through a straw. Then the boy rolled the old man a joint.

He told us he was an acrobat. He came from Tiznit, a town in the south, across the Anti-Atlas Mountains, where all the best Moroccan acrobats come from. When I asked where he learned to speak English, he said, "In New York. I perform there every year."

"Where?"

He was so smart and handsome and confident around foreigners, I thought he might be a member of a government-sponsored troupe brought to the U.S. on a cultural exchange program. But he said, "Washington Square. Do you know it?"

I did. It's possible I had watched him, one of a dozen street performers tumbling on an asphalt stage for dimes and quarters.

"Have you been to Tiznit?" the boy asked.

"Yes, on the way to and from Goulamine."

"So you know the desert."

I told him Linda and I had just driven down the Ziz Valley to Erfoud and farther on to the sand dunes at Merzouga, near the Algerian border.

Pausing between tokes, Bowles jerked his head up. "You didn't cross it, did you?"

"No, I wish we had. I haven't been to Algeria for twenty years. I'd like to see it again."

"I would too. But it's dangerous there now. They're killing foreigners." He recalled a trip to Colomb-Bechar, back in the forties, when he first noticed the Sahara was changing. "They nailed up a sign in Place des Chameaux. It said 'Chameaux Interdit.'" Paul laughed dryly. "Camels forbidden in the Place of the Camels."

When Linda mentioned that we had seen Bertolucci's *The Sheltering Sky,* Bowles didn't wait for our verdict. He peremptorily delivered his. "It was awful."

"I didn't think it was that bad," Linda said. "Visually it was wonderful."

"It should never have been made into a movie," he said. "It's not a cinematic novel. It's all inward. The action takes place almost entirely within the characters. I tried to convince Bertolucci to film one of my other books. But of course he didn't listen. I think he made *The Sheltering Sky* because he got it cheap. John Malkovich told me he hated the character he played. I asked why he took the part. He said, 'I did it for the money. A million dollars.' I suppose I'd do it for that too."

As the Moroccan boy cleared away the soup cup and the lid of kif, we took that as our signal to leave. John Hopkins promised he would be back soon. Linda and I added that we would too.

"You know where to find me," Bowles said. "I'll be here."

I doubted that and thought all four of us were lying. Linda and John and I wouldn't come again, and Bowles wouldn't be alive if we did. But months later, events conspired to bring me back to Tangier. The *New York Times* commissioned me to do an article about the city, and John Casteen, the president of the University of Virginia, asked me to introduce him to Paul Bowles. The Alderman Library held some of Bowles's papers and was eager to acquire more. Even if that proved impossible, Dr. Casteen wanted to explain to Bowles what the university had in its archive and how it was handling the material.

Since Paul now had a fax machine, he sent word that he would be pleased to receive us. But at the last moment, a medical emergency caused Dr. Casteen to cancel his trip and send Karin Wittenborg, UVA's head librarian for special collections, in his place. With several hours to kill before the meeting, Ms. Wittenborg, who had never been to Morocco, took a walk with me around Tangier.

It had grown and changed a great deal since my first visit in 1972. It had changed since my last visit. Stark modern towers sprouted on the outskirts of the city, and a stonehenge of them staggered downhill on Boulevard Pasteur. Rumor had it that this construction splurge was financed by drug money. If so, the cash flow must have slowed to a trickle. Many of the buildings remained half-finished, their steel girders dripping rust stains down the facades as if pitons had been abandoned by climbers.

Beyond the Ville Nouvelle, however, Tangier looked much as it always had—as long as you excluded the signs in the souk for fax, photocopy, and Internet facilities. From the Grand Mosque, murmurous with prayer, we strolled through the jumbled geometry of the medina. Its salt-white houses and green tile roofs were cobwebbed with TV antennas. In the Casbah, Barbara Hutton's villa had been divided into two separate dwellings. Neighborhood kids romped around the gates, regaling tourists with tales about the late heiress's six husbands and notorious profligacy. She had once paid to have part of a house knocked down to let her Rolls-Royce pass through a narrow street.

The Grand Hotel Villa de France, where Matisse stayed during his Moroccan sojourn, had been closed and had fallen into disrepair. The views he painted from the window of room twenty-five were now fanged with shattered glass, and the garden had gone to jungle. Some believe the landmark hotel will be restored. Others fear it'll be razed. I banged at the barricaded gate to summon a guardian and bribe him to let us in to look around. The gate rang like a gong, but nobody responded.

Ms. Wittenborg and I wound up at Haffa, a cliffside café where Jean Genet, Brion Gysin, and passels of expats had congregated. Half the city's population used to be foreigners. These days they make up less than 1 percent of the permanent residents. On the top terrace of a series that descended like giant steps toward the sea, Ms. Wittenborg and I took a table and speculated what had brought outsiders to Tangier in the past and why it didn't attract them now. Was it simply that Sin City, as it came to be called, had gone global and Tangier-style entertainments no longer required relocation to North Africa? Even in small towns like Charlottesville, drugs, sex, and rock and roll were readily available.

Still, the place held its appeal for me. Far below, wind combed the Straits of Gibraltar into white-capped waves, and birds beating their wings were suspended in midair, seemingly attached by invisible strings to their shadows in the sea. It was pleasant to sit there and chat with UVA's librarian, but I thought it wise to warn her about Bowles's condition and his apartment. Although I had no way of knowing the value of his remaining papers, or the state of his finances, if the university made a purchase, I wanted Paul to get the best deal possible.

En route to his place, we bought a box of chocolates. John Hopkins had advised me that Bowles had a sweet tooth. A man named Abdelouahid let us into the apartment, which smelled more strongly than ever of smoke. Whistling down the chimney, the late-afternoon wind scattered ashes from the fireplace over the floor.

Paul was in bed, bundled up in pajamas and asleep under a thick purple duvet. I signaled that we would wait until he woke up. But Abdelouahid shook him by the shoulder, and he twitched awake in an instant. His gaunt face had a fresh scar on the upper lip and a white rime of whiskers along the jawline. The halogen lights above his head gave him constant trouble. Shading his eyes with a shaking hand, he explained that he suffered from glaucoma.

Ms. Wittenborg presented him with an inventory of the manuscripts, letters, and papers in the University of Virginia's Paul Bowles archive. He let the specially bound folder fall to the duvet without looking at it. I set the box of chocolates beside his bed, next to an unopened box that an earlier visitor or importuner had brought him. I began to regret that I had come. There seemed something ghoulish and sordid about our presence. While Ms. Wittenborg was the soul of discretion and never pressured Bowles, I felt like a character from *The Aspern Papers,* a trespasser with a sharp eye to main chance at an old man's deathbed.

When Ms. Wittenborg apologized for John Casteen's absence, explaining that he had to be rushed to the hospital to have a hernia operation, Bowles said he had had the same operation years ago here in Tangier, administered by a Polish doctor who agreed to treat him only on the proviso that he check out of the hospital within an hour. If he stayed longer, the doctor feared Paul would catch a staph infection. To ensure that Bowles would be ambulatory in short order, the doctor used local anesthetic. Afterward, he hustled him off the operating table and into a waiting taxi.

"But a thunderstorm knocked out the electricity all over Tangier," Paul said, turning animated as he talked. Like many writers, he seldom seemed so happy as when telling a story. Still it was a struggle; his voice sounded like a dry gourd with pebbles rattling around inside it. "The elevator in my building wouldn't work, and I was in no shape to climb four flights of stairs. By now the local was wearing off, and I was in pain.

If I didn't lie down, I knew it would get worse. Finally, four men carried me up the steps in a chair. But when we came into the apartment, I found the roof had leaked onto the bed, and they had to stretch me out on a couch. Then they . . ." Like a comedian embarrassed to be chuckling at his own joke, he groped to regain his composure. ". . . Then two American women, TV people, showed up to do a filmed interview. When they saw the agony I was in, they kept kissing me. I don't know why. I was defenseless, and my driver had to escort them out. They came back later to do the film, but they didn't pay me enough."

With this closing line, he might have been setting down a marker, showing he was well aware of his value. As a follow-up anecdote he described how Peggy Guggenheim had visited him regularly on the two-acre island he owned off the coast of Ceylon. "You reached it by walking through the ocean at low tide. During the monsoon season it was unreachable, and the wind blew the tiles off the roof. Peggy complained that the price of visiting me was getting her bottom wet."

Apart from the box of chocolates, Ms. Wittenborg and I had paid no price, just our close personal attention, for the pleasure of his company. For the moment it appeared to be sufficient for Bowles to have people listening to him. But when the conversation returned to UVA's interest in obtaining the rest of his papers, he replied that he didn't believe there were any left. Dealers and middlemen had pawed through the collection, brokering sales to any number of universities in the States. Vague about names and places, he soon tired of the subject.

Ms. Wittenborg mentioned that the Alderman Library was about to mount an exhibition titled "The Psychedelic Sixties." Photos and manuscripts from the Bowles archive would be displayed along with items from Allen Ginsberg's, Lawrence Ferlinghetti's, and William Burroughs's collections.

Bowles said he saw no connection between him and the Beats. They were his contemporaries, more or less the same age. That was the only similarity.

"But they all lived in Tangier," Ms. Wittenborg pointed out.

"That was coincidental. They came here because of Burroughs. People claim they came to see me, but that's a mistake."

"But what a flattering mistake."

He frowned. "Flattering to whom?"

"Flattering to you."

"I don't see anything flattering about an erroneous assumption."

To get us back onto neutral ground, I told him, "We took a walk around town today. We even visited Malcolm Forbes's mansion."

"It's a museum now, isn't it?" Paul asked.

"Yes, for his toy soldiers. There are some interesting photographs, one of Malcolm decked out in motorcycle leathers."

"I hear the house is for sale," Bowles said. "Who knows what it'll turn into next?"

"I suppose you've seen a lot of changes in Morocco," Ms. Wittenborg said.

"I haven't seen much of anything for a long time. But I know every young person in the country wants to escape to Europe or to the States. There's no money or opportunity here. The place is like a jail to them."

And yet Bowles, who had the money and freedom to live anywhere, stayed on in a room with the window blacked out, in a single bed set amid the debris of a frantically rootless life. His world seemed to have shrunk to the circumference of his skull.

Mention of jail called to mind his worst fears, and he admitted, "I was always afraid that Congress would pass a law forbidding Americans to travel. And I was just as afraid that Morocco would decide not to let me live here anymore."

He sighed. He could rest easy now. He was here to stay. He dropped his hand to the purple duvet. His eyelids drooped shut. Karin Wittenborg and I said good-bye. He thanked us for coming and waved without looking as we walked out of the room.

Paul Bowles lived for almost two more years. In the end, he was blind and could neither read nor write. On November 7, 1999, he was moved to a hospital and died of a heart attack eleven days later. John Hopkins called me in London and said, "The last literary light in Tangier has been snuffed out." Paul's apartment had been sealed and the locks changed because, as the Moroccan adage goes, "Nothing attracts robbers like a corpse."

"There'll be a memorial service eventually," Hopkins said. "But his body is being shipped to Europe. Paul asked to be cremated, and that's impossible in Morocco. He'll be buried in the United States."

None of this seemed right, especially the notion that nothing of him would remain in Morocco. On the other hand, Bowles had described the typical character in his books as somebody who "slips through life, if possible without touching anything, without touching other people." In an attempt to bring his fiction and his existence into rough congruency he claimed that he had conducted his own life in that fashion. "If you discover you're affecting other people, you have to stop doing whatever you're doing."

But when I think back to the alienated outsider who lived in an American-style high-rise apartment, the chronicler of chaos and violence who was so gentle himself, the dapper little man who lounged on a carpet with Linda and me listening to tribal music, the gent who dressed like a college prof and tooled around town in a Mustang convertible, I realize that like most human beings he was a horde of contradictions. Nowhere more so than in the fact that despite his stated desire to touch nothing and nobody and never have an effect on anybody, Paul Bowles touched and affected so many people with his work.

THAT winter of 1972, after meeting Paul Bowles, we drove to Marrakech, then down to the desert on the far side of the High Atlas Mountains, to research settings for *The Toll.* My second novel, *Waking Slow,* was scheduled to appear on February 19, the day I turned twenty-nine. To be alive and young then, to be married to a woman I loved, larking through Morocco, should have been veriest heaven. And in most respects, it was. Never again would I meet so many remarkable people in such a short period, nor would I visit such extraordinary places and have experiences that would shape my fiction for years to come. But as in any journey, the emotional weather wasn't always equal to the outer landscape.

I was anxious about the book I wanted to write as well as the one that was about to be published. More than anything, though, I was worried about money. As enjoyable as these footloose adventures were, I didn't imagine living like this for the rest of my life. Linda and I wanted kids and a home where we could raise them and I could work in more or less stable circumstances. Then, too, I couldn't expect anybody to keep bringing out my books unless they generated some revenue.

Ever alert for opportunities to pick up extra income and stretch our savings, I stopped at the U.S. naval base in Kenitra and filled out an application to teach college extension courses to sailors. The commanding officer wasn't encouraging. In fact, he recommended hasty departure from the country. He said the political situation was uncertain after last year's attempted coup, and like Bowles, he warned about the dangers of driving. One of his men had been convicted of vehicular homicide and was serving a seven-year sentence. To make matters worse, the man was not the responsible party. His wife had run over a child who darted into the street. In panic, she fled the scene and returned to the base in hysterics. Since she was in no emotional state to deal with what she had done, her husband volunteered to turn himself in and claim he had hit the boy. Only after he was in police custody did he discover the kid was dead and he was headed for prison.

Although this cautionary tale increased my anxiety, we stayed on in Morocco and pushed south to Rabat. According to an article I had read in the *New York Times,* writers and artists who registered at the Moroccan Cultural Ministry could obtain 50 percent discounts at hotels throughout the country. This was the kind of economy we depended on to keep us afloat; the fact that it required a week of blundering through a bureaucratic maze was insignificant. I had lots of time, very little money, and couldn't afford the luxury of pride. Once I found the right office, Mohammed Sefrioui, a novelist whose work I knew in translation, courteously thumbed through the copy of *Man in Motion* I had brought along as proof of my literary bona fides and supplied me with an impressively stamped document.

After our trip across the mountains to the desert, we settled in Marrakech for the rest of the winter. We didn't consider staying at La Mamounia, where Churchill had painted oils in the hotel's walled gardens. Back then, a double room at La Mamounia ran more than fifty dollars, and even at half price, it was out of our range. We registered across the street at the Chems Hotel, which was set in the candle-shaped shadow of the Koutoubia Tower. Thanks to the artist's/writer's discount, it cost five dollars a day.

Oddly enough, the Chems was at that time the production headquarters for an American movie, *Two People.* While the director—Robert Wise—and the stars—Peter Fonda, Estelle Parsons, and Lindsay Wagner—lived at La Mamounia, lower-echelon actors and crew members made do with more modest digs. Within days we knew most of the people in the film, and in a repeat of the Lana Turner legend, Linda was "discovered" in the hotel coffee shop.

Since Lindsay Wagner was exceptionally tall by Moroccan standards—nearly five foot ten—the film company had had difficulty finding a local hire as her stand-in. Noticing that Linda was Lindsay's height and that they both had the same slender elegance, a producer delivered what sounded like a bad line of dialogue: "Honey, how would you like to be in a movie?"

To his credit, he was candid in describing the job. As its title implied, the task consisted of standing in the space that the star would occupy once the crew finished the time-consuming process of setting up the camera and lights. The salary was eleven dollars a day in Moroccan currency. To me, it seemed a godsend.

Or to be precise, Linda was the godsend. Far more than a wife, lover, and best friend, she played multiple roles in my writing career. She was always the first reader of my work, the best critic and chief encourager, and a nonpareil typist. (I didn't and still don't know how to type.) Now with her job as stand-in, she became the family breadwinner.

When the same producer learned that I was a novelist, he invited me to read the script of *Two People*. Foolishly, I imagined he was interested in my suggestions, perhaps a rewrite. Who knew? This might prove to be the break that every novelist—or was it only characters in novels?—dreamed about. In the movie world, weirder good fortune befell people every day. Hairdressers and whores, mailroom clerks and cigarette girls were forever stepping out of the shadows and into the limelight. As my fevered mind piled one implausibility atop another, I fantasized that the film folks would be so pleased by my rewrite recommendations, they'd option *Waking Slow*. In those days, the fast track to literary celebrity ran through Hollywood, and a book was deemed a success only when it was transformed into another medium.

To my delight, the script of *Two People* needed prodigious revision. Peter Fonda, fresh from the success of *Easy Rider,* played a deserter from the Vietnam War who chooses exile in Morocco rather than the traditional haven of Sweden. (Nobody wanted to shoot the film in Sweden, the producer explained, where the weather was crummy and production costs prohibitive. The Moroccans had guaranteed a sweet rate of exchange.) But after several years of skulking around in the medina of

Marrakech, the Fonda character decides to surrender and face the consequences of his idealism.

The American Embassy in Rabat sends a low-level employee to take
custody of the deserter. Rather than clap Fonda into leg irons and dump
him aboard a military transport bound for Leavenworth, the kind flunky
treats him to lunch and discusses the arrangements Uncle Sam has laid
on. In a spasm of generosity, the government provides a train ticket to
Casablanca on the Marrakech Express, a first-class ticket on Air France
to Paris, and another first-class flight to New York. What's more, it's all
on the honor system. Traveling alone, Fonda will have to turn himself in
once he lands in the States.

When I pointed out to the producer that this royal treatment would
destroy even the most gullible moviegoer's sense of credulity, he claimed
that the plot had to happen this way. Otherwise, how was Fonda supposed to cross paths with high fashion model Lindsay Wagner, who is in
North Africa for a magazine shoot with her agent, Estelle Parsons? And
how were Fonda and Wagner going to spend a single bittersweet night
together at the Hotel Crillon if they didn't have a layover in Paris?

As I suggested a few simple expedients for tidying up these implausi-
bilities, the producer turned apoplectic:"Don't tell anybody I showed
you the script. Bob Wise likes it, and after *The Sound of Music* and *West
Side Story,* that's all that counts. If he wants to make a personal statement
about Vietnam, who are you to say no?"

"What personal statement? As it stands, none of it makes sense."

"Look, kid, if we wanted criticism, we'd have called Rex Reed."

At last it registered that I had been asked for praise, not an appraisal; I
was expected to applaud, not offer advice. Further candor on my part
might cost Linda her career as a stand-in, and we depended on that
eleven dollar per diem. So I shut up and concentrated on *The Toll.*

Every morning I worked at a table in the pool of sunlight streaming
through the double doors to the balcony. From it, I could gaze off at
the ice-capped High Atlas range, forty miles distant. Constructed as if in
imitation of the craggy mountain wall, the nearby town ramparts bristled
with parapets and crenellated watchtowers. Below them, an interlocking
labyrinth of courtyards was cooled by fountains and scented with jasmine
and orange blossoms.

Once I finished writing, I spent the afternoon and evening meander-
ing around Marrakech. The life's blood of the town pulsed through the

medina along an arterial system of alleys that converged in the city's heart, Jemaa el Fna, an enormous square whose name translates as "the meeting place of the dead." Well into this century, it was the scene of public executions, and the severed heads of criminals and the pasha's enemies used to be displayed there on stakes.

These days, it thrummed with life. Drummers pounded out rhythms for dancers and tumblers; blind beggars chanted suras from the Koran; snake charmers coaxed cobras out of raffia baskets. Seen from the rooftop cafés that encircled Jemaa el Fna, the square appeared to be a sundial, with colors changing according to the hour, and the shadows of the crowd lengthening and lacing to form patterns that rivaled those on a Berber carpet. At night lanterns were lit, and people huddled around cooking braziers and cauldrons aromatic of cumin, saffron, and coriander.

With so much to divert me, it should have been simple not to fret about what I wrote in the morning. As Hemingway recommended, I tried not to think about the book and just let my subconscious do its work. But I found my brain obsessively replaying a tape that whispered that I was off to a false start. The novel's early chapters felt stillborn, and the central character, a grad student, for God's sake, was too stilted and intellectual. Still, I slogged on, blaming my jitters on the wait for word about *Waking Slow's* reception.

More than a month after its pub date, an envelope, thin to the point of emaciation, arrived from Albert Erskine. Good news, in my experience, came in fat envelopes. Bad news was as skeletal as a terminal patient. A few scattered reviews drifted like ashes into my hands. By far the most prominent had appeared in the *Washington Post,* my hometown newspaper, done—and done in—by L. J. Davis, who liked nothing about my book. Its cover, its title, the Roethke poem it came from, the protagonist's age, the plot, my prose style or lack thereof, all prompted merciless obloquy.

Stricken, I abandoned the new novel, slid into a ruminative funk, and forsook my view of the Atlas Mountains. Melodramatic as it may sound, I felt as I imagined a pregnant woman would after a miscarriage. Empty and inconsolable, too hurt to recognize symptoms of depression, I focused furious energy on our dirty clothes. Since there was no laundromat in Marrakech, I heaved everything into the bathtub and spent hours scrubbing it clean. Socks and underwear were no problem, but denim shirts and jeans required real elbow grease. I stripped naked, stood under the shower nozzle, and flailed our Levis against the tile walls. Then I wrung out the soapy water and draped the clothes over the balcony rail, where the high desert air dried them as hard as corrugated cardboard.

Most days I visited Linda on the set. I met Lindsay Wagner and liked her. I got to know the assistant art director, Ronald Blunden, who later left the movie business and became my editor at a French publishing house. In the evening we ate dinner with the cast and crew, and occasionally Peter Fonda joined us. He had a sweet, outgoing California girl-friend who was interested in everybody and everything. Peter, by contrast, stayed shelled-in, grinning at a joke he never got around to sharing. At his favorite restaurant, a pizzeria in the European quarter, he generally popped a Quaalude and ordered a pizza margarita, which he admired, laughed at, leaned over and studied at close quarters, then fell asleep in facedown. I never saw him eat anything.

Estelle Parsons kept to herself. With a long list of stage credits and an Academy Award for supporting actress in *Bonnie and Clyde,* she seemed to regard *Two People* as a bit of slumming, a semi-respectable way to visit Morocco and make more money in a month than she could in a year off-Broadway. When she learned that I planned to leave Marrakech for a brief trip down the Dra Valley to the sand dunes on the Algerian border, Estelle asked if she could come along.

"I'll rent a car," she said. "You don't have to drive yours. I'll get La Mamounia to pack us a lunch."

"I was going alone," I said. "Linda has to work."

"That's fine by me. I'm old enough to be your mother—all right, your aunt. If Linda doesn't mind, I don't."

I asked Linda, and she didn't mind. But I didn't ask anybody else, and apparently some people on the film did mind, especially when Estelle neglected to give notice where she was going and with whom. An hour south of Ouarzazate, on the far side of the mountains, she casually mentioned that she was AWOL. With a diva's penchant for the enigmatic, it pleased her to keep her whereabouts a mystery. But I insisted she contact Robert Wise and account for her absence. Again, I had to consider Linda's eleven-dollar-a-day job.

The trouble was finding a telephone in one of the tiny Casbahs that clung like crumbling sand castles to the banks of dry riverbeds. Finally, a postmaster who inhabited a hut that might have been built by industrious mud daubers agreed to send a telegram for us. I didn't see its text until we were back on the road. "I'm in the desert with Mewshaw," was all Estelle had said. I wasn't convinced that this sufficiently clarified matters.

To all appearances, Estelle Parsons had fallen into the dumps more deeply than I had. She lamented that she had nothing to live for except her daughter. Once her girl was grown, what was the point in going on? Her career, she claimed, gave her little pleasure. She had accomplished what she set out to do and didn't care to repeat herself.

For the next few days, her behavior struck me as very strange. Perhaps I just didn't understand movie stars. She urged me to stop at a humble restaurant with a wood-burning oven and a pounded earth floor. Estelle ordered an omelet and never ate a bite of it. But rather than risk insulting the owner, she wrapped the omelet in a Kleenex and stuffed it into her purse, leaving behind a clean plate.

At every village, she was eager to shop for handicrafts. Actually, "shop" is the wrong word. She snapped up whatever people shoved in front of her. She didn't bargain, as custom called for. She didn't dither and debate while she and the seller sipped glasses of mint tea. She had no patience for the choreographed protocol of the Moroccan marketplace. Paying the first absurd price that was quoted, she bought beaded necklaces and earrings, silver pendants and breastplates, camel halters and hemp bags, djellabas, burnooses, and kaffiyehs.

Nothing I said dissuaded her. Nothing I did held off the frenzied hordes of artisans and shopkeepers. At times, she bought until there remained nothing more to buy. At other times, I had to rev the engine of the rental car and make a mad break to stop the riot of commerce.

When I accused her of destroying the region's traditions, not to mention inflating its economy, she explained that she received thousands of dollars of expense money in local currency, much more than she had any need for. Since she couldn't export dirhams or exchange them for dollars, she preferred to buy handicrafts.

That made a certain amount of sense. What didn't make sense was what Estelle did as we recrossed the Tizi n' Tichka pass to Marrakech. She ordered me to stop the car and nodded to the heaped goods in the backseat. "If there's anything Linda would like, keep it. Throw the rest of it beside the road."

"Why?"

"Because I don't need it."

"But you just bought it."

"I've got enough things," she said. "I've got enough everything. Somebody'll put this stuff to good use."

Although this struck me as the crudest, least efficient form of income redistribution, I did as instructed. Scooping up handicrafts by the armful, I piled Estelle Parson's impulse purchases on the shoulder of the snaking band of macadam that curled across the Atlas Mountains.

As we rode into Marrakech, she was elated. So was I. A heavy load seemed to have been lifted, a channel unblocked. Going back to my new novel the next day, I began to reconceive it, shunting the grad student to the periphery of the story and inserting a Vietnam veteran and former soldier of fortune at its center. Though not altogether conscious of it at the time, this was the first step in the process of shedding academic paraphernalia. I wanted to get away from the sort of small, quiet novels I had been taught to admire and start producing work that more closely approximated my experience and sensibility.

As for L. J. Davis's annihilating review of *Waking Slow,* I wish I could declare that it ceased to matter. But I didn't achieve that height of Olympian detachment until several years later, when my agent called to say a Hollywood producer had optioned the film rights to *Waking Slow* and wanted me to do the screenplay. I protested that there must be a mistake. With the novel long out of print, how had anyone heard of it?

My agent suggested that we sign the contract and ask questions later. Once we had a fully executed deal, he gave me the green light to satisfy my curiosity.

"You're too modest," the producer told me. "People know your books. They respect them."

"Who?" I asked.

"Come on, you're fishing for compliments! Your name is out there."

"Where? Where did you hear about *Waking Slow*?"

The producer said he had read a flattering reference to my work—so flattering that he ordered a gofer to scour the Beverly Hills library. A copy of *Waking Slow* turned up, and the producer asked for coverage— i.e., paid someone to read and report on it.

I pressed him about the source of the "flattering reference," and he remembered that it was in the *Saturday Review,* in a piece about Ward Just's latest novel, *Nicholson at Large.* Digging up the back issue, I discovered that the author of the article was none other than my old tormentor, L. J. Davis. He didn't care for *Nicholson at Large* any more than he had for *Waking Slow.* Damning the book with a wicked double carom shot, Davis wrote, "The best that can be said about Ward Just is that he writes about as well as Michael Mewshaw on a bad day." To somebody not privy to Davis's opinion of me, maybe this sounded like praise.

The irony was that his antipathy to my work resulted in a movie deal and a screenwriting assignment. That the film never got made didn't leave me any less grateful, and I've always wanted to thank L. J. Davis, perhaps send him a finder's fee. It's not every reviewer who earns money for a fellow author with a gratuitous jab of his poison pen.

In mid-April, when *Two People* finished shooting in Marrakech, the production moved to Paris. Because Linda and Lindsay got along well, Robert Wise proposed that Linda become her permanent stand-in. He even offered to pay her union wages, thirty-eight dollars a day plus expenses, and begged us to live with Lindsay in the apartment that had been rented for her on Rue du Bac. Since Lindsay was barely twenty-two, Wise believed a couple of mature codgers of twenty-eight and twenty-nine would exert a "family influence."

The apartment belonged to *Time* and *Life* photographer Ernst Haas, and in every room, on every flat surface, prints, transparencies, and sheets of his snapshots were displayed as if for a retrospective of his career. In his studio I resumed writing *The Toll,* and with Lindsay and Linda on set most of the day, I assumed the role of house-husband, shopping for meals, toting clothes to and from the cleaner's, and taking messages for Lindsay. Although gossip spread that we were involved in a ménage à trois and cavorted in Haas's king-size bed, the truth was that Lindsay let us have the leopard-skin upholstered master suite while she slept in a bunk bed in a cramped back room. The worst—or rather the best—I can say about our domestic set-up is that in that pre–Bionic Woman phase of her career, Lindsay showed a California beach girl's disregard for formality and flounced around the flat stark naked. When I complained that this ruined my concentration, she took to wearing a robe.

I have often wondered . . . Oh, why bother speculating about Lindsay? In a factual chronicle of recollected time, my sexual fantasy life is of little significance. Of that winter in Marrakech and spring in Paris, the crucial point is that I completed a draft of *The Toll* and came away with the setting, theme, and plot of another novel, *Land Without Shadow,* which deals with a film crew in Africa and a love affair between a movie star and a college professor.

GRAHAM GREENE

Antibes

A FTER *Two People* finished shooting, Linda and I moved from
Paris to Auribeau-sur-Siagne, thanks again to the generosity of Philip
Mayer. There I learned that Graham Greene lived less than fifteen miles
away, in Antibes. I got his address, predictably enough, from a priest and
wrote Greene a letter introducing myself as a Catholic and a novelist who
had been influenced by his work. I harbored no illusions that he would
answer. The priest had warned me that he was extremely wary of fawn-
ing readers, fellow writers, and religious zealots. But Greene replied by
mail, inviting Linda and me to his apartment for drinks. He supplied a
telephone number and suggested I call to arrange a day and time.

For the rest of his life, whenever I rang him, the first words out of
Greene's mouth were never *hello* or *how are you?* He barked, "Who is
this?" and the serrated edges of suspicion didn't soften until he recognized my name.

Neither this nor his other idiosyncrasies dampened my enthusiasm.
More than a mere admirer or another of his millions of acolytes, I longed
to become Graham Greene. By temperament and sensibility, not to mention talent, I knew early on that I could never be Joyce or Faulkner or

Proust, but Greene seemed within my grasp. Like him, I was a conventional realist, wedded to facts, fascinated by places as much as people, and convinced, as Lawrence Durrell wrote, that we are all children of our landscape. Having inherited a large measure of bleakness from my bipolar mother, I also identified with the sad inhabitants of Greeneland, and I shared his rootlessness and his interest in seedy, dead-end destinations that matched my mood. It seemed to me his books proved that a Catholic writer could square religious dogma with the demands of craft, and reading *The Power and the Glory, The Heart of the Matter,* and *The End of the Affair,* I marveled at how he managed to create characters paradoxically imbued with resolute faith and lingering doubt.

As Linda and I drove into Antibes that night, it was no longer as tender as in F. Scott Fitzgerald's time, and the rich didn't seem so different from you and me. During summer, when half of Europe descended on the Côte d'Azur, tourists rattled into town in plebian Renaults and Fiats as well as Rolls-Royces. They stayed, half a dozen to a room, at cheap condos and pensions that had cropped up around the Hotel du Roc. Their rubber dinghies bobbed brazenly in the paths of mighty yachts, and their bodies, basted with Bain de Soleil, had the impudence to turn as bronze as any jet-setter's.

As we advanced with the ant army of rush-hour traffic, the streets were clotted with cars, choked with exhaust fumes, and ripe with the aroma of seared meat. On Avenue Pasteur, a sterile modern apartment building took up an entire block. I parked and pressed a buzzer beside the name Green. Was the final "e" deleted for disguise? I wondered.

From an antiseptic lobby of the sort that lends the appearance of impermanence and impersonality to air terminals, we boarded an elevator, and Graham Greene greeted us at his open door. Well over six feet, he stooped at the shoulders, not as if bowed by years, more as if to incline an ear and listen closer. His eyes alone betrayed his age, then sixty-eight. Large and moist, those brimming eyes always seemed on the verge of spilling over.

I apologized for being late and explained that we had stopped along the way at an exhibition of Nicholas de Staël's painting in St. Paul de Vence.

Greene led the way into a small apartment comprised of a living/work space, a bedroom, a bathroom, and a kitchen. "There's where he killed himself." He pointed to a terrace, but he was gesturing beyond it, to the ramparts of Antibes. "It doesn't look high enough," he said, "but it worked."

The three of us stepped outside to have a look. Although we stood four or five floors above street level, the noise was so raucous we had to raise our voices to be heard.

"The traffic goes on until all hours," Greene complained, "and everyone in the building has a barbecue on his balcony. They keep me up half the night. Some mornings I'm almost too tired to work."

What time did he start writing? How long did he stay at it? As always, I was eager to hear about an author's work habits. Although my continuing desire to meet writers might strike some as starry-eyed or, far worse, as star fucking, the fact is I wanted to learn from them. Since I wanted to learn not just how to write but how to live as a writer, these encounters, in my opinion, were essential, and nothing was too trivial to merit attention.

"I'm usually awake by six and keep going until I have a hundred words," Greene said. "I have to be strict with myself or I'd never get anything done. I used to write five hundred words a day, but as I got older, I found that was too much. I cut down to three hundred, then to a hundred just to keep my hand in."

His current novel was one he had abandoned years ago and only recently picked up again. He wasn't confident he could complete it or whether he would publish it if he did. "I put the book away when that Kim Philby business blew up. There are similarities between my plot and the Philby affair, and I didn't want anyone to think I had drawn on that. There has already been enough nonsense about my friendship with Philby. Perhaps now the novel can be read on its own terms." The title, he told me, was *The Human Factor*.

"When I was young," he went on, "I liked to bring out a new book every year. It was a reaction against the Bloomsbury people, most of whom seemed content to do a few things, build a reputation, and rest on it. Now it takes me years to finish a book, and sometimes it still isn't right."

It puzzled me that practice didn't make the process easier. "You'd think once a writer had been through it a few times and developed confidence in his talent—"

"One has no talent," Greene interrupted. "I have no talent. It's just a question of working, of being willing to put in the time."

He sounded every bit as paradoxical as his characters, whose weaknesses and flaws miraculously strengthen them, who flee God only to race into His arms, who become saints because they are sinners. I had difficulty accepting that Greene believed he lacked talent, but given the doubts I had about my own ability, I found it reassuring to think that, like him, I might succeed through hard work.

The three of us went back inside. The living room walls were lined with books. There were no photographs or personal memorabilia. Perhaps his Paris apartment or his villa on Capri housed more of his belongings, but I doubted it. In a memoir of their friendship, Shirley Hazzard wrote that Greene "was not attached, through habit or memory, or aesthetically, to the rooms and houses and neighborhoods of his life."

As he mixed us Scotch and Perrier, he said, "You Americans like ice, don't you?" Linda and I nodded that we did, and he dropped a single cube into each glass.

Despite his reputation for being taciturn, Greene was loquacious on this occasion and joked that "It's gotten so I hate to say who I am or what I believe. A few years ago I told an interviewer I'm a Gnostic. The next day's newspaper announced that I had become an agnostic."

Communicating via a succession of vignettes, skipping from topic to topic, he was an accomplished raconteur and drew a listener along with the same skill as he did a reader. Greene often alluded to his novels, not boastfully, but to pin down dates, make comparisons, and discuss places. Where other people would use their own experience as a benchmark, he used his fiction. But on reflection it didn't seem so strange to me. After all, writers spend more time with, and arguably have a more intense relationship to, the characters and events in their books than to the ones in their lives. Since for them the imaginary is real, why shouldn't their novels serve as reference points?

While Greene wasn't much given to self-dramatization, he deployed his hands to good effect. Usually he kept them clasped on his lap, then let them fly up to emphasize a point. It was impossible not to notice that his fingers were crippled by what might have been arthritis or Dupuytren's contracture. It was also impossible to forget the stories he told that night, for they seemed to me the secret history of the twentieth century's most riveting incidents and men.

When I expressed admiration for a painting that hung on the wall behind the sofa, Greene said it was a gift from Fidel Castro. With an unerring tropism for troubled spots in the world and troubled places in the human heart, he had gone to Cuba when Castro and his men were fighting in the mountains. Through intermediaries, he contacted the rebels and arranged an interview. When it went well, Greene asked if there were some way he could repay the favor, and Castro told him, yes, bring warm clothes. It was cold in the Sierra Maestre at night, and his troops were freezing.

Since he feared Batista's police were following him, Greene didn't see how he could smuggle in supplies. But Castro convinced him they only needed sweaters, pairs of socks, and trousers. Greene could wear them in layers, and if he got stopped at a checkpoint, he could claim he was cold. Weren't the English always shivering, even in the tropics? So Greene came back bundled up like an Eskimo and molted the spare clothes. After Castro overthrew Batista, he presented Greene the painting in gratitude.

He still frequently traveled through Cuba on his way to and from Latin and South America, and I asked whether it had changed. "Oh yes," he said. "For the average Cuban it's a far better place. But it's too bad about Havana. It used to be such a lively city." He mentioned the nightclubs, bordellos, and sex shows. "Now it seems sort of dreary."

Linda brought up Haiti, where we had honeymooned and met Aubelin Jolicoeur, a Minister of Culture and Tourism who appeared in *The Comedians* as Petit Pierre. Although Greene suspected that Jolicoeur spied on him and reported to the Tonton Macoute, he acknowledged grudging affection for the nattily dressed little fellow.

"Did you know I put Duvalier into the publishing business?" Reaching up to a bookshelf, he passed me a pamphlet that Papa Doc had paid to have printed. Composed of forged documents and lunatic slander, it portrayed Haiti as a tranquil and progressive paradise, and Greene as a despicable racist and liar.

"I'm really rather proud of it," he said. "I went to a lot of trouble to get a copy, and I wouldn't part with it for anything. I wish Papa Doc had come over to the British West Indies. I would have introduced him to what may be a branch of my family, descendants of ancestors who owned plantations. They're black. One little boy has my name."

Since it was the summer of Richard Nixon's campaign for a second presidential term, and once again he was running on unspecified promises to end the war, it was inevitable that we talked about Vietnam. Greene had gone to Indochina as a journalist before the fall of Dien Bien

Phu and the French retreat, and in *The Quiet American* he prophetically defined the tragedy taking shape for the United States years before most Americans had heard of the place. But he had little appetite for the topic now. He said that he had loved the Vietnamese and the city of Saigon, which he remembered as smelling flowery and freshly laundered each morning. He had no desire to go back and see what had become of it. He did, however, do an amusing imitation of General Diem's hysterical, high-pitched laugh and rejected as absurd the U.S. government's claims of noninvolvement in his assassination.

When I mentioned meeting reporters who insisted that they had rented his apartment in Saigon, Greene said, "I never had an apartment. I stayed at the Hotel Continental." He reveled in the thought that a crooked real estate agent had conned the American press.

As for his own greatest journalist coup, an interview with Ho Chi Minh, he told us that he became so nervous beforehand he smoked opium to mellow out.

Having read a great deal about Greene, including his autobiography, *A Sort of Life,* I wondered why these anecdotes had never made it into print. Was he saving them for a second volume?

Greene swore there would be no more memoirs. "Interesting experiences, fascinating people you meet in extraordinary places—of course, that's all very enjoyable. But they don't make one a better writer, and they don't always make for good books. I sometimes think failure and boredom, the feeling of loneliness, of being flat and empty, have more influence on a novelist."

Doubling back to *The Quiet American,* I asked whether the character of Pyle had been based on General Edward Lansdale, an infamous spook and intriguer during the Cold War. Greene gleefully explained that the model for Pyle was a U.S. Embassy official whose wife he had seduced. With a child's delight in taunting—or as Shirley Hazzard put it, "a playground will to hurt, humiliate, and ridicule"—he apparently liked to stick in the blade and twist it.

Given what I thought I knew about Greene, it scarcely surprised me that he slept with other men's wives, but the casualness with which he discussed this, the absence of any Greene-like guilt or the slightest twinge of sympathy for the cuckolded husband, did bring me up short. And so did his mention of his present mistress, Yvonne Cloetta. She was married to a Swiss, Greene said, who either didn't suspect, or couldn't bestir himself to object to, his wife's infidelity. Coming from a buttoned-up British gentleman with an Oxbridge accent, an aging novelist supposedly chary of personal disclosures, these were surprising revelations. They sounded more like the indiscretions of a Californian with a propensity for "oversharing."

There were a couple of sculptural maquettes on a coffee table in front of the couch where Linda and I sat. One of them was easily identifiable as a Henry Moore reclining woman. "Moore gave it to me," Greene said as he topped up our drinks. "I'm told it's worth fifty thousand pounds."

Linda picked up the other maquette, a metal-plated, vaguely phallic piece, and hazarded a guess that it was by Brancusi or Jean Arp. Greene declared that he had no idea. He had bought it from a chemist, what we would call a pharmacist.

"But it must have come with papers," Linda said.

Greene replied that the papers it came with recommended using it twice a day in the event of itching and inflammation. He suffered from hemorrhoids, and this was a medicine applicator. "It's so decorative, I couldn't bear to throw it away."

Linda placed it back on the table and resisted a powerful urge to wipe her fingers on Greene's shirtfront. Though doubtless we were the butt of a joke, it was difficult to guess its point. Was he testing our tolerance? Gauging how far he could go with us? Or were we being punished for having overstayed our leave? For having heard what Greene now regretted telling us about Yvonne and her husband?

It would have helped had I known then what I later learned from Shirley Hazzard's memoir: "Readiness to hurt even, or especially, those who were fond of him and wished him well, had become a reflex in Graham. . . . Evidence of the pain he caused gave reality to his own existence, restoring him to his 'better' self."

In this case, his "better" self reappeared before Linda or I could speak, much less stalk out of the apartment. He said he'd like to see us again. He was leaving soon for a trip through Spain with a priest he knew there, but he promised to call us when he came back. Meanwhile he wanted me to have a signed copy of one of his novels. The next time we got together I could give him one of mine. He turned to the bookshelf again, craning his neck to check titles.

"Here's an edition of *The Quiet American* that was never released," he said. A one-of-a-kind, it had a hand-painted cardboard cover glued over a paperback. Pen poised, he asked, "What's the title of your latest novel?"

"*Waking Slow.*"

He scrawled an inscription and handed the book to me. I didn't look at it until we were in the elevator, on our way to the lobby. It was ten o'clock. We had been with Greene for over three hours, and both of us were lightheaded from hunger, Scotch, and the zigzags of the conversation. I opened *The Quiet American* and burst into laughter. Linda looked at what he had written and laughed too. Tiny, spidery letters spelled out, "In exchange for *Walking Slow*. Affectionately, Graham Greene."

In our giddy condition, the mistaken title struck us as hilarious. Everything did, even the business about the maquettes. But we agreed that we would probably never see him again. Much as I wished it were otherwise, I couldn't imagine him keeping his promise and phoning us.

When, to our surprise, Greene did call, it occurred to me that much as he professed to crave solitude, he was lonely and liked company. In this respect, as in so many others, the man was a buzzing hive of contradictions. I would learn over the years that as his moods vacillated, he often swung from one emotion to its polar opposite. To complicate the cycle, he felt he had to protect himself against his own and other people's friendliness, balancing pleasure and punishment on a scale that bounced up and down like a seesaw.

When I invited him for dinner, he accepted, then said, "The problem is transport. I don't drive."

Three blocks from Greene's flat, a train took on passengers at Antibes and deposited them minutes later in Cannes, at a *gare* where buses departed for Auribeau. Although Greene had slogged through jungles in Liberia, Mexico, and Malaysia, crossed the Sinai desert during the Six Day War and hurried to Prague in 1969 to support Dubcek during the Russian invasion, I didn't expect him to make an uncomfortable commute to our place. I volunteered to fetch him and drive him back, and counted myself lucky to have him alone in the car for a trip that lasted half an hour each way.

Greene looked less than comfortable in the passenger seat. Long-legged and stoop-shouldered, he hunched forward like a stork, squinting through the windshield at the busy road. He buckled his seatbelt with reluctance, perhaps because it wrinkled his floral, tropical-weight shirt, maybe because it made him feel trapped. "Dreadful—" he pronounced it *dwedful*—"this traffic."

"I don't mind it," I said. "I like driving."

"I prefer to fly."

I confessed that I was afraid of flying.

"Why?" he asked. "At least when a plane crashes, you're not crippled for life. You die."

"I guess that's what I'm afraid of."

"I'd rather [*wather*] die."

With the evening off to a doleful start, I attempted to cue one of the anecdotes that Greene enjoyed telling and I enjoyed listening to. But when I asked what had brought him to Antibes, he grimly replied, "Death duties. I had to get out from under English death duties."

It took me a moment to realize that he was talking about taxes, not a form of capital punishment. When I asked about Africa, he described the Mau-Mau uprising in gruesome detail. Since he had recently traveled to South America, I asked about that, and he described widespread torture in General Stroessner's Paraguay, and terror in Pinochet's Chile, where on his first night in Santiago an American voice—Greene assumed it was the CIA—warned him by telephone, "We're waiting for you."

I told him I admired his courage. No other living author had more frequently put himself on the spot and in danger, or had written as bravely about the bankruptcy of colonial and post-colonial regimes, the menace of unrestrained intelligence agencies, and the repression of political and religious beliefs, whether by the left or the right.

Greene shrugged off the compliment. He said he was a coward who suffered from a long list of phobias. "I'm terrified of water, for example." He had spent months in Tahiti, skin diving every day to conquer his fear, but the effort had been futile.

"For somebody afraid of water, isn't it a triumph of courage to go into the ocean?"

Greene shook his head. It didn't matter. He was still a coward. In a sense, this seemed a repeat of his attitude toward his talent. Inverting the biblical injunction, he insisted on being judged not by his works, but by the weakness he felt within.

Talking to Graham Greene at such times was like playing chess in a mirror. Every gambit was reversed, every attempt to elicit a predictable response got turned around, every commonplace exchange of informa-

tion led to a conundrum. Yet once we reached the house and he had a
drink, he relaxed and was easier to talk to. During dinner he gallantly
praised Linda's cooking. She thought she had overdone the roast beef,
but he said,"Oh no. One gets sick of being served raw meat in France."

With Philip Mayer and his family returning to Auribeau at the end of
the summer, Linda and I planned to move to Spain. Greene tried to talk
us out of it. He detested Franco and recommended that we relocate to
Brighton. I assumed he was joking. I remembered Brighton—the gray-
shingle beach as excruciating as a bed of nails, the chilly sea iridescent
with oil slicks, the tatty shops and hotels, the pinch-faced population.
But Greene spoke of it as a sunny resort, an international playground
with an ideal climate from October through December.

Linda served dessert, and Graham came back for a second helping.
"What's a wap?" he asked. He might have been mimicking the sound of
a wet rag splatting to the floor. Neither Linda nor I had a clue. "James
Baldwin called me last week," he said. "Apparently he and Margaret
Mead did a book called *A Wap on Race*. Since Baldwin lives near me in
St. Paul de Vence, his publisher proposes that he and I do *A Wap on
Religion*."

"Oh, you mean a rap," Linda exclaimed.

Now it was Greene who appeared baffled. "That's what I said."

"'Rap' is a black street term for talk," I told him. "You know, a lively
conversation."

Greene giggled. "I'll let Baldwin wap alone. I don't have anything to
add. There's so much I don't understand about American writers. For
instance, why do they marry every woman they sleep with? I'm still married to the same woman. I wonder about Norman Mailer. Is it Puritanism
that makes him marry so many times?"

"Whatever else Mailer is, I doubt he's a Puritan," I said.

"I've read how much alimony he pays," Greene marveled. "It's unimaginable. I've always thought some writers have the mark of Cain on
them. Malraux has a facial tic, and Moravia has a limp. Maybe Mailer's
curse is marrying. He just can't stop himself."

While Linda and I spent that fall in Spain, Graham and I kept in touch.
He liked to receive mail, he told me, and looked forward each day to
the postman's arrival. A faultless correspondent, he answered promptly, if
briefly, with letters he dictated onto tapes that he dispatched to his sister,

Elisabeth Dennys, in England. She typed them onto pre-signed pages of pale blue stationery and sent them off in distinctive blue-gray envelopes.

By now he had read *Waking Slow* and wrote me that he liked it. He called it "the best black comedy I have read in years." He also read the manuscript of *The Toll* and bluntly wrote that he didn't care for it. He said he had always hated Hemingway and considered his fiction an unconvincing fake. But it wasn't just the echoes of Papa in my novel that offended him. The sex scenes struck him as sophomoric wish fulfillment, and he especially objected to the word "panties." Surely there was a better, less blatantly titillating term for women's underwear. He suggested "step-ins." I stuck with "panties," deciding that in matters of diction even an author of Greene's august stature could occasionally go wrong.

The next spring, when Linda and I passed through Antibes, we ate lunch with Greene at a restaurant that served shepherd's pie—a plate of pub grub in a Provençal setting. The Cannes Film Festival was in progress, but Graham couldn't be bothered taking a short trip up the coast. He still liked films, and as one would predict from his old reviews in the *Spectator,* he watched them with passion and no small expertise. He had just seen David Bowie in *The Man Who Fell to Earth* and urged us not to miss it. But he claimed he no longer cared to be around movie people.

In the next breath, however, he confided that he had made a surreptitious screen debut in François Truffaut's *Day for Night*. As the film's French title implied—*La nuit américaine* is the technical term for shooting night scenes in daylight—the story deals with the way cinematic verisimilitude depends on deception, and how artful illusion leads to truth. When one of the characters in a movie within the movie dies, an insurance agent flies down from London to determine whether the project should be canceled. The insurance agent plays a small role, but a pivotal one, and when Truffaut was dissatisfied with the available professional actors, he put out a call for an Englishman of a certain age. Under a pseudonym, Greene auditioned for the part. Truffaut was favorably impressed. Here was precisely the sort of shabby genteel *rosbif* he pictured in the role.

It wasn't until they screened the daily rushes that somebody recognized the bit-part player and groaned, "My God, that's Graham Greene."

At first Truffaut was furious that during his lighthearted exploration of illusion and reality he had been the stooge of his own illusions. Then he was embarrassed. He phoned Greene, apologized, and offered to cut the scene. But Graham wanted to be in the movie. In that case, Truffaut promised, he would get a credit. No, Greene was adamant that he remain anonymous.

The anecdote was *echt* Graham Greene—the gleeful schoolboy subterfuge, the elaborate practical joke that might not seem funny to its target, the insistence on ongoing secrecy. Since he had a new novel about to be published, Greene might have been forgiven for calling a press conference or leaking the story to a friendly reporter. But he had no intention of doing that and pledged us to *omertà*. Months later, when the movie and *The Honorary Consul* came out almost simultaneously, Graham was far from the book-chat circuit, traveling in South Africa to meet black rebel groups and anti-apartheid activists.

At the age of thirty, I was stunned that a man of sixty-nine still had the urge, not to mention the energy, to snoop around the dangerous, unraveling edges of the Third World. But once I read *The Honorary Consul,* what seemed to me even more remarkable was that Greene was still performing at the height of his powers. The new novel might be regarded as a companion piece to *The Power and the Glory* and an index of the political and religious changes Greene had undergone in the previous four decades. By contrast to the whiskey priest in *The Power and the Glory,* who perseveres in his faith despite the persecution of a left-wing revolutionary dictatorship, the idealistic priest in *The Honorary Consul* becomes a rebel and abandons the established Church, which has allied itself with a right-wing military dictatorship.

Though the turnabout astounded some critics, "It shouldn't have," Greene told me. "My sympathy was always with individuals, not dogma. The book doesn't contradict what I wrote earlier. It's rather a relief not to be told that my best work lies thirty or forty years in the past. Every time I pick up a newspaper and read about another political kidnaping, I think *The Honorary Consul* may have been a few years ahead of the times."

This, I thought, was the very least that could be said about the book. While so many writers of Greene's generation had burned out, died young, committed suicide, slipped into obscurity, or ossified into literary landmarks, he had continued to engage current issues as well as the ultimate ones of life, belief, and death. In my opinion, no twentieth-century author—not Hemingway, Malraux, Camus, or Sartre, all Nobel laureates—could make the kinds of claims that, tellingly, Graham never made for himself. When it occurred to me that I might reintroduce him to an audience that believed it knew him, but really didn't, I drafted a proposal to do a profile of the man and his literary achievements.

It got turned down everywhere. Not, I presumed, because Graham Greene was of no interest, but because I was. *The New Yorker*'s rejection observed that it preferred to publish the work of writers it admired, not profiles of them.

After my agent tired of submitting the proposal to magazines, I sent it around on my own to smaller, more modest publications. Meanwhile, I saw Greene whenever I was in Antibes, and by now he brought Yvonne Cloetta along when we ate at his favorite restaurant, Félix au Port. A petite, pretty woman twenty years his junior, sleek and shapely, with prematurely silver hair, she reminded me of the hood ornament on a classic car, a perfect miniature. She owned a golden spaniel called Sandy that Graham doted on as much as Yvonne did, and when they went for drives in her Opel, the dog rode in his lap.

The three of them once joined us for lunch in Auribeau at Philip Mayer's villa. Graham admired the property, the pool, and tennis court. He wanted to know what we paid for it, and when I told him that Philip only expected us to cover its upkeep and the utility bills, he spluttered, "Why, that's nothing."

"It comes to about $750 a month." I might have added that this was almost more than we could afford.

"That's nothing," he repeated. Then, just as bluntly as he asked about the rent, he blurted that he didn't like to let people live in his house on Capri or in his Paris apartment. A place that was inhabited by a succession of strangers, Graham explained, soon became a home to nobody.

When introduced to the other guests—a couple of attractive American women and an ambitious academic—Greene was attentive to the ladies and more animated than I had ever seen him. Toward the academic he adopted an air of polite indifference. The man invited him to lecture at his university, but Graham said he never did that sort of thing. (In fact, while Greene seldom accepted such invitations, he later agreed to appear at the University of Texas on condition that Yvonne and he fly to the States on the Concorde. With me serving as nervous middle man, negotiations broke down when the university said it would pay Greene's Concorde fare but suggested he pick up the tab for "additional guests" out of his honorarium.)

During lunch, there was an awkward moment when one of the
American women asked whether Greene "ran with the English crowd
in Nice." Drawing his head back, he gave her a gimlet-eyed stare. "I
don't run with any crowd."

Graham had a temper. In calmer moments, he joked about his tendency to fly off the handle. When his American publisher objected to
the title *Travels with My Aunt,* he said he fired off a telegram: "Easier to
change publishers than title." Graham found that very amusing.

After two years of effort, I finally got an assignment to do an article about
Greene. But before I proceeded I asked his permission and pointed out
that the piece would be based on our previous conversations. Greene
expressed some misgivings when he learned I was writing for *Playboy.*
Although he had traveled to South Africa at their expense, he knew that
Playboy interviews could be intrusive. Before he gave me the go-ahead,
he set one condition. I had to promise not to mention Yvonne.

I agreed, then spent months cobbling together a profile that reads to
me in retrospect like a Valentine long on praise, short on prying, and
utterly devoid of irony. With no journalistic experience or editorial input
to guide me, I made decisions I would never consider today. For purposes of unity and coherence, I compressed incidents and conversations
that transpired during many different meetings into a seamless narrative,
and in an act of deference, I deleted unsavory details such as Graham's
hemorrhoid apparatus. Otherwise I included verbatim virtually every anecdote he ever told me and ended on an operatic note: "Antibes may
have changed since Fitzgerald, and all those who came after him,
prowled this coast searching for some vision of grace and dignity that
would endure after innocence ends. But Graham Greene has lasted and
will last."

Playboy rejected the profile as too literary and too lacking in revelations. Where was the bite, the buzz, they asked? What about the mistress
everybody knew Greene had? What about the dozens of women in his
past? They paid a kill fee of three hundred dollars and cut me loose.

Abashed to have botched the job and doubly dismayed to have let
Graham down, I submitted the profile to other magazines, first through
my agent, then on my own. From the fall of 1975 until the spring of
1977, I collected a fat sheaf of rejection slips. Still, I kept at it, and in the
end placed the article in *The Nation* for seventy dollars and *London Maga-*

zine for thirty pounds. With no small relief I sent Graham a copy, hoping he would understand that I had persisted out of deep personal regard and professional respect for him.

His response hit me like . . . In this instance, simile serve no purpose. His letter tells its own tale:

Antibes

14th September 1977

Dear Mike,

I only saw a copy of your article in *London Magazine* just as I was leaving for Panama and so I can only express my real horror at it now on my return. I don't think that any journalist has done worse for me than you who are such a promising novelist. I very much resented the inaccuracies and the bits of dialogue which I had never spoken put between inverted commas. At least a journalist doesn't attribute his mistakes to his victim. I have annotated every page of *The London Magazine* and I propose to sell it for a large sum if I can. The first inaccuracy, in the first line, describing Antibes as a village when it has 50,000 inhabitants was amusing but what followed was not amusing. I never told you that de Staël jumped off the Fort Carré—he jumped off the ramparts. I have never taken five hours to write a hundred words. I very much doubt if I said that I had no talent. It doesn't sound like me at all. Considering the other things you put in my mouth I think this is another of your novelist's inventions. I never said that I thought that *The Honorary Consul* might have been a few years ahead of the times as my best news story is that I found a similar kidnapping happened in Argentina when I was there and I thought I would have to abandon the book. I have never been offered a sinecure at any university. I was not warned my first night in Santiago by the CIA. No one has ever been stupid enough to propose that I should do a promotional tour. I probably said that I was afraid of drowning but [. . .] I have never scuba dived in my life. I probably told you that I did practise with a mask which is a very different thing in Tahiti. All your account of Cuba is completely false. I have only met Castro once long after the revolution. The idea that I would wear double layers of clothing in Santiago in a hot December is absurd. You could have found an accurate account of the affair in the Introduction to the Collected Edition of *Our Man in Havana*. There is not a word of truth in what you have given of the Cuban affair. No little boy in St. Kitt's has my name. One little girl may be a cousin. Your whole account of the affair with Truffaut is untrue and not as I gave it to you. How unutterably silly it is to suggest that I should have called a press conference about the affair. I never went to my meeting with Ho Chi Minh "stoned." I had merely had a couple of pipes of opium in the old town and as my ration was normally ten pipes I was certainly not stoned. You write that I have the ability to make the reader understand and follow the compass, but it must be a pretty dangerous compass if the one manufactured by you.

I am sorry to be angry about this article but it gave me a great deal of pain for its inaccuracies and its absurdities especially when the absurdities were put into inverted commas. I can see that a novelist is far worse than a journalist. I don't think any journalist has made so many mistakes in so few pages. I am sending a copy of this letter to Norman Sherry because I do not want any would-be biographer to be misled by all these inaccuracies. I think we had better not speak of this deplorable article ever again.

Yours,
Graham

It took me two weeks to compose myself before I composed an answer to Greene. His letter would have been distressing under any circumstances, but it was particularly galling after what I had gone through to get the piece published. Then, too, it arrived during the dispute with Eleanor Clark over my review of *Eyes, Etc.: A Memoir*. Buffeted on both sides by writers I had praised, I fought back. While I wish I had been more temperate, less retaliatory, and above all briefer, I felt at the time I hadn't expressed half of my hoarded-up grievances.

Rome
October 6, 1977

Dear Graham,

Needless to say, I am sorry you reacted as you did, and although I can understand how you wouldn't want to hear any more about it, I don't believe you can honestly expect me to remain silent.

Your horror, resentment and anger at my article could not have been greater than my astonishment, disillusionment, and yes, anger, at your letter. Repeatedly you accuse me of inaccuracies, false-hoods, misrepresentations of fact and erroneous quotations. You don't come out and call me a liar, but the word hovers over almost every sentence, even when—perhaps in politeness, perhaps in sar-casm—you attribute everything to my novelist's inventiveness.

It seems not to have occurred to you that when we talked there were two novelists in the room. I should have kept that fact fore-most in my mind and not been so gullible. It also seems not to have occurred to you that we were not alone. Linda was with us. Her memory on most details in the article, especially of the anec-dotes you told, is the same as mine. My notebooks, many of my letters, some of your letters to me, and various article proposals that I began making in February of 1973—all of them safely preserved at the University of Texas along with your own papers—will pro-vide additional corroboration of what I wrote. Of course you can always claim Linda is lying and I falsified my notes and that I in-vented everything. But what imaginable motive would we have? Why would I write an article which was entirely favorable about you, continue for two years in my efforts to get it published, and finally sell it to *London Magazine* for the grand sum of £30 if I knew it was full of falsehoods? If the information and, more spe-cifically, the anecdotes, didn't come from you, where did they come from? Quite frankly, some of them are so good, if I had in-vented them, I would have used them in my own fiction—which is perhaps what you should have done with them.

It is interesting that after accusing me of misquoting you, you proceed to misread and misinterpret much of what I wrote. It is almost as if you hoped to catch me on one or two small factual errors so that you could claim everything was wrong. If one thing was mistaken, then everything had to be. I don't know how else to explain your niggling and your refusal to comprehend what is on the page.

To start where you did—I referred to Antibes as a village only in the sense that it had changed and was therefore no longer a vil-lage, no longer the sort of place Fitzgerald and Hemingway had frequented. Every sentence in the first two paragraphs conveys an impression of Antibes' size, congestion, etc.

As for the ramparts de Staël jumped from, do you mean the ramparts of the town or of the fort? It's unclear from your letter. It was also unclear that evening when you pointed out your window and said precisely the words on the page. I'm sorry to have made it seem you didn't know where de Staël killed himself. The mistake is mine, but the words are yours.

As for your work schedule, I questioned you closely and you said you worked five hours a day and usually did a hundred words. Now perhaps you do a hundred words in a certain time and then use the rest of the five hours to review what you've written. And perhaps things have changed since we spoke about that. At that time, July 1972, you said you thought *The Honorary Consul* would be your last novel. You seemed to have very little hope of finishing the new novel [*The Human Factor*] that comes out this winter. You mentioned that you were doing a hundred words a day just to keep your hand in. I was particularly struck by this and much admired your meticulousness and staying power.

Doubt all you like, but you did say "One has no talent. I have no talent." It's not the sort of quote one forgets when one is a young unknown novelist talking to an older, renowned writer. And frankly, it does sound like you. Although of course you have a sense of yourself and of your great worth as a novelist you do tend to shrug off compliments and to speak on occasion self-deprecatingly. What you said certainly didn't tempt me to agree that you have no talent.

As for *The Honorary Consul* being ahead of the times, I believe you have been much too literal-minded and have misread the passage. It was clear from the context of our conversation—and clear, I think, to any reader—that you weren't claiming *The Honorary Consul* dealt with an unprecedented event. You were pointing out, in response to my comment about the book's timeliness, that the great spate of political kidnappings didn't come to dominate the daily news until the early '70's, but that you had been writing about these topics much earlier.

You're right, nobody is offered a sinecure. He's offered a job, or in the case of the university, a position or lectureship, which turns out to be a sinecure. When I asked whether you had had offers from universities, you said you had turned them all down. At our house at lunch, I listened as a professor offered you a position. You passed it off so quickly, perhaps you've forgotten. If sinecure is the word that offends you, I'm sorry. I should have said you had had offers and refused them. But the point remains the same. I was praising you for not turning into an academic circuit rider, as have so many American and British authors.

"I was not warned my first night in Santiago by the CIA." This claim comes as such a stunning denial of an anecdote which you told at least twice in my presence, I don't really know what to say. Is it possible you were warned not the first night, but some other night? Not in Santiago, but in some other city? Or are you disavowing the entire incident? The reason I remember the story so well is that it didn't make much sense. In fact I asked you whether there wasn't a chance it had been a misunderstanding. A wrong number? Why would the CIA tip its hand? You interpreted the call as simple intimidation.

In June 1973 I asked whether you'd be coming to America for the publication of *The Honorary Consul*. You said Michael Korda at Simon and Schuster wanted you to help promote the book, but you had no intention of doing so. You then told an amusing anecdote about being on an awful book chat show in London, and said you'd never do it again.

After I complimented you on your courage, you brought up your fear of water—something you also deal with in *A Sort of Life*. I know the difference between scuba diving and using a snorkel and mask. But the word scuba, which has a specific meaning, is misused all the time, and that may account for why I misheard what you said. It's possible you said you practiced with a scuba mask and I took that to mean you wore air tanks and dived. Sorry for the mistake. But does it change my point? A man who is afraid of drowning, yet makes himself go into the water, is no coward.

Concerning the Cuban anecdote I am altogether baffled. I have reported exactly what you told me. It is ludicrous to assume that I made it up. Even if you're not willing to give me any credit for decency, honesty, or morality, I hope you'll grant that I'm not dumb enough to have concocted such a story. Since I was trying to enhance your reputation, why would I tell such an extravagant lie and thereby injure your reputation? How on earth could I have thought I'd get away with it? After all, I sent you a copy of the article.

You write, "The idea that I would wear double layers of clothing in Santiago in hot December is absurd." Who said anything about Santiago? Not I. And my article contains no mention of "in hot December." I remember precisely what you told me and nothing you say in the introduction to *Our Man in Havana* will make me forget that.

The same applies to your story about St. Kitts. Is it possible that your own narrative genius got the best of you? That you indulged in a little tall tale telling, never thinking I'd repeat the story in print? How would I even have thought to have given you a branch of black relatives? And why?

Ditto the affair with Truffaut. Perhaps to put the best interpretation on this incident—and on many others—you don't remember what you told me.

I did *not* suggest you should have called a press conference. Far from it. I praised you for not doing anything of the sort, and I contrasted your behavior with other writers who would have milked the incident for every drop of publicity.

There doesn't seem to be any decent way of ending this letter. I can only repeat the same litany of questions—why would I have made up quotes and anecdotes you now claim are false? If I had made them up, why would I have sent you a copy of the article?

If you have annotated every page of *London Magazine* and mean to publish it as a way of undercutting my article or accusing me of gross distortion and inaccuracy, I'm afraid I'm not going to let that go unchallenged. Although I'm well aware my name doesn't carry the weight yours does, I do have a witness and I do have various documents which should corroborate what I wrote.

You and I may not speak "of this deplorable article ever again," but I believe a lot of other people will if you go ahead and press the issue. For your sake, I hope that you don't. Both Linda and I have a great deal of affection for you, and I hate to think of this unpleasantness dragging on to no purpose.

Yours,
Mike

Antibes

28th October 1977

Dear Mike,

I am not accusing you of being a liar—I am accusing you of being a bad reporter who should use a tape-recorder, because your memory is far from being as trustworthy as you seem to believe. Perhaps I should not have dwelt on all the small errors like turning my little black cousin Claudette in St. Kitts into a small boy (I assure you that I am unlikely to make such a mistake) and the "ramparts" which only have one meaning to an Antibois into the Fort Vauban, and a simple mask into a scuba outfit which I would never have the courage to use. But such small errors, with which your Truffaut story too is packed, are only a matter for irritation and an indication of your untrustworthy memory.

The Cuban story is another affair. By defending it you suggest I am a liar—either to you, or to the public in the version of the story which is printed in my Introduction to *Our Man in Havana.* Your account also makes me into a rather boastful name dropper. I only met Castro once for some three hours in 1966 long after the revolution. It was not he but one of his agents in Havana who asked me to take a suitcase of sweaters and warm clothes to Santiago.

Why Santiago you ask? Perhaps you are confused by all the Santiagos in my life—in Cuba, in Chile, in Spain, in Panama. The answer is because the city was Batista's military H.Q. and there was an internal customs at the airport. I would have been able to explain away the warm clothes I was carrying in a suitcase as I was on my way to spend Christmas with my daughter in Canada. The idea that I wore them on top of my own clothes is quite incredible—the heat being somewhere in the nineties. Anyone with a knowledge of Cuba would put down the story you recount as a lie—a lie of mine, not a mistake of yours. The number of false stories in circulation about me through untrustworthy reporting is large, and I have every reason to point out untruths when they occur to Norman Sherry who is working on a biography and working very hard in the interests of accuracy. Of course I don't mind your sending him a copy of that rambling and rather offensive letter of yours. He will be able to judge.

Yours
Graham

Professor Norman Sherry
Alan Ross, Esq.

Rome

November 15, 1977

Dear Graham,

I'll start this letter just as I did my letter of October 6 by saying I'm sorry. I'm sorry first that you found my letter offensive. It was meant to explain, not offend.

Secondly, I'm sorry you thought it was rambling. It addressed itself point by point to the subjects raised by your letter of September 14.

From personal experience and from seeing *Roshamon,* I realize the futility of disputing matters and memories which depend largely on point of view. I can only say that my account of the Cuban story was not intended to portray you as a liar or as a name dropper, and I'm sorry if anyone gets that mistaken impression—although I rather doubt anyone will.

At the risk of irritating you further, I would like to point out an example of how small things—matters of emphasis or intonation, elliptical statements or imprecise antecedents—help promulgate the false stories which you decry. On Sept. 14 you wrote in your letter that on St. Kitts "One little girl *may* be a cousin." By Oct. 28 the subjunctive mood has disappeared and you write of "my little black cousin Claudette." If a disinterested party read only one of these sentences, he would likely draw a much different conclusion about whether you had black relatives on St. Kitts than if he had read the other. That is to say if he heard you speak about your "little black cousin Claudette," he would feel a lot more confident when he told someone else, "Graham Greene has a little black cousin." And yet, judging by your earlier letter, this might be wrong, since you leave the impression she may or may not be your cousin.

I'm not quibbling or splitting hairs here. I'm just saying that all of us make statements which lead to mistaken conclusions, especially when we assume the other person already knows what we're talking about. It seems to me that in the case of the Cuban story, you assumed I was familiar with the Introduction to *Our Man in Havana*—which I wasn't—and this may have led you to delete transitions and particulars which you thought I knew. If you'll read page 41 of the article, you'll notice I mention the jarring and disjointed nature of our conversation, i.e. that the logic of the vignettes was "cartographical." Thus while you supposed I knew you were talking about one of Castro's agents, I assumed you were referring to Castro himself, since the anecdote had been spurred by my comment about a picture which you explained he had given you.

You're right, a tape recorder would have eliminated the possibility of errors, but if you'll recall, I had *not* come to interview you that night or any other time. And it wasn't until years later that I decided to do an article based on those conversations—a fact which I apprised you of and to which you raised no objections.

Finally I'm sorry you think of me as a bad reporter. Actually, I'm not a reporter at all, but rather a novelist who was writing, not a piece of journalism, but rather a personal homage to you. I regret that it has caused you inconvenience, irritation, and pain. Perhaps my reasons for writing the article don't much matter to you, but they do to me and nothing of your reaction can diminish my respect for your work, my admiration for your courage and commitment, and my personal regard and gratitude to you.

Yours,
Mike

cc: Prof. Norman Sherry
Alan Ross, Esq.

Antibes

                                                    30 November 1977
Dear Mike,

Let's forget all about it. I hope you are having a good time in
Italy.

A happy Christmas to you both.

                                                    Yours ever,
                                                    Graham

As swiftly as it boiled up, the storm subsided. Nothing had been resolved,
but Greene had lost interest in the argument. I derived no solace from
this. His suggestion that we forget all about it, his signing off with Christmas wishes, didn't strike me as capitulation. After the sad imbroglio with
Eleanor Clark, I feared the end of another friendship.

Months later, when an Italian magazine asked permission to reprint
the article, I seized on the opportunity to reestablish contact with
Greene. This was our chance, I wrote him, to set the record straight. I
wouldn't publish the piece again without his approval and without cor-
recting the errors he had objected to.

Graham replied that it was good to hear from me. As far as he was
concerned, I was free to republish the article as it stood. He claimed he
couldn't remember what his objections had been. He hoped I got a lot
of money for the piece.

A decade later, as I copy-edited a collection of my essays, I once more
invited Graham to read the original article and make changes. Again he
said he couldn't recall any errors and gave permission for the profile to
be included in *Playing Away*.

It crossed my mind then that Greene, like any crafty double agent,
recognized the advantages of laying a minefield of misinformation. As if
to bear out my suspicion, Norman Sherry prefaced his second volume of
The Life of Graham Greene with a cautionary quote from Graham: "If anybody tries to write a biography of me, how complicated they are going
to find it and how misled they are going to be." According to Sherry, in
his efforts to distort the record, Greene went so far as to jot false entries
in his diary.

Fortunately, this was the first and last row Greene and I ever had. Our
relationship resumed as if nothing had gone wrong. He never referred to
the incident, and the closest he came to an explanation or apology was a

comment he made one unseasonably warm winter day when we ate outdoors at Félix au Port. He observed that as he had grown older his mood
swings had flattened. No more manic highs or bleak lows. He attempted
to draw a straight line in the air, as if to demonstrate his smooth disposi-
tion and emphasize a demarcation between present and past, but because
of his arthritic fingers, he traced a jagged arc.

In his late seventies, Greene told me of an arrangement he had with
the Bodley Head. He was still writing—he would continue writing into
his eighties—but some doubt had crept into his mind, and he demanded
absolute candor from his publishers. If his books no longer held together,
if they sounded gaga, he insisted that the Bodley Head say so. Was this, I
wondered, an admission that he suspected he didn't always make sense?

Personally, I never noticed any diminution in his mental acuity. Even
if he did sometimes round the rough edges off the truth, he remained a
masterful raconteur and never lost that splinter of ice in his novelist's
heart. (Shirley Hazzard speculated that Greene's "splinter" was "the tip
of an iceberg.") He also never lost his stomach for literary brawls. In
1979, when *The New Yorker* ran a lengthy laudatory profile of him, Graham promptly repudiated it. Dispatching a tart letter to the *New States-
man,* he characterized the article as the "product of Mrs. [Penelope]
Gilliatt's rather wild imagination. . . . It will be safer . . . to assume that
almost anything there I am made to say is probably—to put it kindly—
inaccurate."

Though miffed that *The New Yorker* had gone on to publish a profile
of Greene after refusing mine, I felt almost sorry for poor Penelope. It
was no picnic to have Graham breathing fire down your neck. But then
I read Gilliatt's piece and began to breathe fire myself. She opened with a
description of Greene on the terrace in Antibes complaining about noisy
neighbors who ruined his sleep. That sounded familiar, as did her description of Graham: "He bends his head a little, not in the stoop of age
but in attention, so as to lose nothing."

The similarities continued as Gilliatt discussed his daily writing schedule, his travels to Dubcek's Prague and Allende's Chile, and his capacity
to grow with the times rather than rail at them. When I came to a quote
from Greene, "I have no talent. It's just a question of working, of being
willing to put in the time," two possibilities presented themselves. Either
this was plagiarism or one of Graham's sadistic practical jokes. I didn't
put it past him to regale Gilliatt with the same tales he told me and entice

her into repeating them. To sow the same misinformation twice and deny it both times would have constituted a delicious coup for him.

As I read the article's final paragraph, the uncanny echoes increased until Gilliatt was lifting my words nearly verbatim. Greene, she wrote, had "been alert to the bankruptcy of colonial regimes, the threat of intelligence agencies with uncontrolled powers, the suppression of private and religious beliefs. He is moved most by characters who have to be strong because they are weak, who have to be good because they think themselves sinners." While willing to accept that Graham could have fed her some of the same anecdotes he gave me, these expository passage smacked of piracy, pure and simple.

I phoned Elizabeth Pochoda, then literary editor at *The Nation,* and asked whether the magazine cared to join me in complaining to William Shawn. But *The Nation* had no desire to ruffle *The New Yorker's* feathers. The literary community was small, and no one wanted to go to war with Mr. Shawn.

I consulted an attorney, who analyzed parallel sections from my article and Gilliatt's, and concluded that it looked like plagiarism. The question was what kind of compensatory damages we could claim. Since I had sold my piece to *The Nation* for seventy dollars, *The New Yorker,* which had sufficiently deep pockets to contest the case forever, might maintain that they owed me no more than an apology and a minuscule permission fee. The only way to win a substantial settlement—the only kind that interested an attorney working on a contingency basis—was to prove that *The New Yorker* had appropriated copyrighted material that it knew belonged to me and that it did so with disregard for my proprietary interests. Without evidence to that effect, the lawyer recommended I send a list of parallel passages to Mr. Shawn and trust him to do the honorable thing.

When I did so, I got the quickest answer I've ever gotten from a magazine editor. Shawn called me at home, and when he found out I wasn't there, he tracked me to a friend's house. Defining the problem as "unconscious plagiarism" on Penelope Gilliatt's part, he revealed that although she had had a long, illustrious career as a staff writer and film critic for *The New Yorker,* she had been suffering for some time from severe alcoholism and unspecified drug use. When she screened movies, *The New Yorker* had to send along a minder to ensure that Gilliatt got the plots straight. This had all been very unpleasant for him, Shawn said, and for the magazine, not to mention for Ms. Gilliatt, and now for me. If I would tell him what I wanted, he would see what he could do.

"I want an acknowledgment that *The New Yorker* used my material. And I want whatever you normally pay for a profile."

"That depends on many factors. The writer's seniority. The subject matter. The quality of the article."

"Let's make it simple," I said. "I want what you paid Ms. Gilliatt."

"I'd be glad to pay one thousand dollars. As for running an acknowledgment, I wish you'd reconsider. Ms. Gilliatt's in a precarious state. I'm afraid another humiliation would be too much for her to bear. If she sees an acknowledgment in the magazine, there's a chance she'll do something self-destructive."

I didn't know what to say. Mr. Shawn filled the silence. "It's a moral choice. I leave it up to you. But I'd be willing to double the check if you'd forego an acknowledgment."

I had no idea what *The New Yorker* paid for profiles, yet while I was convinced it was far more than two thousand dollars, I felt grubby quibbling about money with the man reputed to be America's most gentlemanly editor. I accepted his offer. "But even without an acknowledgment," I added, "I need some assurance that the profile of Graham Greene will never appear in any *New Yorker* anthology or collection of Ms. Gilliatt's work."

"I'll put that in a letter, along with a check for two thousand dollars. I really don't think Ms. Gilliatt knew what she was doing. You've made the moral choice, Mr. Mewshaw. There's nothing else to tell you except how sorry I am."

There were, in fact, a few things Mr. Shawn might have told me. He might have mentioned that there had been a second plagiarism claim against *The New Yorker* over the profile, this one by Judith Adamson, whose article in *Sound and Light,* "Graham Greene as Film Critic," Ms. Gilliatt drew on without attribution. In that case, too, Shawn agreed to pay a settlement, but not a printed apology in the magazine.

He might also have told me what Renata Adler later wrote about the Greene profile in her memoir *Gone: The Last Days of the New Yorker.* "Over the years, Mr. Shawn had several times been put on notice that Ms. Gilliatt plagiarized. In this instance the checkers had noticed that Ms. Gilliatt's piece tracked, to an extraordinary degree, an article in *The Nation* by Michael Mewshaw. They had called this to Mr. Shawn's attention.

He called it to the attention of Ms. Gilliatt. She was incensed. Of course, she said, Graham Greene had said to Mr. Mewshaw the same sort of things he said to her—evidence not of plagiarism but of accuracy. This did not quite meet the facts. Her profile tracked Mr. Mewshaw's in details that could not have come from Graham Greene. After a tirade or two from Ms. Gilliatt, Mr. Shawn made his decision. He ran the piece."

So *The New Yorker* should have been liable for punitive damages. Mr. Shawn's excuse of "unconscious plagiarism," his talk of "a moral choice," were a strategic deception that he repeated to the *New York Times* when he announced he had put Penelope Gilliatt on an indefinite leave of absence. Although Ms. Gilliatt filed no more articles or film reviews for *The New Yorker,* her fiction continued to appear in it on a regular basis until her death.

When I next saw Greene in Antibes, he said he had followed the controversy and was delighted by the way it played out. He hadn't noticed the similarities between *The New Yorker* profile and my piece, and it was of no concern to him that he had once been every bit as angry at me as he now was at Penelope Gilliatt. He chortled as though the two of us were in this together, giving "that horrible woman" her comeuppance. In his long battle to the death with boredom, this was just another skirmish. The campaign would continue till the end of his life.

In April 1991, I sent Greene a letter and a day later heard the news that he had died. Nevertheless, within a week, one of his familiar blue-gray envelopes arrived. Like Scobie in *The Heart of the Matter* who receives reversed telegrams—the first saying his daughter is dead, the second that she's been hospitalized—I experienced an absurd pang of hope. But it was a note from his niece, who had taken over his correspondence. Although Graham was gone, she didn't want my letter to go unanswered. She said how much we would all miss him. I certainly do. For as even the husband of one of Greene's mistresses once admitted to him, "You caused pain. Who that ever lived can claim that he didn't? But you also gave joy."

GORE VIDAL

Rome, Los Angeles, Ravello

FROM the mid-seventies until the end of the eighties, Linda and I lived more or less permanently in Italy. More or less permanently, that is, apart from the semesters I taught at the University of Texas. Hired to help start a creative writing program, I was quickly given tenure. It was a good job, and Austin, in that pre-high-tech era, was a funky town, full of Tex-Mex food, country and western music, and some of the nation's last true hippie holdouts. The climate allowed me to play tennis year round, and when I tired of the English faculty, there was a lively crowd at *Texas Monthly* magazine, where I was a contributing editor and book critic.

Still, like Henderson, the rain king in Saul Bellow's novel about yearning and ambition, I heard a single compulsive phrase hammering at my head. *I wanted, I wanted . . .* I wanted to be a writer, not a teacher; I wanted to live a more interesting and intense life; and I wanted to base myself in Europe. With the birth of our son, Sean, in 1975, I suppose I also wanted to show that I wasn't satisfied to settle down like a model citizen and mature husband and father. Taking an unpaid leave of absence every other year, I returned to Rome and used it as a jumping-off point for long trips to Spain and England, North Africa and the Middle East.

Linda and I never consciously planned to expatriate. Always assuming we would return to the States, which we still referred to as home, we extemporized during those fifteen peripatetic years and sublet other people's apartments. When our second son, Marc, was born in 1980, we took him to Rome as a three-month-old and cut bait altogether with the University of Texas.

Like a lot of foreigners in the city, we didn't bother about visas or resident permits. We lived between the lines, off the books, in legal limbo. Officially, we didn't exist. We never opened an Italian bank account, never bought furniture, never feathered our nest. We kept our possessions to a minimum and could pack all we owned into a Volkswagen Derby and move whenever circumstances, our mood, or our bank balance dictated.

The VW itself didn't belong to us. It belonged to an art professor from the University of California who arrived in Rome at regular intervals and reclaimed it for a few weeks. With the passage of time, he forgot his car, and we drove it for a decade, unbothered by traffic cops, who couldn't rouse themselves to object to its out-of-date Dutch license plates. Since we had no right to sell the VW, we let it be recycled through the foreign community after we left Rome. On subsequent visits, I've seen it on the streets, rusty and ragged, driven by ever younger and more impecunious strangers. Sight of it drenches me in nostalgia, and I hope whoever has it now is half as happy as we were.

Of course a life of finagling and subterfuge wouldn't appeal to everybody. Linda occasionally experienced acute apprehension, for this improvised existence seemed to her not just to cast us into legal jeopardy, but to erode our identity. Like a jumpy tourist slapping at her pockets to make sure that her cash, keys, and credit cards were safe, she sometimes groped for the security of a fixed point. But I felt that our transience and the pure contingency of the place offered compensations. Rome kept me alert, adrenalized, hungry. It infused my style with its edginess and provided an endless reservoir of stories. Its arcane protocols and ordered irrationality gave it the aura of a secret society that was paradoxically open to anyone who took the trouble to wise up to its ways. Part of the pleasure of living there was learning the ropes and never getting tangled in them—or laughing at yourself when you did. As the natives swore, "Only for death was there no solution."

Then, too, Italy had its more conventional attractions. Although people lamented that *la dolce vita*—the golden age that always seems to end just as *you* arrive—was long gone, we loved the weather, the food, the wine, and the finely woven fabric of self-contained villages that make up a sprawling metropolis that calls itself eternal yet pulses with the frenetic metabolism of a fruit fly.

Eventually I became aware that behind the ornate brocaded public tapestry, Italians pursued their private lives with absolute indifference to the assumptions that foreigners imposed on Rome. That was fine by me. I believed I inhabited the same hidden space as they did, and my eyes slid over the landscape in an ellipsis that eliminated stock footage. St. Peter's, the Coliseum, and the Forum exerted little claim on my attention. I focused on neighborhood cats sleeping in the sun, chunks of white marble that were veined with green moss like slabs of Gorgonzola cheese, the delicate purple flowers that tufted the Aurelian wall, anonymous statues of classical figures, their uplifted hands gloved in gray lichen, their feet shod in dead leaves.

During those years, most of my creative, social, and recreational interests revolved around the American Academy in Rome, an institution that describes itself as "the foremost American overseas center for independent study and advanced research in the fine arts and humanities." Although this might sound like coarse chest-pounding, and although wisecracking critics have dubbed it the Club Med of the art world, the academy does number among its past members twenty-eight Pulitzer Prize winners, nine MacArthur fellows, four U.S. Poets Laureate, and two Nobel Prize winners. Located on the Gianicolo, the highest of Rome's seven hills, the academy's main building, designed by McKim, Meade & White, accommodates about seventy-five writers, painters, composers, and classicists per annum. While the community can sometimes suffer a deadly case of ego gridlock, generally the result is a collegial spirit and high achievement showcased in a series of concerts, lectures, and exhibitions.

At times I was affiliated with the American Academy in a formal capacity as a visiting artist. At others, I simply rented an office there or holed up in the stacks of the library to write. I hope I'm not deluded in believing that I also learned a lot on the academy tennis court, hitting balls with the likes of Gay Talese, Galway Kinnell, Kenneth Koch, Brad Leithauser, Oscar Hijuelos and David St. John. Poets, it occurred to me, played in short bursts of brilliance; prose writers tended to be baseline grinders with a passion for marathon matches.

Whatever our genre, we all delighted in the paradisiacal views. Plunked down amid a copse of umbrella pines, the court was banked by a backdrop of ivy at one end and the Aurelian wall at the other. As afternoon sunlight poured golden-green through a grape arbor that paralleled the western sideline, players could become so engrossed in the sweeping progress of filigree shadows across the red clay (later replaced by a hard surface), they lost track of the score.

Not all of the academy's educational opportunities were quite so pleasant, particularly its lessons in brinkmanship, artistic pique, and marital discord. Once, at a reception, I watched a woman shake hands with Mary McCarthy and graciously say how good it was to see her again— only to have the Dark Lady of American Letters smile a glacial smile and deliver a line of her famously disciplinary dialogue: "I've never met you before in my life."

In the mid-eighties, novelist William Gaddis, best known for his novel *The Recognitions,* and a two-time National Book Award winner, spent several months as a resident at the academy, a position that carried a single requirement: He had to give a reading of his work. An attentive if not especially large crowd turned out, and Gaddis, seated in an easy chair, leafed through a copy of Gogol's *Lost Souls* while we waited in vain for late arrivals. Finally, he closed the book on his finger. "I was going to read a section from the novel I've been writing here. But then I happened to look in the academy library, and I discovered that it doesn't have a single copy of any of my books. I stopped at the USIS library. It didn't have any either. I searched all the English-language bookstores in town, and none of them carries my work. This has persuaded me that no one in Rome has the slightest interest in what I write. So I've decided to entertain you with a chapter from *Lost Souls.*"

The audience accepted its punishment in silence, grateful, I guess, that Gaddis didn't choose to read Gogol in the original Russian.

Ana Mendieta, a diminutive Latina sculptor of Cuban ancestry, arrived at the academy with Carl Andre, an older, rotund fellow who was a far better known sculptor. Both of them specialized in floor installations. But whereas Carl's minimalist hallmark was bricks and boards and stones laid out in geometrical patterns, Ana arranged earth and straw in the vague shape of female genitalia. One art critic called them "mud pussies." After Ana's Prix de Rome fellowship ran out, she and Carl stayed on and rented an apartment around the corner from our place on Via di Santa Maria in Monticelli. The four of us had a celebratory dinner the night they signed the lease. As usual, Ana was loud and animated, and Carl silent verging on sullen. Rumor had it that he was jealous of her growing reputation.

That summer, on a visit to New York, Ana jumped or was pushed out of a thirty-fourth floor window, and Carl was indicted for her murder. Waiving his right to have the case decided by a jury, he stood trial in front of a judge—wags referred to this as a "minimalist trial"—and was acquitted. Carl emerged from the episode as a pariah at the American Academy, while Ana evolved into a feminist icon.

My boys' most cherished memory of the academy was the 1982 Christmas party, where the annual play starred English architect James Stirling as Santa Claus and Poet Laureate Mark Strand as Mrs. Claus. Novelist Mark Helprin, in the role of the Wicked Witch of the North, swung down on a rope from the roof. Frank Stella painted the scenery, and I've always wondered whether the sets for that performance, squirreled away in some dank cellar, might be worth millions.

My own most vivid memories are of the writers I crossed paths with in Rome—Joseph Brodsky, Nadine Gordimer, Joseph Heller, Pete Hamill, Muriel Spark, Francine du Plessix Gray, Donald Barthelme, Giorgio Bassani, Alberto Moravia, Luigi Barzini, and Italo Calvino. But the one I came to like best was, surprisingly, Gore Vidal. I say surprisingly because so many people mistakenly regard him as cold, remote, and impersonal, when not downright imperious.

From the first he was hospitable to Linda and me, and invited us for drinks at his apartment. The evening was hot, the air heavy with humidity, and though it was late October, a summer thunderstorm felt imminent. We caught a bus crammed with commuters, and it careened downhill into Trastevere. It was rush hour—one of the four traffic jams that Roman drivers endure each day—and cars had stalled on Ponte Garibaldi. I didn't mind. The bridge offered mesmeric views of the Tiber, flowing dark and turbid below us, and of the dome of St. Peter's, gleaming like a bishop's miter off to our left.

Back then I was more familiar with Vidal's nonfiction, primarily his essays in the *New York Review of Books*. And of course I knew him—or imagined I did—from his appearances on TV talk shows in the States. For a popular, best-selling author, he seemed never to dumb down, and even as he meted out stern punishment to the likes of William F. Buckley or Norman Mailer, he maintained the composure of a natural patrician. But when I read *Myra Breckinridge,* an iconoclastic, gender-bending novel that simultaneously exploited and exploded traditional narrative devices, I recognized that Vidal was also a significant innovator, not to mention a very funny man.

We jumped off the bus at Largo Argentina, a fenced-in sunken square crowded with truncated pillars, fluted columns, a tall brick tower, and cypress and pine trees that sprouted from a bedrock of ruins. It was one of those parts of Rome where some ancient buried secret appears to have burst through the surface of the modern city for the explicit purpose of reminding you that there is no end, no simple explanation, of the place. And no explanation of its citizens either. Dozens of crazy old crones had shown up for the evening shift, carrying bowls of pasta to feed the mangy cats that slunk in the ruins.

At the corner of Corso Vittorio Emanuele and Via di Torre Argentina, a gray-and-mustard-colored palazzo had been divided into shops on the ground floor, offices and a language school on higher stories, and apartments above them. Vidal occupied the penthouse. When I pressed the intercom, a crackling voice instructed us to take the elevator "all the way to the top." But the elevator, a cage about as big as the holding pen in a county jail, wasn't functioning, and Linda and I had to climb flights of stairs whose iron railings and scalloped steps called to mind a Piranesi prison sketch. The hall reeked of garbage and cooking oil, and behind one door a man was screaming as if he had been driven mad by the babble of televisions throughout the building.

Gore Vidal called from the highest landing, urging us on and explaining that kids from the language school must have broken the elevator again. He wore a blue blazer and gray flannel trousers, an outfit I would see him in so often, I began to regard it as his uniform. Despite a reputation for vanity, he was self-deprecating about his appearance and joked that he used to be the handsomest man in Rome. Now he was "reduced to just another classical ruin."

The three of us passed through a high-ceilinged salon where a fluffy toy Yorkshire terrier leaped out of an armchair and yapped at our heels.

It wasn't until we were outside on the terrace that we caught our breath and cooled off. Vidal asked what we wanted to drink, then shouted over his shoulder for two Scotch and sodas.

Sipping a glass of white wine, he identified the church domes visible from where he stood. "That's Sant'Andrea della Valle," he said, "the setting for *Tosca,* Act One. And there's St. Ivo, the one with the corkscrew on top. And that's St. Peter's."

Above us, flocks of swifts wheeled against the sky—circumflexes of black against overcast gray. Wind had gusted up, harping through pots of flowers and rattling a vine-laced trellis. Vidal stepped over to the railing. Linda and I followed him and glanced down at the traffic in Largo Argentina. Cars, buses, and cabs swerved around the ruined temples with the indifference of scavengers scuttling past meatless bones. The racket of their horns and tires dinned at our ears; a haze of exhaust fumes stung my eyes and grated my throat.

Vidal gave no sign of being bothered by the noise or the pollution. He told us that the Largo had been one of Mussolini's urban-renewal projects, another effort to prove that Fascism had recaptured the grandeur of Rome. In profile, Vidal's face might have been the silhouette on an ancient coin—a high, brainy forehead, prominent nose, and slightly swollen, slightly insolent mouth. At the age of fifty, he had given in grudgingly to gravity and showed a bit of loose flesh at the midsection.

A servant, Indian or Sri Lankan, brought our drinks, and we went inside as it started to rain. The salon was a hodgepodge of styles and eras and decorating motifs—gilt-framed mirrors, Neapolitan sideboards, antique marble busts, a stone lion, oil paintings of the Coliseum, Indian wood carvings, and an Aubusson tapestry of three Dutchmen slaying a wolf. Displayed on end tables were photographs of Princess Margaret, Jack and Jacqueline Kennedy, and Tennessee Williams.

Vidal poured himself a refill. In those days, I never saw him drink anything stronger than wine. He subscribed to the theory that no amount of it was as unhealthy as hard liquor. "That's the killer," he said, "hard stuff." And this theory was related to a second one about sex: "Think how many American men kill themselves with two or three drinks before dinner, then wine with a heavy meal, then jumping right into bed. My father had a heart attack in middle age. It didn't kill him, but he never was the same man again. The trick is to have sex in the afternoon, and save the booze and food for later."

As the storm intensified, the shutters to the terrace banged back and forth. Vidal didn't bother to close them. "That's it," he said with finality. "Summer's over. Now it's winter." He settled into an armchair, and the dog, called Rat, cuddled next to him.

A short, freckled man with sandy hair darted into the salon and shut the doors. "I don't guess it occurred to you," he said to Gore.

"I was just saying that it's the end of the season." He introduced Howard Austen, his companion of many years. Like Vidal, Austen wore a blue blazer, but with faded blue jeans. He had about him the grit and spunk of New York City. Once an aspiring singer, he had a throaty voice and a brash presence that put newcomers on notice that they would have to take him on his terms or not at all. Though he respected Gore, he was by no means daunted or deferential the way so many people were in his presence.

When Vidal crossed his legs, Howard said, "What the hell? Do you know you have a hole in your shoe?"

Vidal examined his sole. "Well, it was good enough for Adlai Stevenson."

A bedraggled woman came in shaking an umbrella that had blown inside out. Skinny and infirm, she had on ill-fitting clothes that added to the impression of a lady down on her luck, shrunken by age and ill health. She described herself as an actress too sick to work. "I wouldn't have survived," she said, "if Gore hadn't helped me."

He passed this off with an indolent whisk of the hand. Though not immune to compliments about his books, he had no interest in gratitude or praise for personal charity. Any such discussion seemed to embarrass him, and he quipped, "No good deed goes long unpunished." He preferred to discuss politics. When I asked who he thought would win the '76 U.S. presidential race, he said, "Teddy Kennedy. Every declining culture deserves a King Farouk."

While the actress, Linda, and Howard fell into conversation, Gore and I talked shop. Ever the rank beginner eager to learn from an older author, I asked when Vidal wrote, where, and how.

"In the morning," he answered with crisp efficiency. "At a table. Longhand on yellow legal pads, just like Nixon, when I'm doing fiction. Typewritten when I'm working on an essay or filmscript." He kept at it three or four hours a day, he said, and didn't let houseguests or social commitments interrupt. It nettled him to be depicted as a *flâneur* or *boule-*

vardier who went to too many parties, spent too much time in Holly-wood, and was on a first-name basis with too many nonliterary celebrities. To date, he had produced a dozen novels, five plays, several collections of essays, countless film and TV scripts, and a handful of mysteries under a pseudonym. His historical novels, in particular, were time-consuming enterprises that required years of research, all of which he did himself. He wasn't one of those wealthy authors who hires legions of grad students to do their donkey work. When he embarked on a book, he said, "I go into training. I check into a hotel, give up alcohol, fast for a few days, and clear my head. I'm no romantic. To write what I do, I have to be able to think. Anyway, Henry James and Edith Wharton led far more active social lives than I do, and it never harmed their writing."

And as I would often hear Vidal repeat with glee, no number of dinner parties could possibly dry up a writer's creative juices as quickly as a steady diet of teaching freshman composition and cruising from one campus literary conference to another.

It was nearly nine by the time the rain stopped, and Vidal suggested that we go out to eat. He knew a neighborhood pizzeria that served "the best pizza in Rome. The kind with thin crust and not too much cheese on top."

As we walked through the warren of streets between Largo Argentina and the Pantheon, the cobblestones, lit by shop windows, gleamed like the scales of a carp. The stores on Via dei Cestari resembled the celebrated designer boutiques on Via Condotti, but instead of Gucci shoes, Valentino gowns, and Bulgari gold, these specialized in religious vestments. Mannequins decked out as priests and nuns modeled this season's cassocks, surplices, and sensible canonical underwear.

In Piazza della Minerva a monumental extravagance erupted from the pavement, as skewed as a dream from the deep subconscious. Atop a tall pedestal there perched a marble elephant that bore on its back an upright Egyptian obelisk. "Bernini," Vidal identified the sculptor. An indifferent high-school student who never attended college, Vidal had transformed himself into a polymathically educated man who took for granted that everybody shared his obsession with knowledge of all sorts.

At the pizzeria, he proclaimed that "The best Italian food is simple. Anytime they get fancy or try something foreign, they foul it up. Rome is the only city in the world where a Chinese restaurant opens with great fanfare and by the second week it's serving bucatini all'amatriciana."

He ordered a salad and a plain pizza margarita, explaining that he had to watch his weight. But soon he was eating off everybody else's plate. He couldn't resist french fries and swiped them by the fistful from Linda and the actress. Gobbling food with the same ravenous appetite as he devoured political news, literary gossip, and medical lore, he asked me about a mutual friend who had been diagnosed with multiple sclerosis. He was anxious to know the symptoms of the disease, its prognosis and etiology. "I take my hypochondria *very* seriously," he said.

Although Vidal did much of the talking, he wasn't averse to being interrupted and didn't reject opposing points of view with the kind of peremptoriness his TV persona might lead one to expect. He also had the saving grace of good humor and sprinkled every conversation with polished throw-away lines. "What are the three saddest words in the English language?" he asked, then after a beat answered his own question. "Joyce Carol Oates."

During his prep-school days at Exeter, he had been dubbed "the Senator" by classmates, partly for his debating skill and seigniorial aplomb, partly because his grandfather, T. P. Gore, had been a senator from Oklahoma. But he delighted in puncturing his own aura of self-importance and refused to duck potentially discomfiting questions. When I asked why he had dropped his father's first name and adopted his grandfather's last name, he said he wanted to ease out from under the double burden of being known as Eugene and Junior, both of which he detested. He swore that he loved his father. He just didn't care to be saddled with the same name. Then, too, he admitted he had harbored political aspirations and believed the Gore name would win votes.

Since he characterized the American political system as a tool and an extension of U.S. corporate greed, I asked if he ever felt guilty about his wealth. Whereas a different man might angrily brush off such a question from someone he had just met, Vidal gave it a moment's thought and calmly replied, "Why should I? I've never exploited anyone. I give fair value for what I get."

But when he got million-dollar advances, didn't that leave less for other writers?

"There's no such thing as unilateral socialism," he said. "I work within the system we have. I guess I was born with certain advantages. But I wasn't raised in a bell jar, I wasn't pampered. I've supported myself—and others—since I was seventeen. I didn't inherit my money, as some people believe. Everything I have, I earned."

When the bill came, Vidal wouldn't let anyone pay a share. "That's how I know I'm not rich. I pick up bills. Rich people never pay. No matter how much money they have, they let other people pay. That's why they're rich."

Years would pass before Gore Vidal let me pick up a tab. But it was only a few days before I saw him again. The expat community in Rome was small, and the same cast of characters cropped up at American Academy receptions, U.S. Embassy functions, and private cocktail and dinner parties. On occasion, however, because of his politics, his sexuality—"bisexual, like everybody else," he insisted—or his feuds, Vidal couldn't be invited, and this caused awkwardness for his friends.

Mickey Knox was a blacklisted actor, banned from working in Hollywood because—depending on the story you chose to believe—he once had Communist party connections or because he slept with an important producer's wife. Born in Brooklyn, he was a feisty little fellow whose name director Oliver Stone gave to the psychopathic protagonist in his film *Natural Born Killers*. Now an exile in Hollywood-on-the-Tiber, he had resuscitated his career by playing bit parts, working as a dialogue coach on international productions, writing dialogue, notably for Sergio Leone's *The Good, the Bad, and the Ugly,* translating scripts, and serving as an all-round Mr. Fix-It for film people who passed through Rome. Since Vidal knew many of the same people, it was natural that he and Mickey became friends.

But Mickey was also good friends with Norman Mailer, whom he had known since childhood. They married sisters and were brothers-in-law for a brief time, and Mickey appeared in a couple of Mailer's movies, *Wild 90* and *Beyond the Law.* Trapped squarely between two of the most fractious authors of the generation, Mickey had attempted without success to act as a peacemaker.

Earlier in their careers, Vidal and Mailer had been close acquaintances, and when Mailer stabbed his wife, Adele Morales, Gore was one of the few members of the literary establishment to stand by him. After Mailer was released from police custody and Adele from the hospital, Vidal invited them both to Edgewater, his home in upstate New York, where they could recover in privacy. Subsequently, he introduced Mailer to Jean Campbell, the woman who would become Mailer's third wife.

But they had a falling out in the early seventies, when Vidal wrote of *The Prisoner of Sex* in the *New York Review of Books* "There has been from Henry Miller to Norman Mailer to Charles Manson a logical progression."

Irate, Mailer didn't wait long for revenge. In November 1971 he confronted Vidal in the green room before the Dick Cavett Show. Norman head-butted Gore, and Vidal punched him in the stomach. Once they went on stage, things got really rough as each man fell back on his most vicious weapon—words. Since then, they hadn't seen or spoken to one another.

Cantankerous as he could be himself, Mickey Knox wasn't without diplomatic skills, and he had a history of bringing disparate groups together at his apartment on Via Gregoriana for what he described as his "famous chili." You might say he ran the closest thing in Rome to a salon—although he possibly thought of it as a saloon. When Ed Koch was mayor of New York, Gay Talese made a point of introducing Mickey to him as the mayor of Rome. But in Mailer and Vidal he had two constituents who refused to do his bidding and bury their animosity.

In the winter of 1976, when Norman flew into Rome to write a screenplay for Sergio Leone's *Once Upon a Time in America,* Mickey was obliged to orchestrate events to keep his two friends, now enemies, separated. Sparing everyone his chili, he set up a dinner for Mailer at Dal Bolognese on Piazza del Popolo. Mickey brought along the actor Stacy Keach and Keach's wife. Linda and I came with *Playboy International* editor Donald Stewart and his Italian wife, Luisa. Having known Mailer for more than a decade, Don had interviewed him for *The New Yorker* and signed him up to do articles for *Playboy.* What's more, Don had been there the night Norman stabbed his wife, and he had helped carry Adele downstairs to the ambulance. A former classmate of Don's at Harvard, Edward Hoagland, en route to Africa on assignment for *Harper's,* was also at the dinner.

The evening limped off to a bad start. Mailer was late, and the waiters were soon pressuring us to order. To keep them happy, we had a round of drinks, then a fiasco of Chianti. Marinated in good cheer, Mickey Knox told Edward Hoagland how much he admired his op-ed pieces in the *International Herald Tribune.* Hoagland, plagued by such a severe stutter that his face was seized by spasms, said he had never written for the *Herald Tribune*. Mickey had mistaken him for Jim Hoagland.

Stacy Keach asked a waiter to describe Dal Bolognese's specialty, bollito misto. Practicing his English, the waiter said that it was a dish of "mixed boils." Mickey, Don, and I guffawed with laughter that was swiftly silenced by a fierce glance from Luisa. Her handsome face conveyed more emotion with one flared nostril than many a woman could express with her whole body.

There followed an hour of resolute drinking and desultory waiting. I was a great fan of Mailer's fiction and had done a grad-school seminar paper on *Barbary Shore* and *The Deer Park*. But alcohol on an empty stomach must have made me giddy. How else explain my reaction to Mailer's entrance? I burst into giggles, which I hurried to hide by slugging down another glass of wine.

Trailed by a strikingly tall young woman with long, straight auburn hair, the tough guy of American lit looked like a tiny tot in a Halloween costume. With a wrinkled khaki safari coat unbuttoned over his potbelly, Mailer might have been Livingston, lost a long time in the jungle, or Doughty just back from Arabia Deserta. Wherever he had spent the past six months, there hadn't been a barber. Ringlets of unruly white hair framed his plump face.

He introduced his companion. A shy, sweet girl in her twenties, Norris Church seemed bedazzled by Mailer. Formerly Little Miss Little Rock, she had been an art teacher in Russellville, Arkansas, and might have remained there had Norman not stopped by to lecture at the local college. Twenty-eight years her senior, he plucked the loveliest rose from that briar patch, brought her to New York, and renamed her. Barbara Norris magically metamorphosed into Norris Church. And no more schoolmarm, she became a model. Now here she was in Rome and just couldn't believe how nice everybody was being to her. Even the hairdresser at the hotel treated her warm and friendly and made a big fuss. Her fondest hope was to model some Italian fashions.

While Mailer was catching up with Don Stewart and Mickey Knox, I talked to Stacy Keach about his role in the film *Fat City*. To the character of an aging, down-and-out prizefighter battling alcoholism, Keach had brought what struck me as an extraordinary degree of authenticity. But Mailer overheard and broke in to say he hadn't seen the movie. He

had, however, read the Leonard Gardner novel that it was based on, and
Gardner got it all wrong about boxers.

Rolling his shoulders, feinting with his fists, Mailer objected that the
internal monologues of the fighters lacked verisimilitude: "They don't
think the way Leonard Gardner thinks they think. For him it's bang! a
boxer takes a punch to the head and thinks, God, that hurts. I've never
been hit harder in my life. Boom! that left hook almost busted my rib."
Mailer shook his frizzball of hair. "That's not how a boxer's mind functions. They get hit and hurt so often, it's part of the business, just a blip
on the radar screen. They don't remember the pain of any one punch.
They're too preoccupied with technique, with how to cover up and
counterattack. Their mind's not a stream of consciousness, it's pure muscle memory."

Case closed, he swung back to Mickey and Don. Mailer might have
been right. But he could not have looked or sounded less like a man with
firsthand knowledge of fighting. In contrast to Mickey, whose voice was
jagged with the echoes of Brooklyn streets, Norman spoke with the Irish
brogue of a whiskey priest and looked about as threatening as a teddy
bear.

After dinner, we decided to stroll up to Via Veneto. Except for tourists under the sway of Fellini's *La Dolce Vita* and hustlers of melodramatic
sexual proclivities, the street was dead. Clubs and cafés that had once
swarmed with celebrities had deteriorated to the level of kitsch. We
wound up at Jerry's Luau, an ersatz Trader Vic's, with a Kon-Tiki village
motif. A waterfall trickled through rubber philodendrons, drinks arrived
festooned with tiny paper parasols, and corny Polynesian music carried
the tremolo of steel guitars through a staticky speaker system.

Mailer ordered Cent'erbe, a bitter Italian *digestivo* manufactured from
one hundred herbs. It was meant to be sipped slowly from a thimble-
sized glass. Norman knocked his back as if downing a straight shot of
bourbon at the Last Chance Saloon. He demanded a refill, then another
and another. To the astonishment of the bartender, he guzzled half a
dozen cent'erbes as he lectured us about bullfighting, masculine initia-
tion, grace under fire, and living life close to the horns. To listen to him
on the subject of boxing had been borderline, but to hear Mailer maun-
der on about bullfighting verged perilously close to parody. So many
writers I had met were refreshingly unlike their images, but Mailer had
remained a prisoner, not of sex, but of a fictional character he had per-

mitted to body-snatch him. When I had had enough, I announced that I was tired, I couldn't hold my liquor, and the little wifey and I better hurry home and relieve the babysitter.

Thereafter, on the subject of Mailer vs. Vidal, I sided with Gore. I continued to side with him even after I learned that behind my back he referred to me as Youngblood Hawke, the lumbering, cartoonish figure from Herman Wouk's roman à clef about Thomas Wolfe.

That same spring, before I started *Land Without Shadow,* a novel about a film company shooting in a Saharan location plagued by drought and famine, I flew to North Africa to gather background information about the setting and to refresh my memory about movie making. My first stop was in Tunisia, where I hung around the set of Franco Zefferelli's *The Life of Jesus Christ* (script by Anthony Burgess). Since the cast and crew had been marooned for months in the small coastal town of Monastir, any outsider was welcomed with astonishing warmth and pumped for news about events in the real world. I found myself sharing the English newspapers with James Mason, eating dinner with Rod Steiger and Ian Holm, and having drinks with Anthony Quinn and Laurence Olivier. Spry and surprisingly eager to participate in the nightly gab-fests and games, Sir Laurence competed with the other actors to see who could perform the saddest exit, the most original entrance, and funniest double-take. Off screen, Larry, as he instructed us to call him, always wore white gloves and apologized for not shaking hands. He explained that he had recently completed a course of chemotherapy for cancer, and his fingers felt raw and morbidly sensitive.

From Tunisia, I intended to cross into Algeria to the Grand Erg Oriental, an expanse of sand dunes sculpted by wind into wavelike crests hundreds of feet high. In a rental car, I headed west over a dry lake bed, its sun-bleached surface rippling with heat mirages and blinding salt crystals. To add to the eeriness of the trip, a bus labeled SPIES bore down hard on my rear bumper and followed me for miles. Although I learned that Spies—pronounced "speece"—was a Danish tour group, I couldn't help feeling I was under the combined scrutiny of the CIA and the KGB.

To shake them, I stopped in Tozeur, where things turned increasingly surreal. As I explored the oasis, I was attacked by a pack of dogs and barely made it back to the hotel without being bitten. Hurrying to the bar for a stiff drink, I discovered that it had been taken over by a contingent of midgets. George Lucas, who was shooting a *Star Wars* sequel in this lunar landscape, had imported the little people to play androids and Ewoks. I met Lucas and asked to visit the set, but he told me it was closed to the press. When I protested that I was a novelist, not a reporter, he said that was all the more reason to keep me away.

Pushing on to the frontier, which appeared to be little more than a faint scribble in an infinity of dust, I had no trouble leaving Tunisia. Customs officials waved me right through. On the Algerian side of the border, however, authorities decreed that I could enter the country, but the rental car couldn't. Determined not to be thwarted so close to my goal, I left the rental car behind and caught a ride in a *louage,* a kind of long-distance taxi that connects remote towns in the Sahara.

The Peugeot that picked me up had grease smeared over its fenders and hood to prevent blowing sand from chipping off the paint. A brass hand of Fatma, an amulet to ward off evil, swung from the rearview mirror, and I soon realized how desperately we needed good luck. As the driver barreled along, he kept one hand on the horn, the other on the radio dial, and steered with his knees. He slowed down only to drop off a passenger who was lugging two large raffia baskets stuffed with baguettes of bread. The man marched straight up the nearest dune, toward nothing I could see. He might have been a character out of a Samuel Beckett play trudging into desolation. Then again, maybe he meant to open a bakery at the top of the dune.

Even with the windows shut, I heard sand buzzing at the glass, and I tasted grit in the air. Periodically, the dunes encroached on the road, and bucket-and-shovel brigades attempted to clear the asphalt. But their task was Sisyphean. The sand went wherever it wanted, smothering cultivated fields, encircling whole cities. The archipelago of oases that survived reminded me of the desert islands seen in cartoons, some of them with just a single palm tree at the center.

I spent several days in El Oued, the fabled city of a thousand cupolas, where the writer Isabel Eberhardt lived—and then died, in keeping with her histrionic personality, in a flash flood in one of the world's most arid areas. Having heard its praises sung by local people, I made it a point to visit the Souf museum, which resembled the cluttered storeroom of an eccentric pack rat. Beyond the predictable samples of native carpets, antique jewelry, and handicrafts, the most riveting objects were venomous snakes the size of earthworms, intestinal worms the size of boa constric-

tors, scorpions the size of ten-dollar lobsters, and horned beetles as big as
Princess telephones. In one corner drooped what appeared to be the
business end of a feather duster—in fact, the last ostrich from this part of
the Sahara, shot by a French Legionnaire in 1937.

Among the miscellany of indigenous lizards, lethal spiders, and centipedes, the prizewinner was a wine glass filled to the brim with formalde-
hyde. In it fat gray blobs floated like rotten grapes. Perhaps Algerians had
no trouble making sense of the display, but for out-of-towners they provided a thoughtful card identifying in three languages "Blood-Engorged
Camel Ticks."

I returned to Rome with a surfeit of material, far more than I needed
for my fifth novel, *Land Without Shadow*. A decade later, I dug back
through my notebooks of that trip to North Africa and wrote a comedy
called *Blackballed*. Though I didn't recognize it at the time, my work had
started to fall into a pattern that mimicked my emotional makeup. Struggling to cope with my depressive tendencies, I was attracted to stark settings and grimly violent stories, as if they might inoculate me against my
feelings. When that didn't work—sometimes they only deepened my
sadness—I went to the opposite extreme and tried to wring laughs out
of pain. As I began to get journalistic work, the contrast in tone, not to
mention content, from one piece to the next grew more pronounced.
When I wasn't writing about political terror, parricide, or family turmoil,
I wrote about tennis, travel, and the pleasures of fatherhood. Editors and
readers could be forgiven for never knowing what I would turn out.

At the end of the summer in 1977, Linda and I and our son, Sean, then
two years old, moved into the ground-floor apartment of Villa Chiaraviglio. The largest and best accommodation at the American Academy, it
had three bedrooms, a kitchen the size of an amphitheater, a living room
with a wood-burning fireplace and a vaulted ceiling that soared to a
height of twenty feet. Double doors in back opened onto a brick-paved
terrace. Beyond its balustrades stretched a garden of palms, lemon and
orange trees, and oleander bushes and shrubs that a team of topiary artists
pruned into ovals, pyramids, and obelisks. From their shredded leaves,
the scent of spring oozed all year round.

A gravel path of white pebbles, each of which appeared to have been
set in place by hand, ran parallel to an aqueduct that fed the Fontanone
dell'Acqua Paola. In *Rome and a Villa,* Eleanor Clark described this foun-

tain, with its water-spouting gargoyles and Corinthian columns, as an example of "the baroque at its most serene and loving." The esplanade in front of it offered a panoramic cityscape of towers, arches, lanterns, and loggias undulating toward the Alban Hills like one vast lesson from an architecture manual.

Viewed from the Gianicolo, Rome seemed to be somnolently baptized in dense golden light, but despite the city's luminescence, Italians had taken to calling that time *Anni di Piombo,* the Years of Lead. Radical political activists had gone underground and declared war on the state. The best organized and most virulent band among them was the Red Brigades. Under the banner of *tanto peggio, tanto meglio*—so much the worse, so much the better—its members vilified the official Communist party for rejecting revolution in favor of respectability, and they systematically went about provoking a backlash from the government. In their clotted jargon, "Violence was to be the coagulant of the movement's subjective energy."

Even the American Academy, in its palmy isolation, wasn't spared. During its annual spring show, a smoke bomb cleared the building and closed the exhibition. But much worse befell cities and factories and universities up and down the Italian peninsula. Labor disputes and student demonstrations degenerated into riots. There were bombings, kidnappings, knee-cappings, and a number of assassinations.

Yet to an American, accustomed to our homegrown variety of random violence, these events begged to be put into perspective. During an average week in Houston or Washington, D.C., more people were murdered than the Red Brigades killed in a decade. And despite sensational headlines in the local press and in overseas dispatches that made Rome sound as anarchic as Belfast or Beirut, life continued, apart from increased annoyances and inefficiencies, much as it always had. Although *The New Yorker* reported that after dark nobody ventured outdoors "except for muggers and nervous bachelors walking their new Dobermans," every piazza was thronged with crowds; every sidewalk was a proscenium devoted to *commedia dell'arte.* Kids clattered around on motorbikes until dawn, and all the best restaurants and cafés were crammed to the rafters with customers, many of them the same journalists who, after an evening of alfresco bingeing, posted stories to the States portraying a city under siege. When I asked Gore Vidal his opinion of these apocalyptic alarms, he replied that "a revolution in Italy is about as likely as a pogrom in Tahiti."

Despite my previous failed efforts at magazine writing—autumn of 1977 was the hellish season of my disputes with Eleanor Clark and Graham Greene—I proposed to do a piece for *Harper's* titled "Two Cheers for Italy." While conceding the country's social and economic woes and its culture of political corruption, I planned to subject recent news accounts about the Red Brigades and other urban terrorist groups to reanalysis. Editor Lewis Lapham liked the idea, and I went to work.

Which is to say I went to lunch, I went to dinner, and lavished my expense money on Italian economists and sociologists (preferably English speaking), on university professors, counterterrorism experts, and embassy officials from various foreign delegations. Among my "sources" were American reporters, theoretically in Italy to cover the story of the country's imminent collapse, in fact relishing its age-old attractions. They saw nothing contradictory, no cause for cynicism, in this. If things didn't pan out—if the government didn't fall and the Red Brigades failed to commandeer Palazzo Chigi—the reporters still got paid. Meanwhile, there was tennis to be played, new discos to dance in, the same cheap and reliable *trattorie* to eat in.

What none of us ever encountered in the course of our rounds was a bloody-clawed, fully-fanged terrorist. A few Italian journalists had been foolhardy enough to try to contact the Red Brigades and had had their kneecaps blown off. One was shot point blank in the head and left to die in front of his wife. At most, the rest of us saw slogans spray-painted on monuments: "*la mitra è bella,* the machine gun is beautiful" and "Americans, you will return home in caskets." On the marble embankments of the Tiber, somebody had had the leisure to render a line in lovely purple calligraphy: "As long as the violence of the state is called justice, the justice of the proletariat will be called violence."

While I was on assignment for *Harper's,* an editor at the *New York Times Magazine* called and asked me to penetrate a terrorist cell. She wanted an investigative report from the inside—"to show the human face behind the mask." I thought this was a joke, a cruel and dangerous one in which allusions to "kill fees" amounted to sick humor. Not a single antiterrorist agent, much less a freelance hack, had managed to infiltrate a Red Brigades *covo.*

"That's the beauty of it," the editor said. "It's never been done before.

You do it, and an article is just the beginning. You'll get a huge book contract and probably a movie deal."

"Why not give the assignment to your Rome correspondent?" I asked, knowing full well Henry Kamm would howl at the idea.

"Don't say no, Mike, until you've thought it over and talked to people. All the years you've lived in Rome, you must have sources."

"I wouldn't know where to start or who to ask."

After a pause, the editor posed a tantalizing question. "Who knows more about the Red Brigades than you do?"

The question reverberated in my brain for years until finally I started taking notes for a novel about a reporter who invents an account of his adventures in the Italian terrorist underground.

In point of fact, quite a few people knew more than I did about the Red Brigades, and friends arranged for me to meet them. Donald Stewart introduced me to Robert Katz, a scholarly looking, biblically bearded American who was generous with advice. Having published books on a broad spectrum of topics from Giordano Bruno to Pope Pius XII and the Nazi occupation of Rome, he would go on to write perhaps the best and most accessible study of the Red Brigades, *Days of Wrath,* later the basis for a successful Italian TV documentary. In a fairer world, Katz would be far better known, but he has had habitually bad luck, having suffered the rare, perhaps singular, misfortunes of losing a libel suit to a dead man (actually, he lost to Pius XII's family) and later getting knocked down and bitten by a muzzled German shepherd.

Mickey Knox took it upon himself to put me in touch with William Murray, who flew to Italy at intervals to file a "Letter from Rome" for *The New Yorker.* We met for dinner at Gigi Fazzi's, and like most social events *all'italiana,* this one was free form and ad hoc. Unlike evenings in France, which tend to be solemn, high-church ceremonies, it was as raucous as a fundamentalist revival, with each course accompanied by the clatter of plates and cutlery, and outbursts of praise and blame from customers.

William Murray brought his wife, Alice, and I was with Linda. Robert Katz showed up with his wife, Beverly, and Don Stewart and Luisa came too. The decibel level at our table rendered conversation difficult, and most of the discourse consisted of shouts and sign language. So when Mickey Knox and William Murray began bellowing at one another, nobody took special notice. For all we knew, they might have been debating the World Series. Each man leaned into his remarks, rocking back and forth with the flow of the discussion, and as they talked, Mickey mixed a salad for the nine of us in an enormous wooden bowl. Slicing and dicing, he dropped in chunks of tomato, celery, onion, mozzarella, and carrots, which he garnished with basil, thyme, oregano, and cloves of garlic. Eyes squinted—against the onions, I guessed—he glared at Murray as he got on with splashing oil and vinegar, then tossing the whole soggy mulch.

Just when he was about to serve our plates—or so I supposed— Mickey hefted the bowl in both hands. Suddenly Murray hollered loud enough to be heard by the rest of us, and we got our first inkling that they were arguing and on the brink of fighting, not simply chatting. "Mickey, you've been abroad too long," Murray shouted.

"I ain't never been a broad." With that the Mayor of Rome heaved the contents of the bowl in the general direction of his old friend. But his aim was awful. Gobs of greasy vegetables splattered William Murray and everybody else at the table. Shreds of lettuce and purple radicchio spackled our hair. Olive oil dripped from our chins and puddled in our laps. Chunks of vinegary mozzarella left snail tracks on shirtfronts and dresses.

Livid, Murray drew himself up to his full indignant height, dropped a fistful of lire next to his plate, and strode out of the restaurant with as much aplomb as he could muster. He hadn't been gone a minute before Don Stewart broke the silence with a line that should be chiseled on his tombstone. "Waiter! Waiter," he called out. "There's a salad in my fly."

For a week, Mickey and William Murray were on the outs. Then they made up, and we all met for dinner again. Exercising the sort of hindsight that focuses exclusively on happy and entertaining moments, I'm tempted to claim that the evening was typical of our time in Rome, but if honest, I have to admit that those years also held some major disappointments.

After editing my first four novels, Albert Erskine responded tepidly to *Land Without Shadow* and offered a $7,500 advance. That was what he had paid for my previous book as well as the one before it. At my agent's suggestion, we submitted the manuscript to other editors to test the market and give Albert a chance to reconsider. When Doubleday bid twice what Random House would pay and sweetened the deal with a two-book contract, Albert refused to budge, leaving me little choice but to switch houses.

This wasn't, of course, an unusual story. As the book business went corporate, the relationships between many authors and editors eroded. Gradually publishing became a branch of the entertainment industry where a Hollywood boom-or-bust mentality prevailed, and the bottom line was often the only one people read. But this is like observing that more marriages end in divorce these days. While that may be true, it doesn't mean that breakups hurt less or don't cause lasting damage. After a decade of working closely with Albert, visiting him and his family in Connecticut, and babysitting their house in the summer, I considered him a friend, a father figure, and it saddened me to feel cut adrift.

When I flew to New York to meet my new editor, I stopped by at the *New York Times* to pick up a batch of books to review. There I bumped into Anatole Broyard, who invited me to lunch. He said he had something to discuss with me.

In addition to doing book reviews, Anatole taught creative writing, and we decided to eat at P. J. Clark's, on the way uptown to his class. As voluble and energetic as ever, he set a brisk pace from Times Square to Third Avenue and never quit talking. Having reviewed *The Toll* enthusiastically, he had been ambivalent about my next book, *Earthly Bread,* and asked when I intended to get around to "the big expatriate novel" he believed I had in me.

Flattered by his attention and the idea that he cared what I wrote next, I assumed this was why Anatole invited me to lunch—to discuss my work. But after we ordered, he asked, "Why the hell did you leave Albert Erksine?"

The question and his tone caught me off guard. "I wouldn't put it that way. It wasn't a question of leaving him."

"But he's not your editor anymore. Why?"

"It was an economic decision." I tried to cut the subject short.

"What do you care about money?" Again his bluntness, the slight edge of belligerence, grated.

"I've got a wife and a son. It's cheap in Rome, but if I had to live on what Albert paid, I'd go broke."

"Come on, Mike. Albert told me who your father-in-law is. You don't need the money."

Stunned—no, stung—I didn't know what to say, and it annoyed me that Anatole appeared to feel I owed an explanation. It was nobody's business, neither Albert's nor the *New York Times* book reviewer's, that Linda's father was the CEO at Westinghouse. I wondered how many other people mistakenly presumed that he financed us. I wouldn't have minded being regarded as a rich kid, if that were actually the case, but it galled me to be simultaneously penniless and envied.

"I live," I informed Anatole, "entirely on what I make writing and teaching from time to time."

"You're not rich?" Clearly he disbelieved me.

"Far fucking from it. Did Albert tell you I was?"

"Yeah, he did."

As soon as Broyard and I finished eating, I phoned James Wilcox, who had been Albert's assistant. Now writing his own fiction, he admitted that it was taken for granted at Random House that I had independent means. The subject even came up at sales conferences when first printings and promotional budgets were discussed. "Albert told us it didn't matter to you," Wilcox said, "whether your books sold or not. You were set."

Short of publishing my bank statements and annual tax returns, I realized there wasn't much I could do in my defense. But I sent Albert a letter expressing regret that we no longer worked together and equal regret that he had been under the illusion I didn't need to earn a living. He never replied.

During that same December trip to New York I delivered the article on Italy to *Harper's*. It was scheduled for publication in February. The galleys returned in record time, and I came into the *Harper's* office to correct them. But then Lewis Lapham demanded that I shorten the piece by 50 percent and accept $1,000, instead of the contractually stipulated $3,000, in full payment. Since it was either do this or accept a $500 kill fee and have the article go unpublished, I capitulated.

Without letting me know in advance, *Harper's* didn't run the article in its February issue. Then the March issue appeared on newsstands, and the piece wasn't in it either. To my inquiries *Harper's* remained stonily unresponsive. Only weeks later, after Aldo Moro, the former Italian prime minister, had been kidnapped by the Red Brigades, was I informed that "Two Cheers for Italy" would be shelved until the situation resolved itself.

During that period of uncertainty and political turmoil, we invited Gore Vidal and Howard Austen to dinner at the Villa Chiaraviglio, and for the first time they let us reciprocate their hospitality. The other guests were John D'Arms, the new director of the American Academy, and his wife, Teresa, the daughter of Evelyn Waugh. With Sean now a boisterous and very verbal three-year-old, Linda decided it would be prudent to hire a babysitter. Mary Walsh, a former editor of the *Daily Texan* at the University of Texas and a future producer at the CBS Evening News, arrived after a full workday at the *Daily American,* bathed Sean, changed him into pajamas, and read him a story before bed.

But Sean refused to sleep or stay in his room. Wound tighter than a two-dollar clock, he kept running and sliding on the marble floors in his footed pajamas, shouting, "I want to see Gore Vee-doll! I want to see Gore Vee-doll!" As he pronounced it, the famous name sounded like one of the violent Japanese characters he watched on cartoon shows.

Mary and Linda, talking in tandem, persuaded Sean to accept a deal. If he quieted down and sat still in the living room, he could stay up to say hello to Gore Vidal. After that, he had to go to his room and sleep.

Enthroned on an overstuffed chair, his blond mop of hair tinted red by the light of the fireplace, he waited with surprising equanimity, hands poised on the high arms of the chair, his legs extending only to the edge of the seat cushion. When the D'Armses showed up, he barely acknowledged their presence. He was beginning to nod off, his head wobbling on the skinny stalk of his neck. With luck, Mary Walsh could soon swoop him up, put him to bed, and join us for dinner.

But Sean refused to forsake his vigil, and when Gore and Howard arrived he snapped wide awake. Notoriously indifferent to kids, Vidal had nevertheless been asked to serve as a godfather so often that he quipped, "Always a godfather, never a god." Bestowing a wintry smile on Sean, he said, "Aren't you a pretty little girl."

"I'm a boy," Sean protested.

"Well, then," Gore replied, "aren't you a pretty little boy."

As he turned away, Sean chirped, "Gore Vee-doll."

Gore turned back to the pretty little boy, who proclaimed in clearly enunciated syllables, "I want to eat you."

The reaction. . . . No, initially there was none. Everybody froze. For the first and only time in my presence, words failed Vidal. Reduced to dumb miming, he demonstrated to Sean that he could wiggle his ears.

Then he preformed a trick with his fingers that made it appear as if he had detached the last joint from his thumb. This set Sean giggling, and the rest of us joined in, laughing in relief.

Mary grabbed Sean and hauled him off to bed. I poured Gore a glass of wine and Howard a vodka on the rocks.

"It's interesting how alcohol affects different writers," Vidal observed, as if that's what we had been talking about. "Whenever I read Faulkner and he starts rambling on about 'the ancient avatar of the evening sun slipping down the crepuscular sky,' I know he must have been hitting the sauce when he wrote the passage. On the other hand, your sainted father," he said to Teresa Waugh D'Arms, "became meaner and more concise the drunker he got. In every sentence, there was a dagger."

Again we all laughed, and I hoped that Vidal would never mention what had happened. He didn't that night, but the next day, he telephoned. "Who was that dwarf you hired to get the evening off to such a rousing start?"

On May 9, 1978, fifty-four days after Aldo Moro's kidnapping, I boarded a bus on the Gianicolo and traveled downhill to the *centro storico*. Beyond Ponte Garibaldi, traffic stopped dead on Via Arenula, and streets in every direction were clogged with pedestrians and cars. In itself, this wasn't an uncommon occurrence. I figured that strikers or demonstrators had blocked the area. But as I climbed off the bus, I heard the crowd murmurously repeating a single word. *Moro,* they whispered. *Moro. Moro.*

Gleaning snippets of information as I advanced on foot, I shouldered my way into the Jewish Ghetto. Moro was dead. Police had found his body in the back of a Renault parked on Via Caetani. For fear the car was booby-trapped, the *carabinieri* were keeping people away. But I pressed forward, making my way through a maze of medieval alleys, many no more than an arm-span wide. There were checkpoints at Piazza Mattei, a square with a central fountain where naked bronze boys hoisted bronze turtles into a shimmering basin. I flashed my credentials for the Italian Open tennis tournament, a card marked *Stampa* (Press) in bold black letters. The cops took a cursory look and let me cross to Via Caetani, where I moved to within yards of Moro's corpse. A priest was bent over the back of the Renault administering the last rites.

News accounts and dozens of books have claimed that Moro's body was left equidistant between the Communist and Christian Democratic party headquarters. The Red Brigades were said to have chosen the location for symbolic purposes, intending to condemn both parties for their "historic compromise." But, in fact, the car was parked in front of the American Studies Center, and if there was symbolism, it could as easily have been against the United States for its constant intrusion into Italian affairs.

After the priest finished, a forensic team arrived to process the crime scene. I watched them for a long while. I stayed on, not just in ghoulish curiosity, but out of a sense that I was in the presence of events that exceeded comprehension and that as a novelist I should notice everything, down to the minute and incongruous details. At one point, a street vendor carrying buckets of olives and garbanzo beans blundered onto the scene and set down his wares as though this were a good place to do business. The *carabinieri* chased him off. They had tears in their eyes. By the time I left, people were already bringing flowers, huge sprays as well as potted plants, to mark the spot where Moro's body had been.

Weeks later, *Harper's* notified me that "Two Cheers for Italy" couldn't possibly be published as written. They asked for a rewrite that dealt with Aldo Moro's kidnapping and assassination, and its causes and effects, with an inevitable shift in the article's emphasis.

I pointed out that I had met the contractual deadline more than six months ago, had cut the piece to their specifications, and agreed to a greatly reduced fee. While they might reasonably have held off publication after Moro was abducted, they had never explained why the article hadn't run as scheduled, *before* the kidnapping. Under the circumstances, I thought it only fair that I receive additional payment. I suggested the $2,000 that would have brought my total fee up to the figure called for in the original contract. *Harper's* dismissed this idea and me with a brusqueness that indicated no desire for further communication.

After this, a sensible, or simply less masochistic, man might have chosen to stick to fiction. But I was determined to support myself with my writing, and in those days nonfiction seemed like a short cut to that goal. With the noisy ascendancy of the New Journalism, lots of novelists were trying their luck with magazine work, hoping to reach a wider readership and then turn its attention to their fiction.

So I continued to shoot off article ideas. In one proposal I pitched a reappraisal of Gore Vidal that would refute the conventional picture of him as an icy, meanspirited, selfish, America-hating, narcissistic sexual deviant. The *New York Times Magazine* was intrigued and, after some discussion, gave me an assignment.

Vidal, however, was reluctant to cooperate. He swore the *Times* would never print anything positive about him. For the past thirty years, he said, ever since his second novel, *The City and the Pillar,* presented a nonjudgmental portrait of homosexuality, "The Good Gray Geese of American literature," as Gore called them, had decided that he must be "a bad person." For the *Times,* this mattered far more, he claimed, than whether he was a good writer, and as a result, his books got harsh reviews or none at all.

"You have to keep in mind that it wasn't just the usual fag-baiters who were after me," he said. "During the McCarthy era I was viewed as a dangerously outspoken leftist—not only a threat to the sanctity of the American family, but out to destroy the Republic. When I began spending a lot of time in Italy, that inflamed suspicions all the more. I mean, what kind of real man and real American would want to live anywhere except the home of the brave and the land of the free?"

I argued that times and the *New York Times* had changed, and in the end, Gore agreed to be interviewed on the condition that I let him read the piece before it was published. Locked in litigation with Truman Capote, he needed to make sure the manuscript didn't misquote him and deepen his legal jeopardy.

Given what I had gone through with *Harper's,* Graham Greene, and Eleanor Clark, it seemed sensible to me to let him check the manuscript for accuracy. I was adamant, though, that I wouldn't change anything except factual errors. My opinions and conclusions had to remain as I wrote them.

We arranged to meet in Los Angeles over the 1979 Christmas holidays. In one of my cyclical efforts to replenish the bank account, I was teaching at the University of Texas and couldn't leave Austin before the semester break. Then because the *Times* paid only five hundred dollars in expenses—not enough to cover airfare, much less a rental a car in LA—I drove across country and economized by bunking in a friend's unheated pool house. This was another peculiarity of journalism that I had to accustom myself to. Frequently, I got the impression that the prestige of a publication was inversely proportionate to its pay scale. In effect, the best newspapers expected freelance authors to finance them.

In addition to his apartment in Rome and a villa on the Amalfi coast, Gore had a house in the Hollywood Hills. He stressed that he didn't consider himself an expatriate. "The more I stayed abroad," he said, "the more intensely interested I became in the United States; the more clearly I saw it." As co-chairman with Dr. Spock of the People's Party in the early seventies, he had traveled the length and breadth of the country campaigning against the Vietnam War. So he claimed it should have been no surprise when he bought a whitewashed Spanish provincial on Outpost Drive and settled there for half the year.

Vidal answered the door wearing his standard uniform—a blue blazer and gray flannel trousers. "Let me give you the tour," he said, and walked me around the property, which was screened off from the street by high cypress hedges. He pointed to a patio where the swimming pool used to be. Then he led me up a flight of steps to a terrace where a new pool had been installed. As we gazed across the ultramarine water at the red tile roof of the house, he observed, "It's like the setting for a Raymond Chandler murder mystery, isn't it?"

Inside, the living room was a head-on collision of Andalucia and the Far East. There were Moorish arches and banquettes, a Persian carpet, a rattan coffee table, and a Japanese screen. The books and magazines lying about—*The Nation,* William Golding's *Darkness Visible, An Illustrated History of the Civil War, Jerry Brown Illustrated,* a collection of photos of China, and a volume titled *L'Amour Bleu*—seemed as eclectic as the décor and suggested the broad range of his interests.

As I set up a tape recorder, Gore avoided eye contact. It didn't strike me as conceivable that after thousands of interviews he suffered from stage fright. More likely he averted his eyes because of what he imagined he might see in mine. Though we had known each other socially for five years, perhaps he suspected that he would spot some inkling of animosity, some intimation that I meant to drag him over the coals, if not with my questions, then later in what I wrote. It cannot be pleasant to realize, as all celebrities must, that the friendliest journalist may turn into a betrayer or a torturer.

Before we started, he hurried to the kitchen and brewed us each a cup of strong Italian coffee. "This stuff has killed more writers than liquor," he said. "But I can't live without it." Then he settled into a chair, and his dog Rat snuggled in beside him.

When I asked what he was working on, and his synopsis of current projects took ten minutes, I understood why he needed coffee. He had just finished *Creation*—fifteen hundred pages in longhand—a novel that required him to master the teachings of Buddha, Confucius, and Zoroaster. Then he had started research on Abraham Lincoln in preparation for a six-hour NBC teleplay. Now his publishers wanted him to write a novel about Lincoln to coincide with the miniseries. Meanwhile, he had been doing a filmscript for *Dress Gray,* Lucian Truscott's book about the murder of a homosexual cadet at West Point.

Gore was born at West Point, on the grounds of the U.S. Military Academy, where his father, Eugene Sr., an All American and an Olympic athlete, had returned to coach the football team and teach aeronautics. I had trouble picturing Gore as the happy son of a soldier/athlete/football coach and science prof, but he again swore abiding love for his father. His mother, he admitted, he hated.

As I checked off a list of questions, I was conscious of addressing his alleged character flaws. How did he react to the accusation that he was a mandarin from a privileged family, out of touch with America and its democratic values?

Vidal grinned and held the expression so long, it etched vertical grooves in one cheek. Though he allowed that growing up at Merrywood, with Hugh Auchincloss as his stepfather, had its advantages, it wasn't an unalloyed joy—a fact that Jacqueline Kennedy Onassis, who later had Auchincloss as her stepfather, could confirm. In any event, his golden youth hadn't lasted long. After high school, he served in the Army as a private during World War II.

As for his being out of touch with the country, he didn't accept that. He had studied the nation's history and politics all his life. That was the basis for his books. What Americans didn't like was that he declined to take them at their most flattering evaluation of themselves, and he rejected their opinions of him. "Americans prefer their writers obscure, poor, and, if possible, doomed by drink or gaudy vice"—none of which applied to him.

"Your critics might consider that evidence of egotism and narcissism," I said.

He tilted his head to one side. "Strange. I suppose I'm as egotistical as the next person. But narcissism? In what way? With the exception of *Two Sisters,* I've never drawn directly on my life for fiction. I sometimes talk about myself in essays, but only as a way of confessing my point of view. On television I talk about politics or the state of the world. Frankly, I don't find it very interesting to analyze myself."

But didn't his frequent TV appearances create the image of a publicity hound and relentless self-promoter?

"No. Usually I don't even mention my books. I ride my hobbyhorses, and they tend to concern the commonweal." For instance, he once appeared on the Johnny Carson show carrying a model of an ecologically improved toilet system that could conserve thousands of gallons of water. "What other writer would do that, waste precious air time when he could be plugging his work?"

Did he really believe he got bad reviews, or none, because of his sexual preferences? That smacked of paranoia.

Again he inclined his head and smiled. "Anybody who's not paranoid isn't in full possession of the facts. When I was nearly broke in the late forties and early fifties, and it had become clear to me I could not get a good review anywhere, I published a series of mysteries under the pseudonym of Edgar Box. All of them were favorably reviewed. But when they were reissued under my name, some of the same magazines that had praised them were quite negative, even nasty. What would you infer?"

"You think things haven't changed since then?"

"Not much."

Although it's difficult to gauge whether Vidal's sexual outspokenness has hurt his career, it's true that candor about the subject has never helped him. When the vogue was for two-fisted authors of irreproachable masculinity, he proclaimed that he was bisexual. When fashions changed and an admission of homosexuality might have been marketable, he continued to insist that he was bisexual. But it's wrong of Vidal to complain that he hasn't gotten good reviews. Each of his books is emblazoned with encomiums, one of them, amazingly enough, from Norman Mailer.

Still, even those who admired his honesty and supported his politics and his writing sometimes objected to his attitude. Why, I asked, was he so often perceived as meanspirited, prone to put down friends and savagely punish enemies?

Vidal contended that he rarely attacked people. He attacked their ideas and behavior—a crucial distinction, he stressed—and he chose his targets with care, deflating the pompous, unmasking the fraudulent, and confronting the criminal. He didn't go after defenseless prey. In some instances, he was accused of being cruel when he meant to be funny and in other cases "when I'm simply being candid. Honesty isn't a quality greatly admired in a literary community that views all criticism as conspiratorial and personally motivated. So many writers are caught up in a frenzy of mutual back-scratching. I'm not."

Finally, I asked why at this stage in his career he worked so hard. Was it thwarted ambition? A desire to prove his critics wrong?

He trotted out a canned answer that I had heard in rough draft the previous winter as "The brain that doesn't feed itself eats itself." Now it had been refined into "The mind that doesn't nourish itself devours itself. Middle age is a period of melancholy and boredom. To hold them at bay, I keep busy."

"Would you feel guilty," I pressed him, "would you be unhappy, if you weren't working?"

"Of course," he said, with no trace of a smile. "After all, I am a Puritan Moralist."

This would become the theme and title of my article—"Gore Vidal, Puritan Moralist." I made the case that for a man of supposedly dubious morality, Vidal's most serious failing as a writer was his determination to infuse his fiction with the same ethical concerns, the same polemical tone and didactic spirit, that inform his nonfiction. While his essays manage to be stylish and, at the same time, instructive, his weaker novels are too explanatory, too manipulative, too eager to demonstrate that it's absurd to regard sex as the sole measure of morality. Impatient with the novelist's task of moving by implication, he nudges the reader along and too often depends on adverbs and adjectives to hammer home his points.

But at his best, I wrote, Vidal dramatizes his ideas in the dynamic interplay of characters, and creates scenes of exceptional imagination, wit, and seriousness. In reasonable circumstances he would be recognized as an author and cultural commentator of singular importance. Instead, for too many Americans, he was best known as a talk-show guest.

Otherwise slavishly faithful to the transcript of Vidal's quotes, I confess I tinkered with one comment about Norman Mailer. Asked whether he had read *The Executioner's Song*, Gore said, "No, life is short and Mailer is too long." I couldn't help rounding off the joke: "I take that back. Mailer is short too."

After Vidal read the manuscript, he telephoned from Los Angeles and told me to turn to the page, to the very line, I had fiddled with. Rather than upbraid me for putting words in his mouth, he said, "After 'Mailer is short too,' let's add, 'Isn't it ironic that our would-be most masculine writer has come to resemble—in appearance, if not art—Colette?'"

Although he took exception to my estimation of his fiction, he never suggested that I change my opinion. He did, however, object that I had made one factual error.

"It's in the paragraph that begins, 'For a man in his mid-fifties, Vidal looks remarkably well.' The next sentence, 'His hairline has receded a bit,' that's wrong. My hairline hasn't changed. Don't take my word for it. Look at old photographs. You'll see that I'm right. You said you'd correct factual errors, didn't you?"

After consulting snapshots on his early books, I wasn't convinced and so left the passage as it stood. Then I mailed the piece to the *New York Times Magazine,* along with a note to Ed Klein, the assigning editor. With suits and countersuits pending in the Vidal vs. Capote case, I mentioned that I had interviewed Capote's agent and lawyer, and that I had allowed Vidal to review the manuscript to verify its accuracy on legal matters.

Ed Klein called back at once to say that he couldn't publish the piece. The *Times* had an iron-clad rule against letting the subject of an interview see it prior to publication.

"You never told me that," I said.

"I didn't think I needed to."

"There was nothing about it in the contract," I protested. "Don't you normally check with sources and read back their quotes?"

That, he said, was different from letting a source read quotes about himself from other sources.

"Are you sure you're not rejecting it because it's positive about Vidal?" I asked.

Klein swore the rule had removed the decision from his hands. Now that Vidal had seen it, the article was dead, and there was nothing to be done about it.

Nothing except inform Gore that I had flubbed another assignment. I had failed him just as I had Eleanor Clark and Graham Greene. My heart sank to my stomach, then they both fell to my feet. I felt I was trampling my own entrails.

When he heard the news, Gore reacted with equanimity, as if his worldview had been revalidated. "I told you the *New York Times* would never run a favorable article about me."

"It's not their fault. It's mine. I shouldn't have shown it to you."

"Don't be ridiculous. Do you think they don't let Kissinger or Carter or Hollywood stars read what they're going to print?"

I could only repeat what Ed Klein told me.

Vidal sighed, not without sympathy, at my ingenuousness, and voiced one of his pet aphorisms. "No good deed goes long unpunished."

It took time—years, in fact—but eventually the article appeared in the now defunct *Washington Star,* in *London Magazine,* and in the *Daily American* in Rome. Gore was generous with praise and claimed that his half-sister Nini regarded it as her favorite profile of him. He objected to just one thing—that I hadn't deleted the line about his hair. "It's not receding."

Back in Rome, he marched me into the guest bathroom and showed me a framed photograph of him as a teenager in an Army uniform. "You see, the hairline has never changed."

I no longer dispute this, nor will I debate whether the *New York Times* bears Gore unending animosity. But I would note that a year and a half later Michiko Kakutani interviewed him, and her profile in the *Times* swarmed with every buzz word I had attempted to refute. "Glib," "cold," "pervasive cynicism," "tart disillusion," "little hope and even less charity," "elitist," "misanthropy," "pessimism," "dismissive . . . of nearly everything"—Ms. Kakutani didn't miss a one.

This incident, like my other botched jobs in journalism, strikes me as important to include in any chronicle of my career. As Graham Greene put it, failure often has far more influence on a writer than success, travel, or exotic experience. The truth is most of us fall short in our work and in our lives, and even authors as exalted as Gore Vidal carry the wounds of disappointment and have cause to feel aggrieved. Whenever I taught, whenever I've spoken to people who aspire to become writers, I've recommended that they cast their gaze on those who have gone before them. If they wanted to be pro football players, I would urge them to visit an NFL locker room and take stock of what they see. Well, much like football players, most writers get their teeth knocked out or their knees shattered and limp around with strange twitches and sad stories.

What Norman Mailer once said about his own literary celebrity being achieved at an early age applies equally to Gore Vidal, whose first novel, *Williwaw,* was a best-seller and made his reputation at twenty. Despite the advantages of success, it isolates authors, and it's not "easy afterward to look upon people with simple interest because generally speaking they're more interested in us than we are in them," Mailer wrote. As a consequence, Mailer observed, a famous writer risks being trapped "in the sarcophagus of his image."

Worse yet, as the sarcophagus stays the same and the author ages, his youthful image persists as a reminder of what he was and a reproach to what he has become. But during the eighties, Vidal seemed determined to embrace and call attention to the differences between him and his handsome, haughty original persona. In restaurants he quit ordering salads and sneaking french fries off other people's plates. He asked for what he wanted and ate it all, and when he grew fat, he accepted that this was how it was meant to be. No more dieting and going to the gym; goodbye to ascetic retreats and fasting before new projects and promotional tours. He continued to drink great quantities of wine and now consumed Falstaffian portions of Scotch and vodka as well. Warned that he ought to cut back—that for a man with high blood pressure, he was ruining his health—he said he didn't care. Having been vilified for decades as vain, he was now caricatured as bloated and slovenly—and he swore he didn't care about that either.

Always iconoclastic and witheringly funny, he started to verge, in the new critical vocabulary, on being transgressive. He became a kind of performance artist who burlesqued the prevailing zeitgeist with his behavior. Invited to deliver the commencement address at St. Stephen's High School in Rome, he encouraged the young graduates *not* to go forth and multiply. He assured them there were a lot more where they came from, the world was already overpopulated, and they should learn to dissociate sex from procreation. At parties at the U.S. Embassy he did deadpan, pitch-perfect impersonations of Ronald Reagan and marveled that corporate America had at last hired an actor able to hit his mark and read the lines that had been written for him.

Since the press and the public had long been so curious, not to mention censorious, about his sex life, Vidal seemed to have decided to become as confessional as a guest on *Oprah*. No more urbane obfuscation or shrewd silence. If people were dead set on invading his privacy, he reveled in shoving the truth down their throats. If they asked intrusive questions, he gave as good as he got. And if they insisted on boring him with their preoccupations, he perked things up with his own.

For decades, he had never deigned to define his relationship with

Howard Austen. While journalists referred to Howard as his constant companion, Vidal said nothing at all—until such time as he decided to make it clear that they weren't a couple. According to them both, they had had sex when they first met, but not since then. As Gore put it to me, "One can always find sex, but one doesn't find friends that easily."

Confining sex to a separate compartment from love or affection, Gore took to speaking of his libido with the utmost detachment. Which isn't to say he couldn't be as comic as he was candid. When I asked him about his comment that the only true thing Truman Capote ever said was that Gore Vidal was a lousy lay, he retorted, "Capote could not have known at firsthand. He also lied about everything on principle. I did think it a good tactic in my youth to spread the word that I did nothing at all in bed to please others, on the ground that unwanted seducers would pass one by. It's not the worst tactic, by the way, though hardly foolproof, as fools found out."

"If famous men have more opportunities," I asked, "was Karl Marx correct that a change in quantity is a change in quality?"

"That's one way of looking at it—though most of us prefer quantity. Groucho Marx at the end of his life was asked if he had it to do all over again what would he do differently. 'Try another position.'"

At a dinner party at our apartment, Vidal listened bemused to Andrea Lee, a *New Yorker* writer, discuss her first novel, *Sarah Philips,* which was about to be published by Random House. Gore and she had the same publisher, Ms. Lee gushed. Not only that, they had the same editor, Jason Epstein. "He really loves me, and he really loves my book."

"Oh, I bet he does." At the time Gore would not have claimed that Epstein loved him and his writing. Their long friendship was foundering on Gore's refusal to stop producing idiosyncratic, inventive novels such as *Myra Breckinridge* and *Duluth* and stick to a strict diet of historical best-sellers.

When Ms. Lee prated on about the prepublication signs that she believed augured well for her book, Gore interrupted. "Has anyone noticed that as a man gets older, his wee-wee begins to grow back into his body?"

"I don't understand," Ms. Lee said.

"When I got out of the shower this morning," Vidal said, "I looked at myself in the mirror and noticed that my wee-wee is growing back into my body."

Ms. Lee reacted in all earnestness, as if this might be a question she could submit to *The New Yorker's* famed fact-checkers. "Don't you think your body is, you know, gaining weight and growing down around your penis so it just looks like it's growing back into you?"

"No, it's retreating," Gore insisted. "I remember Cecil Beaton making a similar observation when he was my age. He asked Greta Garbo and me, 'Has either of you noticed that as you get older your sexual organs get smaller?' And Greta told him—" Vidal lowered his voice to imitate Garbo's—"'Would that I had that problem.'"

Linda organized another dinner at the behest of an American couple eager to meet Vidal. Both had backgrounds in business and finance, but they were avid readers, committed art patrons and opera- and concert-goers. Of all the historical figures they admired, Abraham Lincoln held the place of prominence in their pantheon. Having read Gore's novel about the sixteenth president, they had many, many questions to ask.

Over pre-dinner drinks, when I closed my eyes and listened to the couple, invincibly cheerful and upbeat, I pictured a country club the night before the member-guest golf tournament. Yet no matter how ditzy the conversation, Gore was cordial and never condescending.

But as we moved to the table and Linda was ladling up the soup course, he said, "Do you mind if I ask a question?"

The couple urged him to go right ahead.

"What do gals think about anal intercourse?"

I concentrated very hard on the tortellini floating in my bowl of brodo.

Linda said, "You know, Gore, gals don't talk about anal intercourse."

"Oh, come on, they're doing it."

"They may do it. But they don't talk about it. Not on the first course, they don't."

I kept my eyes riveted on the soup. I didn't want to see anyone's face. I didn't want anyone to see mine.

If I maintain that my fortieth birthday party is remembered by millions, I'm not indulging in mythomania. Most of the guests would have promptly forgotten it, and no one else would have heard of it, had Pat Conroy not transformed the event, as he has dozens of experiences from his own life, into fiction.

Pat arrived in Rome in 1981, and in a role reversal, he called and asked to meet me. "I'm lonely," he pleaded. "I need a friend." The words spilled out in a torrent, but also in italics. The desperation he declared scarcely sounded credible in his broadly comic, country-boy voice. "Come to my house for lunch on Sunday. Bring your family. Bring everybody. I'll give you anything. I'll give you a blow job."

Only an intrinsically strong and stable person, I concluded, could let himself sound so pathetic and needy. Only a truly talented and successful man could plead failure and hopelessness, and make it fun for everybody.

All writers are cannibals—when, that is, they're not vacuum cleaners Hoovering up raw material. But Pat Conroy is especially voracious, and he's quick. Within weeks of our first meeting, we took a driving trip from Rome to Munich for Oktoberfest and talked nonstop for twelve hours. The following spring, when Pat showed me a draft of *The Prince of Tides,* an entire episode had been lifted intact from our conversation and assimilated into the plot, and a polluting nuclear power company in the novel had been named after me. In *Beach Music,* Pat returned to our time on the road to Munich and dredged up another of my anecdotes, this one about a high-school classmate who had been mocked on the football team for being afraid to hit. In the end, he proved everybody wrong by standing up to the school bully and beating him senseless with an axe handle. After that, everybody, even the coach, acknowledged the kid was a hitter.

In no way do I reproach Pat. Stories, as the Greeks observed eons ago, happen to those who can tell them. When Pat told me about a woman in Atlanta who ran over her adulterous husband in the family car, I stole the scene and used it in my fiction before he could use it in his. But in the service of accuracy, I do take mild exception to his description in *Beach Music* of my fortieth birthday party as a glittering Roman gala at the palazzo of Paris and Linda Shaw. The novel's narrator, transparently Pat, arrives at the celebration with his beloved child, an innocent, preteenage daughter, whose beauty and precocious intelligence are praised by none other than Gore Vidal.

In truth, the party took place in our drafty, threadbare *attico,* not in a palace. Still, it was a festive occasion. Sean and Marc folded forty origami birds and strung them from the ceiling. Linda baked a sheet cake large enough to accommodate the requisite number of candles. Dennis Redmont, the AP bureau chief, brought me a ceramic coffee mug fired in the succulent shape of Gina Lollobrigida, and Mickey Knox, never one to come empty-handed, dragged along actors Eli Wallach and Anne Jackson.

Gore Vidal was there, and so was Pat Conroy, but without any of his five daughters. Rather than praise the beauty of Pat's progeny, Vidal remarked that he had read and liked *The Lords of Discipline,* and would have admired it more had Pat dared to declare the obvious.

"What's that?" Pat asked.

"The boys in that military school, all the masochists and the sadists, were having sex with each other."

Conroy did a comic double take. "They were?"

"Of course. It couldn't be clearer that the narrator and his roommate were screwing."

"This is going to come as a great shock to Pig," Pat said of his Citadel roommate, who, like so many real-life characters, found his way into the novel.

In private, Vidal admitted to me that he had given serious thought to Conroy's mass popularity. "He's onto something. He's tapped into an American truth that the rest of us never knew ran so deep. His novels about families show just how dysfunctional our nuclear units have grown."

While Vidal's I-don't-give-a-damn attitude may have liberated him from the "sarcophagus of his image," there was a troubling subtext. For among the things he announced that he no longer cared about was living. With discomfiting, then frightening, frequency, he declared at parties, receptions, and dinners that he was tired and wanted to die. This unnerved Howard, who, in his agitation, sometimes told Gore to stop talking about it and just go ahead and drop dead. At other times, he left the room and didn't return.

One year at Christmas, Don and Luisa Stewart had a house full of guests at their place on Via Margutta. A former artist's loft, with one wall of windows and two opposing walls paneled with mirrors, the living room comfortably accommodated the usual Roman crowd, plus William Gaddis and Muriel Oxenberg, and Gay and Nan Talese.

Vidal loitered with me next to one of the iron columns that supported the tent-like roof. He confided that he was steering clear of Talese, who had been in town for months researching a memoir about his Italian roots, *Unto Thy Father.* Talese had been heard to complain that Vidal sucked all the air out of a room.

"So I stand here," Gore said, "occupying as little space and consuming as little oxygen as possible."

His talk that night was downcast and dwelled at length on how much he had left undone. In 1982, as a Democratic candidate opposing Jerry Brown in the California senatorial primary, Vidal had conducted a provocative campaign, but squandered hundreds of thousands of dollars of his own money and a great deal of energy to capture only 15 percent of the vote. That had killed one of his lifelong ambitions. He would never again run for elective office.

I argued that he wielded more political influence and enjoyed greater freedom to speak out on issues as an author than he would have as a senator. And could he actually imagine trading his life in Italy for the fishbowl of Washington D.C.? He'd lose the little privacy he had preserved.

"If you're speaking about sex," he said, "I would have led a secret life in Washington, no different from plenty of American pols. The problem isn't sex. I should have run sooner. If I had, I'd be a senior senator by now, probably with a wife and a couple of kids. Maybe I'd be president."

When I told him I had even more difficulty envisioning him as a father than as president, he said, "I have a daughter. At least I think I do."

This was another theme he had taken to repeating, and it drove Howard to distraction as surely as Gore's talk about dying. On occasion Vidal sounded as if he had no doubt about this daughter, and he described her mother and the man who had raised her without realizing he wasn't her father. At other times, the child sounded as speculative as his unrealized political aspirations.

When he started in again about wanting to die, I said it saddened and upset me to hear that.

"What do you care?" he asked with a touch of belligerence.

"I like you. I don't want you to die."

"I don't believe that. You're like all young writers. You can't wait for the old ones to die off so you can replace them."

"Whether you're dead or alive, I don't see me replacing you. I'm strictly midlist."

That got a grin out of him. "Okay, maybe you don't want me out of the way. But Edmund White, I bet he'd like to see me gone."

"I don't know about that. Call me selfish. I'd rather you stick around as long as you can."

"It won't be long."

"Are you thinking about killing yourself?"

"No, I won't do that. I'll keep leading my life. That'll take care of things soon enough."

Less afraid of sounding fatuous than of not making an effort, I found myself trying to convince him how much he had to live for. But at that moment his writing, his money and fame, his friends, the admiration of millions of readers, all meant nothing to him. He seemed to me clinically depressed, an occupational hazard for writers, especially heavy-drinking self-medicators.

Although I wouldn't bring it up and have Vidal dismiss the idea as ridiculous, I also believed I knew one reason for his disgruntlement. Despite his insistence that he was a stoic of the meditative Marcus Aurelius stripe, he wasn't invulnerable, he wasn't bulletproof. Acceptance mattered to him, and I had witnessed the petty offenses and rejections that came his way often enough to make him feel undermined.

One winter, the American Academy asked me to invite Vidal to deliver a fund-raising lecture at the Villa Aurelia. After dickering over topics and dates, and apologizing for not doing something original for the evening, he agreed to read from an article that would be published in the States the next spring.

The evening attracted one of the largest crowds in academy history—so large it spilled out of the main hall and into adjoining rooms, where spectators watched on closed circuit TV. Among those in attendance, Italo Calvino stayed on afterward to tell Gore how much he admired *Duluth* and that he intended to write a review of it for an Italian newspaper. Later Calvino's essay appeared as the introduction to the American paperback of the novel.

But behind the scenes, there had been awkward jostling and negotiating. Eager to arrange a dinner for the speaker, the academy director, Sophie Consagra, drew up a guest list that included Linda and me, that year's writing fellow, Mark Helprin, his wife, Lisa, and a female scholar to balance the table with Vidal.

I advised Ms. Consagra that unless I was mistaken, Gore planned to come with Howard Austen. As for Mark Helprin, he was a friend, an affable fellow under the right circumstances. We often had him over to our place, and he amused the boys by doing push-ups with them on his shoulders. But I knew he wouldn't eat with or even speak to Gore. I had already offered to introduce him to Vidal, and Mark refused, explaining that he detested what Vidal stood for. Conservative himself—Helprin would go on to write speeches for Bob Dole during the '92 presidential campaign—he opposed Gore's liberal positions on social and sexual matters, and as an American who also had Israeli citizenship, he considered Vidal an anti-Semite.

Reconfiguring the dinner party, Ms. Consagra replaced the Helprins with the first openly gay couple to reside at the American Academy. Afterward, when Gore and Howard were alone with Linda and me, they fumed about being stereotyped. Did the academy suppose that they wouldn't feel comfortable around straights? Or that straights wouldn't care to be around them? Why pair them off with a couple of queens? Howard referred to them as "Anna Mae Wong and consort." Gore called them a couple of "fagolas." "One either likes men or one likes women," he said. "Not something in between."

Vidal's relationship with U.S. Ambassador Maxwell Rabb was in its way as revelatory as the episode at the American Academy. Gore met the ambassador through Robert Bentley, a First Secretary who knew that Vidal and his Hollywood connections would appeal to Rabb and his wife, Ruth. A genial couple in their seventies, of the same generation and the same slightly baffled bonhomie as President and Mrs. Reagan, the Rabbs had long been starstruck. Not content to watch films with friends in their private screening room at Villa Taverna, they went out of their way to entertain actors and directors who passed through town, and they were more fascinated by celebrities and high fashion designers than by political figures, so much so that they danced dangerously close to causing a diplomatic incident.

In 1984, on the fortieth anniversary of the liberation of Naples, a formal commemoration was scheduled in the city. The U.S. ambassador was, of course, expected to attend. But the date of the event conflicted with a dinner party Gore was throwing in Rome for Joanne Woodward. The embassy staff advised Mr. Rabb against canceling his long-planned appearance in Naples. But after a bit of wobbling, he forgot protocol, followed his heart, and agreed to attend Gore's dinner party.

Later, when Nancy Reagan was about to visit Rome, Ambassador

Rabb included Vidal on the list of guests to a reception for the first lady. But when the White House reviewed the names, it struck off Gore's. Although Rabb had been willing to stand up to the Neapolitans and to his staff, he didn't care to cross Washington in Vidal's defense, and thus Gore became persona non grata.

When I spoke to him about this, Gore shrugged and sounded blasé. Having fallen out of favor with the Kennedys, having figured on Nixon's enemies list, having been eliminated now from Reagan's list, he figured he had scored a hat trick. Still, he couldn't help but be annoyed and, I believe, hurt. People high and low clamored for his company and greedily accepted his hospitality and generosity. But when the chips were down, Gore, as the British would say, was "unclubbable." Whenever I hear him accused of bitterness or bitchiness, I remember these incidents—and I remember what he did for me.

In 1982 I faced an inflexible deadline from a British publisher hellbent on forcing me to break a contract so that he could withhold the rest of my advance. When Vidal heard me complain how difficult it was to write in our apartment with Sean and Marc underfoot, he suggested I finish the book at La Rondinaia, his villa in Ravello. "Drive down and have dinner with us on Thanksgiving," he said. "Howard will show you around, introduce you to the help, then you'll have the place to yourself." They were flying to the Far East, and I could stay as long as I pleased.

Linda and the boys and a babysitter we hired to keep Sean and Marc from breaking furniture or falling off the mountain came with me. Packed into our battered, borrowed VW, the five of us puttered south to Naples, then on to Sorrento and the Amalfi coast. Though the weather was cloudy and cool, the landscape loaned itself to illusions of perpetual summer. Royal purple bougainvillea unscrolled from balconies, and vines of Virginia creeper had turned red and started to shed their flame-shaped leaves. Citrus and olive groves flourished on terraces hacked out of precipitous hillsides.

Painted in pastels and rich earth tones—salmon pink and sienna, pumpkin orange and Pompeian red—towns huddled in mountain valleys and beside tranquil coves. Colonized by Saracens ages ago, the area retained Arabic touches in its keyhole arches, variegated tile domes and labyrinthine streets. Each vest-pocket piazza resembled a room where a party was in progress. Driving through them, I had the sense of entering a sprawling old palazzo owned by a loud and lively family that had offered me free run of the place.

The road to Ravello cut inland and climbed in a series of hairpin curves. On one side, the Lattari mountains sheered up out of the earth. On the other side, the land plunged toward the sea. In every direction, the perspective seemed distorted. Alternately lengthened and foreshortened, the distances, like the light, kept changing.

We parked in the main square in front of a Byzantine cathedral and hiked a quarter of a mile along a footpath to a gate where Vidal greeted us. Wearing a tweed jacket instead of the familiar blazer, he escorted us onto his property and down a majestic colonnade of cypresses. "As you can see," he said, "my wants are simple."

His eight acres had staggering views of a sea full of brightly painted fishing boats and a sky full of scudding clouds. Far below, coastal towns and the automobiles beetling through them looked toylike. Up here, the air was pure and scented with rosemary, lavender, and thyme.

Vidal told me he had first visited Ravello in 1948 with Tennessee Williams at the wheel of a secondhand army jeep. As they careened up the corkscrew road, Williams chose that moment to reveal "I am for all intents and purposes blind in one eye." Between Williams's reckless driving and the splendor of the landscape, Gore conceded that he had had "a mixed first impression" of the Amalfi coast. Now it inspired him, he claimed—inspired him, that is, to write a filmscript "to get the pool finished. That's a powerful inspiration. I always date things by which money, which book, built them."

Hewn out of a mountainside a thousand feet above the Mediterranean, the villa clung to a craggy cliff face as if to defy gravity and graphically incarnate its name: La Rondinaia or The Swallow's Nest. The floor plan of the house, Gore said, replicated a classical Roman layout, with a series of rooms opening off long halls. Yet it also bore hallmarks of the Saracen style—barrel-vaulted ceilings, arched doorways, and windows with filigree ironwork. Moroccan carpets lay scattered over terra-cotta floors. The dining room table was a slab of glass balanced on a trestle of stone, and the chairs had ornate backs crowned with golden rams' heads. Though he had bought them at a Roman antique shop, Vidal theorized that "they were made at Cinecittà for *Ben Hur* when I was writing the film."

Downstairs, where he and Howard had their bedrooms, there was a gym with a sauna and racks of barbells. Bookshelves lined a wall that ran the length of the house. "Read whatever you like," Vidal said, "but put each book back where you found it."

After showing us our quarters on the third floor, he let Howard introduce Linda to the cook while he and I went to his study. Wood burned in a massive tufa fireplace inlaid with arabesque tiles. In front of it, a low table topped by a mosaic gleamed in imitation of the ceramic pulpit in Ravello's *duomo*. Beyond that, there was the wooden table that Vidal used as his desk and where he had written all his books starting with *Burr*. He told me to make space for myself among the litter of his manuscripts and mail, and work where he did.

That was it for instructions, advice, and embargoes. The villa was ours. The next morning Gore and Howard handed over the keys and departed. A few days later, Linda left with the boys and the babysitter, and I was alone and in a position to absorb, as I had done so often in sublets and house-sits, the secret lessons of a place and the people who normally occupied it. This isn't to say that I snooped. That would be contemptible, not to mention cheating. I divined my conclusions from what was around me.

It occurred to me, as it had years ago in the Le Corbusier cottage in Auribeau, how difficult it is to live in a house that's a work of art. Wind whistled through the windows at La Rondinaia, billowing the curtains and chilling the tile floors. Though a man laid a fire each morning in the study, its feeble flames provided more flickering light than warmth, and by mid-afternoon I was freezing and wrapped up in a blanket as I wrote at Gore's table. It rained every day for two weeks, and when storms raked in from the sea, they rocked the house on its foundations, left the phone on the fritz, and blew out the electricity. Several nights I had to read by candlelight, feeling like Abe Lincoln roughing it in a log cabin. Whining that the house was haunted, the cook fled each evening before dark, hurrying toward the gate with one hand extended, her first and little fingers flashing against the evil eye. The other servants followed her example, and I rattled around alone in La Rondinaia, ready to find ghosts in every room.

It came to me that despite its luxurious appointments and spectacular views, the villa was no berth for sissies or sybarites. It was a purpose-built factory dedicated to literature and labor. During the summer it might have been different. I could picture Sting, one or two Rolling Stones,

Susan Sarandon and Tim Robbins rollicking in the gardens. But even then, I'm convinced, Vidal lived here mainly to work, wake up in the morning, and work some more. Much as I appreciated his loan of the place, I was more grateful to get a chance to see that Gore, like any serious artist, fed off the essential ingredients of solitude, silence, and self-discipline. For the famous as well as the neophyte, writing is always a bit like laying bricks.

Less than a year later, Linda and I returned to Ravello. The municipality had conferred honorary citizenship on Gore, and friends flew in from as far away as Los Angeles to mark the occasion. Fred Kaplan, Vidal's authorized biographer, rightly describes this as "a rare event." But by focusing on "formal speeches, grand presentations, and celebratory decorations in the high Italian style," he missed an opportunity to discuss what the wildly disparate crowd revealed about the heterodox subject of his biography.

Yes, there were local and national dignitaries on hand, members of *le beau monde,* including Marella Agnelli, and a clutch of prominent Italian writers—Luigi Barzini, Alberto Arbasino and Italo Calvino. There was grandiloquent speechifying in the gardens of Villa Rufolo, and windy panegyrics to Ravello as an earthly Eden that historically had attracted authors, artists, and composers. There was Neapolitan singing in the square and, inevitably, fireworks. But none of this prepared the crowd for the full weirdness of the proceedings.

Perhaps only an author of Italo Calvino's exquisitely honed sensibility—a creator of metafictions and hypernovels "elevated to the square or to the cube"—could articulate what many of us had in mind. Yet in his oracular homily that evening, Calvino caused head-scratching when he declared, "I must ask myself if we are indeed in Ravello, or in a Ravello reconstructed in a Hollywood studio, with an actor playing Gore Vidal, or if we are in the TV documentary on Vidal in Ravello . . . or whether we are here on the Amalfi coast on a festive occasion, but one in 1840, when, at the end of another Vidal novel, *Burr,* the narrator learns that the most controversial of America's Founding Fathers, Aaron Burr, was his father. Or, since there is a spaceship in *Duluth* manned by centipedes who can take on any appearance, even becoming dead ringers for U.S. political figures, perhaps we could be aboard that spaceship, which has left Duluth for Ravello, and the ETs aboard could have taken on the appearance of the American writer we are here to celebrate."

Calvino would get no argument from me. Among the guests, I would grant that some of them might well have been centipedes disguised as his mayorship Mickey Knox, AP bureau chief Dennis Redmont and his wife Manuela, screenwriter Steven Geller, and Frederick "Freckie" Vreeland, a CIA agent at the U.S. Embassy and son of *Vogue* editor Diana Vreeland. But the people who raised the greatest suspicions were the tanned, muscular young men clad in Versace and Armani, and a tall, mocha-colored woman who made an entrance in a floor-length gown with a silver lamé bodice and a back cut low to the cleavage of her buttocks.

The men, it turned out, were models who had pitched up on the Amalfi coast to do a photo shoot for *Gentleman's Quarterly*. Somebody decided that they would add a smart touch to the ceremony and brought them along. As for the long-stemmed lovely in the silver lamé bib, her identity remained a mystery. I thought she, too, might be a model—fine-boned and chisel-featured, perhaps from Africa, like the high-fashion mannequin, Iman.

Once Vidal's official investiture was finished, the crowd repaired to the terrace at La Rondinaia for a party. Gliding along the cypress allée in her gown, the beautiful black woman stayed tantalizingly ahead of me. Then, as we reached the villa, I lost track of her and got stuck with Italo Calvino. No insult to the maestro, but we had met before at the American Academy and at Gore's apartment in Rome, and he was a solemn, ultra-serious sort and not nearly as pretty as the black swan. Nevertheless, I told him how much I admired *Invisible Cities*.

Accustomed to compliments from far more authoritative sources, Calvino accepted mine with no discernible reaction. The two of us loitered, drinks in hand, at a balustrade that tilted dizzily toward a blue abyss of sky and sea. Gore had taken Calvino's wife, Chichita, inside to show her a photograph of Montgomery Clift, and Calvino gazed in the general direction they had gone.

"Your evocation of place was beyond compare," I said, wishing that I were now in one of the invisible cities he had so vividly evoked.

"Do you read Calvino in Italian," he asked, "or in translation?"

"Translation," I confessed.

"Then you have never read Calvino." With that he said he, too, preferred to peruse Montgomery Clift's photograph.

Feeling foolish and forlorn, I went and watched couples dance on the terrace. One of the bronzed *GQ* hunks had coaxed Linda onto the floor for a slow number. Howard nudged my elbow. "Hey, forget her. Don't get mad. Get even. Lemme introduce you to somebody that's dying to dance with you."

Reclining on a chaise longue, the black beauty peered at me through eyelids at sleepy half-mast. Howard referred to her as Egitta. No last name. Graceful as an egret, she got to her feet. I'm six one. She was a good two inches taller, and when she wrapped her arms around me and pressed close, her pelvis hit me high in the solar plexus.

"Where are you from?" I asked in Italian.

"Rome," she answered in English with an accent I couldn't quite place.

"Where'd you learn to speak English?"

"Arkansas."

"You're from Arkansas?"

"You got something against the South?"

"Nothing at all." It seemed inadvisable to tell her I had taken her for an Ethiopian princess. "Are you married?"

"Yeah, to that teeny-weeny Italian with the beard. But don't let that bother you."

"Any kids?"

She threw her head back in a throaty laugh. "I babysat my brothers and sisters. That's enough kids for me. How about you?"

"Two boys."

"Hey, macho man. You ever feel like getting something on the side?"

"Like what?"

Again, the throaty laugh punctuated by a pelvic thrust. I was torn between the urge to get away from Egitta and the desire to go away with her.

"Are you a model?" I asked.

"No, I'm in the movies." Then, after a gravid pause, "Porno."

As the music died and I debated whether to ask, soft-core or hard? Manuela Redmont raced over and shouted, "Did they get it all?"

Hands on canted hips, Egitta waited for the next tune.

"Well, did they?" Manuela demanded.

"Get what?" I said.

"They keep cutting off his cock." She gestured to Egitta. "And it keeps growing back."

Suddenly I saw Egitta, as they say, through new eyes and noticed what had escaped me until then—the size twelve shoes, the snow-shovel hands, the Adam's apple and five o'clock shadow. It seemed that everyone in Italy except me recognized her as a transsexual star of stage, screen, and TV. I might have said, "You could have fooled me," but I had already proved that. With no notion of the etiquette in these matters, I thanked Egitta for the dance and hastened to mix myself another drink.

At the bar, Steve Geller and Mickey Knox were arguing over Freckie Vreeland's sport jacket, which was draped over the back of a chair. While they both agreed that it was the most appalling item of men's apparel they had ever seen, Geller wanted to wear it as a joke, and Mickey wanted to throw it away. Mickey won and hurled it off the terrace. We all watched as it floated like an unmanned hang glider past orchards and vineyard stakes, over fences and farther on down the mountain toward the sea. And as it fell, things kept falling from its pockets—coins, keys, pens, and pills—so that it lost weight and sailed on long after we expected it to crash land. Sight of that airborne coat, and of Steve and Mickey cheering its flight, was my last memory, my last coherent image, of the night Gore Vidal was made an honorary citizen.

In retrospect, that appears to have been the occasion when Vidal emerged from his gloom and quit saying he wanted to die. Perhaps convinced he was already in heaven, he proceeded to publish another spate of best-sellers and eccentric novels, an award-winning collection of essays, and his autobiography. He even made peace with Norman Mailer, and if that wasn't astonishing enough, Mailer's wife, Norris Church, became so enamored of Gore, the three of them agreed that if she were ever widowed, she should marry him.

In Italy, it is frequently said that nothing is as it appears to be. In this land of *trompe l'oeil,* everything incandesces in a state of perpetual flux—partly what it was in the past, partly what it might become in the future. Some alterations occur with the slow inexorability of one earth plate grinding against its neighbor, and nothing registers until the land buckles and a new crevasse opens. Others transpire in a matter of months. Grand palazzos metamorphose into hotels, churches evolve into supper clubs. Still other changes take place from afternoon to evening, from one hour to the next. A market folds its stands and is supplanted by a restaurant, a famous fountain becomes a footbath or a car wash.

So it shouldn't have surprised me that during a decade and a half I felt the ground shift under my feet. At times I envisioned myself blissfully married to Rome, but in truth, the relationship had never been one of drowsy domesticity and calm conjugal joy. The city was a demanding mistress whose seductiveness existed in precarious equipoise with a penchant for murderous inefficiency and brutal tantrums. Something as simple as mailing a letter or cashing a check could devour an entire day.

High-strung, headstrong, and mercurial, Rome insisted on being accepted on its own terms even as it rewrote those terms and raised the tariff. What had been a cheap, sweet life in the seventies turned expensive and astringent by the eighties. The apartment that had started off costing us two hundred dollars a month now rented for fifteen hundred. As traffic worsened, the rush hours that I once regarded as the equivalent of the running of the bulls in Pamplona, with pedestrians delighted to dance close to the horns, became a maniacally cruel Punch and Judy show. Exhaust fumes ate at the city's marmoreal splendor, and Marc developed allergies that required us to hook him up to an inhaler and have him breathe into a device that resembled an astronaut's mask.

Still, we stayed, convinced that, on balance, Rome offered ample compensations. Who, we reasoned, wouldn't choose to live in close proximity to so much art, history, good wine, and marvelous food? And what writer would willingly relinquish the trove of stories that Italy supplied with the same abundance as it produced flowers in every season, music for every emotion, and obscenities that cancelled out every frustration and disappointment?

We stayed on even after others started leaving. The Conroys had become close friends. Our kids went to the same English-language school, and frequently we got together for family celebrations. Over the years we met in half a dozen different cities. We went sledding in the Gran Sasso, swimming and crabbing in South Carolina, sightseeing in London. But what I remember best are evenings in Rome when Pat and Lenore fixed meals, the food always in vast quantities and of the finest quality, all served with liberal doses of wine and many extravagant, manically amusing anecdotes from Pat. He seemed happy and ebullient as he recounted these stories, some devastatingly funny, some simply devastating, about his bullying, abusive father, a deracinated childhood on military bases, and an aching adolescence that ended—shades of my own life—with his girlfriend getting knocked up by another guy. It was as if he slit a vein and let his heart's blood pour out while saying, "See, it doesn't hurt. This is a joke. I'm laughing and I want you to laugh too." What all this cost him—the eating and drinking, the soul baring and emotional purging—wouldn't become clear until later.

When Lenore was at Salvator Mundi Hospital a block from our apartment giving birth to their daughter Susannah, Pat would drop by after visiting hours to bring reports on the baby's progress, the mother's recovery, and his own tumultuous internal weather. Linda and I were delighted to be Susannah's godparents, but then, when she was two, the Conroys moved back to Atlanta. They quickly decided they were "Rome-sick" and returned—only to leave again the next year, this time for good and bad and forever. In my mind's eye, one moment Pat and I are swaying drunk on the rooftop of the American Academy on New Year's Eve, staring out at a city illuminated by a fusillade of fireworks. Between rocket bursts and cherry-bomb blasts we hear the clatter of plates heaved out of windows as people wish the past year good riddance. The next moment the night sky goes black, and Pat is gone.

Then Steve Geller, the last Expatriate American Café Writer, disappeared. A novelist and screenwriter—he was nominated for an Oscar for his adaptation of Kurt Vonnegut's *Slaughterhouse-Five*—he worked outdoors in Piazza della Rotonda, orchestrating his schedule according to the rising and setting sun. In the morning, he had a table at the Bar di Rienzo. In the afternoon he migrated across the square to the Bar Rotondo. He didn't write longhand in a notebook, like a classic café writer. He typed on a Brother EP44 battery-powered portable. Odder still, he sat next to his dog, an attentive white Maltese that perched on its own chair. When Gore Vidal passed through the piazza, he taunted Geller, "Now I know who does your writing. You're taking dictation. You're ghosting *The Tales of Fluffy*." Now, without Steve and his dog, the piazza looked deserted and bereft.

For reassurance that we were doing the right thing, Linda and I took refuge in the thought that we were staying in Rome for the boys. When they were babies, people on buses always let their mother have a seat. Once they were ambulatory and we took them to neighborhood trattorie, the waiters gave them free run of the kitchen. As they got older, they went to Mass with me every Sunday, and the smell of incense and wine and beeswax candles, and especially the service in Italian, which sounded so much like Latin, reminded me of my own Catholic childhood. Bilingual, they attended a school whose student body might have been assembled in response to a Health, Education, and Welfare directive. All races, creeds, colors, and religions were represented. Cultural differences were occasions for class discussion, not discord. Art was an integral aspect of their lives, and history surrounded them everywhere in the streets.

The problem was how to pay for all this. Since my fiction didn't sell well enough to support us, I tried my hand at journalism again, and despite my sad early track record, I got assignments and gradually better results. Starting in the mid-eighties, I wrote a "Letter from Rome" for *European Travel & Life* magazine. In addition to paying the rent, a regular column taught me to meet a tight deadline and how to deal with editors who, although they had literal rather than literary expectations, helped me develop a new voice and different narrative strategies. Usually told in the first person and often involving Linda, Sean, and Marc, these articles came to seem to me the equivalent of short stories. Far from straight reportage, they depended on character and incident, dialogue and descriptive passages, and when they were collected and published in book form as *Playing Away,* they constituted a kind of piecemeal autobiography.

Looking back, it's difficult for me to explain how hard it had been to get the hang of writing nonfiction. Perhaps it was a holdover from graduate school, some lingering belief in the sanctity of art and the primacy of imagination over fact. For almost two decades I had harbored the intention of turning the case of Wayne Dresbach, my boyhood friend who was convicted of murdering his parents at the age of fifteen, into a novel. In many respects it had come to seem the story of my life, the one I couldn't quit thinking about, the one I had already told many times at boozy, late-night bull sessions, the one I was born to write. But the more I learned about it and the better I got to know Wayne during his years in jail, the clearer it became that it was his story, and after all the abuse he had suffered, the distortions of the initial news reports and the savage inequities of his trial, he deserved to have the truth finally told.

Paroled after a dozen years in prison, Wayne lived with us for a time at the American Academy in Rome, where he narrated his recollections into a tape recorder, and I reviewed police records and the trial transcript. Despite the amateur tattoos on his arms and his habit of drinking beer at breakfast while the academy Fellows and scholars downed cappuccino, he fit in surprisingly well. Asked which institution in the United States he was affiliated with, he told people, "Patuxent Institute for Defective Delinquents."

Unfortunately, when *Life for Death* was published, Wayne's brother Lee filed a lawsuit for libel and invasion of privacy, demanding damages of six million dollars. After two years of litigation, he dropped the suit and settled out of court for twenty-three thousand and the agreement that a few phrases would be cut from the book's paperback version. Interestingly, he didn't demand that I delete Wayne's claim that Lee told him to shoot their parents again to make sure they were dead. But this was small consolation for me. The lawyer bills and settlement wiped out every dollar *Life for Death* earned.

My agent urged me to put the experience to good use. Since I now had a hard-earned education in law, why not do a book about the psychopath accused of killing twenty-eight black children in Atlanta? But I feared I would be typecast as an apostle of cataclysm, and I didn't care to spend the next year studying autopsy photos. So I decided to combine my twin passions, travel and tennis, and set out to cover the men's professional tour. I imagined I would live a Walter Mitty fantasy and return to write a lyrical hymn to the sport. Instead, I discovered a host of financial and ethical improprieties in the game. This resulted in a brief scandal and long-term rule changes once *Short Circuit* came out. Still, there were blissful moments on the tour when I gloried in the thought that I was doing so many things I liked, all at the same time. I was watching tennis, getting a tan, and taking notes for a book. If only the pay had been better.

For a while it appeared that film work might be my financial salvation. The British producers of *Chariots of Fire* and *The Killing Fields* wanted an original screenplay based on the 1981 assassination attempt against Pope John Paul II. According to their high concept, the gun man, a disturbed Turk named Ali Agca, was actually a clever killer-for-hire, like the posh English gentleman assassin in Frederick Forsyth's *Day of the Jackal*. Nothing I said could persuade them otherwise. But on the opening day of his trial when Agca faced the world's TV cameras and proclaimed, "I am Jesus Christ," the Brits concluded he was a jackass, not the Jackal, after all. They dropped me and the project.

Then Italian director Lina Wertmuller phoned to say, "I half read you and I luf your dialogues." In stutters and starts in several languages, it came out that she had written a script in Neapolitan dialect that had been translated into English to attract foreign investors and an international cast. While she had succeeded in securing financing and the services of Harvey Keitel and Spanish actress Angela Molina, she feared the script was unshootable as it stood. "Please, read it," she said, "and I pay you to tell me is this English or what."

Titled *A Complicated Intrigue of Women, Alleys, and Corpses,* the script, I found out, fell into the "or what" category. An update and improvisation on *Lysistrata,* it dealt with a coven of women who vow to stamp out heroin in Naples, not by withholding sex from men, but by killing them during the act with drugs shot straight into their testicles. If this wincingly painful plot weren't problem enough, the screenplay's Neapolitan dialect had been translated into something resembling Esperanto more than idiomatic English. The unintentionally hilarious dialogue consisted chiefly of curses, obscenities, and incessant repetitions of the same four-letter fricative. A case could be made that I was only hired to find synonyms for "fuck."

Compulsively putting on and removing her trademark white horn-rimmed glasses—dozens of pairs of identical spectacles lay scattered about her apartment so she always had several close to hand—Wertmuller peered over my shoulder all during the rewrite, arguing every word. "Screw," "hump," "bang," "pork"—we sounded like a couple of dirty-mouthed school kids, not a director and a writer doctoring a script. Lina's absolute favorite expression for sexual intercourse was "bumping the uglies," a phrase I stole from "The Boys in the Band."

We wasted the worst part of a week debating just two lines. Angela Molina, who is meant to portray a sympathetic character, has a cute little boy about six years old. In one scene, he races across a room and plumps himself down on her lap. Wertmuller has Molina exclaim, like any warm Italian earth mother, "Oh, fuck my ass, but you're heavy." It was damnably difficult to convince Lina that in middle America this was not how loving moms spoke to their children.

Then we clashed over an exchange between Molina and Harvey Keitel. He plays a former lover who wistfully asks what she ever saw in him. Molina replies, "I loved your pirate's chest, and you always smelled like seafood."

"What does she mean by pirate's chest?" I asked.

"She loves his *corpo,* his body." Lina patted her own meager *poitrine.* "He has the chest of a pirate."

"In America a pirate's chest is a box full of gold doubloons. And I can assure you, nobody there thinks seafood smells nice."

"Ma senta bene." She kissed her fingers. "It smells good, seafood."

"Maybe in Italy. Not in America."

"This cannot be."

"Look, Lina, you simply have to choose—"

"Shoes?" She changed glasses and glanced at her feet.

"You have to choose whether you're making a movie for an Italian audience or for an international one."

"You ruin my dialogues," she cried. Off came the glasses, on came an interchangeable pair, and off we went on another lunatic linguistic altercation.

The money for that rewrite wound up being the hardest I almost didn't make. To get paid, I had to go on a sit-down strike in Lina's living room and threaten to tear up the pages I had revised. Eventually a thug showed up and, in standard Neapolitan fashion, forked over a brown paper bag stuffed with millions of lire.

As the struggle to stay in Rome for the sake of the kids started to exhaust us, Linda wondered aloud whether we weren't doing them a disservice by raising them outside their own culture. While she and I could easily reintegrate, the boys might be beached on an ambiguous middle ground, stranded between Europe and the United States, not quite comfortable in either, foreigners wherever they lived. Worse yet, they might become strangers to their mother and me. Already they were ignorant of the myriad shards that compose the national mosaic. They knew nothing about baseball or football, the names of teams, the vital statistics of star players. They didn't even know the difference between an American toilet flusher and a burglar alarm.

In fairness to our younger son, Marc, this statement requires an explanation. During a visit to his maternal grandparents' house, he pushed a button on the bathroom wall, figuring it would flush the toilet. That's how the plumbing functioned in our Roman apartment. But in Pittsburgh, Pa., in an incident that dramatized rich new dimensions of the phrase "culture shock," he set off an emergency alarm that summoned the police.

For months, that clamorous alarm reverberated in my brain, crystallizing the realization that we really did need to move back to the States.

Otherwise the boys were in danger of growing up to behave in the U.S. like the hapless, bumbling tourists they saw in Rome—unable to operate a pay telephone, wary of taxis and buses, perplexed by the currency, hesitant about using colloquial expressions for fear of voicing some incredible barbarity. In short, they were in danger of becoming the kind of comic character their father often was in Italy.

And so we did leave. Yet no sooner had we departed than I regretted it. Rome haunted my dreams at night and ruined my mood during the day. Awake or asleep, I had trouble holding an accurate picture of it in mind. Falling into fragments, the city streamed as haphazardly as eye-floaters through my field of vision, reduced to a jumble of images from the dozen or so apartments we had lived in, confused with telescoped views from various terraces, the Tiber flowing beneath different bridges, the ceilings of grand palazzos glittering with gold scrollwork, candlelit vaults and murals of angels and saints. Heartsick, I struggled to recapture Rome intact, but it was dissolving like powdered medicine in water, depositing a faint residue of distortion on the glass between me and it.

From time to time, I flew back to Italy, ostensibly on newspaper and magazine assignments, in reality to reacquaint myself with the place. During the prolonged period when Francis Ford Coppola was filming *Godfather III* in Rome, Mickey Knox played a bit part and served as a dialogue coach. By sheer happenstance I was there the night he fixed his famous chili for the crew and cast. Gore Vidal was there, too, an honored guest, and as we ate and talked, a handsome young man in jeans stopped near the couch where we sat. His face was familiar, but I couldn't attach a name to it. Afterward I was told he was Andy Garcia.

"Sorry to interrupt," he said. "But before I go, I wanted to say good-bye to my favorite writer."

"Thank you." Gore extended his hand with the practiced grace of a cardinal offering his ring to be kissed.

"I don't mean you. I mean Mr. Mewshaw."

This had all the earmarks of one of Mickey Knox's jokes, a setup to tweak Gore's nose and embarrass me. I made the mistake of asking, "What have you ever read of mine?"

"I don't read much," he admitted. "I have an awful lot of scripts to get through, and I'm sort of dyslexic. But I saw an article you wrote about taking your sons to eat at the first McDonald's to open in Rome, and that's the best thing I've ever read."

With that, Andy Garcia shook my hand, shook Gore's, and sauntered off. It was a moment to cherish. Okay, he hadn't read one of my novels. Still, in this company, it was high praise to hear I was his favorite writer.

But Vidal put a quick end to my preening. "You can have all the dyslexic ones."

Eight years after its publication, *Year of the Gun,* the novel I set during the turmoil of Red Brigades terrorism, was made into a movie. That brought me back to Rome as a consultant, a task that entailed reading the script and telling the director, John Frankenheimer, my reaction. Loathe to sound like those aggrieved authors who object to every change in their artfully crafted creations, I limited myself to one observation. Not a single line of my dialogue, I pointed out, had been retained by the screenwriter. Instead, he had put long expository passages from the book into the character's mouths, with results that were unfortunate for the actors, not to mention the narrative. Frankenheimer listened, nodded, and did nothing. For the rest of my consultancy, I played tennis with Frankenheimer and stayed out of everybody's way. At last, this was a big payday, and I didn't care to louse it up by complaining.

My only substantive contribution to the production related to Sharon Stone. Not caring to hole up in a hotel for three months, she demanded an apartment fit for a star, and I knew just the place. A friend, Peter Schweitzer, a *CBS News* producer, had a sumptuous duplex with a terrace overlooking Trajan's Forum and a walled private garden in back. Since he was a bachelor and often on the road, I believed he might be willing to sublet. Before relocating to the States on a lengthy assignment, Peter had lunch with Sharon Stone on his terrace, and they struck a deal.

It wasn't until the last week of shooting, when I returned to Rome for the wrap party, that I met Sharon. One raw December day she emerged from her trailer swaddled in mink and sought me out. I didn't flatter myself that she wanted to pay her respects to the writer. She was far too savvy to be deluded that an author had any claim to importance. She wanted to talk to me about her absent landlord, Peter Schweitzer.

"I've got a thing for the guy," she confessed, hugging herself against a frigid wind.

"Has he been in Rome?" I asked.

"No. I've seen him just once. But living in his apartment all this time, it's like I've gotten to know him and we've become close. I mean, in the morning when it's cold I wear his robe and socks. I play his records and CDs. I read his books. I look at his photographs. I admire the art he has on his walls. Is there any chance I'll see him again?"

I assured her that this wasn't the impossible dream and gave her Peter's New York number.

She thanked me, but didn't overdo it. High-tailing it back into her trailer, she stayed snug and warm inside while I froze and shivered outside. When it started to rain and Frankenheimer called it a day, I tried to hitch a ride from Cinecittà with Sharon Stone, whose limo passed right by my hotel on the way to Peter's apartment. But she said, "No. I'm not going in your direction."

She did, however, go in Peter Schweitzer's direction, and for a few months they were an item. To observe that she was exigent will surprise no one. When the war with Iraq broke out, and Peter had to fly to the Persian Gulf to report on the Mother of All Battles, Sharon accused him of going there to prove his manhood rather than staying with her and working on their relationship. To punish him, she landed the lead role in *Basic Instinct* and began working on her relationship with fame.

Shunned by Sharon Stone, I phoned Gore and Howard and offered to buy them dinner. They suggested Passetto's, a once popular, now out-of-fashion, restaurant. Vidal, who was writing his memoirs, seemed to be in an elegiac mood, and maybe that's why he preferred old haunts. As we walked through Piazza Navona, the wind blew a spitting mist from the fountains, and the damp tablecloths at Tre Scalini's outdoor tables flapped like laundry. Gore told me he was debating titles for what he referred to as his Me-Mores. Since he had recently played a role in *Bob Roberts* and was scheduled to appear in more movies, he had considered stealing the title from Stanislavski and calling his book *An Actor Prepares*. But he settled on *Palimpsest*. "A word nobody will know," he said. "But then it's a life nobody will know, particularly after reading the book. I just skip around to things that interest me." He had grown weary of reading other memoirs and "finding a stranger masquerading under my name."

At Passetto's, the head waiter recognized Vidal and treated the three of us with deference. But that didn't make up for the restaurant's morose atmosphere. Most of the tables were empty, and among the few diners, none appeared to be Italian.

"It's dead," Howard said, announcing not just the demise of the restaurant but of Rome itself. "It's so bo-o-oring!"

Gore agreed and complained that life here had become intolerable. The air was unbreatheable; it stung his eyes and throat. And they could no longer abide their landlady, who demanded an extortionate rent for an apartment that would have crumbled if they hadn't poured money into its renovation.

"It's not worth it anymore," Howard said. "Not when we use it only three or four months a year."

To my amazement, they spoke of abandoning Rome and moving full-time to Ravello. It didn't seem possible, not after Gore had announced in Fellini's *Roma* that the Eternal City was the perfect spot to await the end of the world. Did this signify that Armageddon had been delayed? Or that it had already arrived?

After the meal, the headwaiter brought a bottle of Stolichnaya vodka. I assumed it was an *omaggio,* the sort of gift or homage that favored customers receive in Italy. But when the bill came, thirty dollars had been tacked on for after-dinner drinks. Vidal was furious. We hadn't, after all, ordered the vodka. I assured him it didn't matter.

It mattered to Gore, though, and as we retrieved our coats, he continued fuming. When he noticed that the hat-check girl was reading a bodice-ripping romance in English, he lit into her. "You shouldn't be reading that drivel."

"What do you recommend?"

"You should be reading . . ." He flung an arm in my direction. ". . . you should be reading him."

"Who's he?"

"He's a famous American novelist. He's in Rome to see one of his novels being made into a movie." Vidal's voice died and he squinted at the girl as if something had just registered. "Are you an American?"

"Yeah."

"Has it come to that?" he demanded. "In my day Italians moved to the States to work as hat-check girls. Now Americans come to Rome and don't even recognize their country's most famous author."

As he stalked out of Passetto's, the poor girl to mumbled to me, "Who are you?"

In retrospect I realize I should have said, "Gore Vidal." Instead, I murmured, "Nobody you'd know," and hurried out with Howard.

Gore had a head start, and we didn't catch up to him until he was on Via Argentina, stabbing his key at a door and swearing. "It's broken. It won't work."

"That's because we don't live there," Howard said.

Baffled, Gore glanced from the key to the lock and back again. Like a man trapped in a bad dream, he appeared to have lost track of where he was and where he belonged.

"We live in the next building," Howard said.

But they didn't live there long. In March 1993, they left Rome for good. This turned more than a page. It ended a chapter, an era, in the city's literary history.

These days when I travel to Rome, I feel like a ghost drifting through a town haunted by the shades of old friends. Soon after Gore and Howard left, Mickey Knox, the mayor, pulled up stakes for Los Angeles, and Bob and Beverly Katz transferred their Italian base to Tuscany. Only Don and Luisa Stewart remain.

Although well aware that the city must have taken other prisoners of love after me, I didn't care to know about them. I preferred to imagine her in reduced circumstances, chastened and lonely. When people complained how gracelessly she was aging, I gloated and congratulated myself for jumping ship before twenty-seven more McDonald's opened, before there was a Footlocker franchise on Via Condotti, before the bizarre fad for Irish and English pubs began to flourish, before the American Academy ripped up its tennis court and replaced it with a bland greensward called the Sid and Mercedes Bass Garden.

On a recent trip, I landed at Fiumicino airport with an excruciating crick in my neck and taxied into Rome with my head cocked at an acute angle. Despite the pain, I thought I was in a perfect position to take the measure of the town and pass summary judgment on it. But I had to concede that for a lady rumored to be on her last legs, she looked spry and lively. Celebrated landmarks and monuments that had for years been webbed with scaffolding and tented under sheets of tarpaulin now had their wraps off. Long-shuttered museums had reopened, and once soot-covered baroque facades by Bernini and Borromini were burnished by light.

These renovations had had a curious secondary effect. The old and the new, the classical and the contemporary, have always overlapped there. But with ancient historical sites being refurbished, buildings constructed this century now appeared older than the Coliseum or Constantine's arch.

At Piazza Barberini, it stunned me to spot a familiar face—a man in goofy sunglasses, a beanie with a propeller on top, and earphones with tinfoil antennae. As long as I could remember, the fellow had lollygagged there pretending to direct traffic with two drumsticks. "When they were little kids, my sons used to love that crazy guy," I told the taxi driver.

"He's not *pazzo*. He's *felice,* happy," the cabby replied, offering the explanation that Italians suggest whenever foreigners view local exuberance as lunacy.

Still expecting to spot evidence of my former mistress's decay, I ditched the taxi and explored the city's back streets on foot. Lots of them were off-limits to traffic, and customers at cafés no longer had to fear hurtling cars and motorcycles. The Spanish Steps had been scrubbed clean, and signs forbade drinking and eating on that splendid staircase from Piazza di Spagna to Trinità del Monte. Foot-weary tourists and backpackers sat on the cool marble, untroubled by tumbleweeds of trash, clanking cola cans, and broken wine bottles.

I can't say when I quit searching for excuses to justify my failed romance with Rome and came to understand that I was falling in love again. Maybe it was on Sunday, when I strolled through streets as dead as church Latin and visited San Silvestro, where Sean had been confirmed. It pleased me that this was still the parish of the Link Community, where Asian immigrants traded gossip with friends before attending a Mass sung in Tagalog. They congregated afterward in the courtyard, perched on splintered columns and Roman sarcophagi and ate spring rolls and rice.

Or perhaps it was the evening I strolled through Piazza Santa Maria in Trastevere, where the usual grubby brigade of guitar pluckers slouched around the fountain. Once, when Marc was an infant and fell sick, I had hurried here to an all-night pharmacy at two in the morning, and as I rushed across the cobblestones with the medicine, a woman walking ahead of me was mugged. Magically, half the guitar pluckers pulled guns, mutating into plainclothes policemen, and captured the thief.

Abrupt reversals of expectation, incandescent transformations, scenes of high hilarity and tearful sadness—these sundry Roman experiences were what had kept me in the city for the better part of fifteen years. Now no matter how intensely I felt the old emotions, I knew it was temporary. So it was with regret, exacerbated by the pinched nerve, that I set off for the airport and another departure.

On the way, thinking it would ease the pain, I stopped at a drugstore and asked in what I presumed to be impeccable Italian for a foam-rubber collar to brace my neck. The cashier promptly fetched a leash and a dog collar. This should, I suppose, have signaled the end, the final, irrevocable break. If we no longer spoke the same language, I should have conceded that the tempestuous affair with Rome was well and truly over. But I saw it as a symbol of a different sort. Wherever I go, I'll always be chained to the city.

And just as surely I'll always feel linked to the people, especially the writers, I met there and in all the other places where I've spent time. Although many of them are now dead, I don't flatter myself that they endure only in my memory or in this book. They live on in their shelves full of novels and volumes of poetry, in the movies and documentaries based on their work, and in the biographies and critical studies devoted to them. But as Shirley Hazzard has pointed out, "When friends die, one's own credentials change: one becomes a survivor"—and as such, there's the imperative to remember and to provide as accurate a record as possible. If nothing else, I trust I have done that.

Of course it might be objected that my emphasis has been wrong, that I've too often focused on the personal and on events that are peripheral to masterpieces and their celebrated creators. But I believe that the public events and the artistic achievements of the writers I deal with have already been adequately examined, and there is value in showing these figures in less formal poses and at more candid moments. As Phyllis Rose remarked in *Parallel Lives,* even "gossip may be the beginning of moral inquiry, the low end of the platonic ladder which leads to self-understanding. We are desperate for information about how other people live because we want to know how to live ourselves."

Although I've learned a lot from these writers, I wouldn't go so far as to claim that they taught me how to live or that I have set my course in life by following their compass. For one thing, that would imply that they bear some responsibility for my shortcomings, and I have no right to blame anybody else for what I've done or failed to do. But I owe them something, a debt I can only repay by being as kind as they were to the next generation of writers.

Looking back at the age of fifty-nine, I see my life as more or less of a piece. Now as in the beginning, it seems improvised, unsettled. Linda and I still don't own a house or have a fixed address except our e-mail. For the past decade, most of our belongings, including books and paintings, have remained in storage bins and in the basements of indulgent friends. Wherever we go—for the last few years it's been Europe in the summer and Key West, Florida, in the winter—we rent everything, including a car.

There used to be a financial reason for our nomadic existence. Traveling light cost less. But now that it's no longer a matter of money, I realize just how crucial it has always been for me to stay free of clutter, to maintain clarity and concentration. While I wouldn't necessarily recommend this to others—perhaps people who have more talent and intelligence have less trouble managing their possessions and domestic arrangements—I'm convinced that I couldn't write any other way.

As to the question of how well I have written, I'm reluctant to reach a conclusion. That suggests to me an ending and the sort of stock-taking that leads to more pain than insight. If honest, however, I will admit that I haven't yet done what I hoped to do. I haven't produced a large and lasting body of fiction, nor have I won a wide readership. But given what I have done, where I have traveled, and what I've experienced, it would be churlish to complain. Then, too, there are the people I've known. Unlike Jean Paul Sartre, who lamented that, "Generally in life, writers are inferior to their books," I have had the great good fortune to meet authors who were every bit as complicated, challenging, and accomplished as their work.